COURTS THAT MATTER

In *Courts that Matter,* Sandra Botero tackles a crucial question: Can courts advance socioeconomic rights? Using a rigorous comparative study of the impact of socioeconomic rights rulings in Colombia and Argentina, Botero argues that such decisions can be significantly impactful when courts deploy certain monitoring mechanisms and when legally empowered organizations in civil society are engaged in the outcome. The book includes case studies of landmark rulings on environmental, health, housing, and other socioeconomic rights and charts pathways for broader applicability through comparison with rulings by the Supreme Court of India. The book demonstrates how Colombian and Argentine highest tribunals have, at times, successfully configured important new political spaces for the effective pursuit of public policy goals, in conjunction and dialogue with other social and political actors. This title is part of the Flip it Open programme and may also be available Open Access. Check our website Cambridge Core for details.

SANDRA BOTERO is Associate Professor of Political Science at Universidad del Rosario (Bogotá, Colombia). She is the coeditor of *The Limits of Judicialization: From Progress to Backlash in Latin America* (2022).

COMPARATIVE CONSTITUTIONAL LAW AND POLICY

Comparative constitutional law is an intellectually vibrant field that encompasses an increasingly broad array of approaches and methodologies. This series collects analytically innovative and empirically grounded work from scholars of comparative constitutionalism across academic disciplines. Books in the series include theoretically informed studies of single constitutional jurisdictions, comparative studies of constitutional law and institutions, and edited collections of original essays that respond to challenging theoretical and empirical questions in the field.

Books in the Series

The Story of Constitutions: Discovering the We in Us Wim Voermans

Democracy Under God: Constitutions, Islam and Human Rights in the Muslim World Dawood Ahmed and Muhammad Zubair Abbasi

Buddhism and Comparative Constitutional Law Edited by Tom Ginsburg and Ben Schonthal

Amending America's Unwritten Constitution Edited by Richard Albert, Ryan C. Williams, and Yaniv Roznai

Constitutionalism and a Right to Effective Government? Edited by Vicki C. Jackson and Yasmin Dawood

The Fall of the Arab Spring: Democracy's Challenges and Efforts to Reconstitute the Middle East Tofigh Maboudi

Filtering Populist Claims to Fight Populism: The Italian Case in a Comparative Perspective Giuseppe Martinico

Constitutionalism in Context David S. Law

The New Fourth Branch: Institutions for Protecting Constitutional Democracy Mark Tushnet

The Veil of Participation: Citizens and Political Parties in Constitution-Making Processes Alexander Hudson

Towering Judges: A Comparative Study of Constitutional Judges Edited by Rehan Abeyratne and Iddo Porat

The Constitution of Arbitration Victor Ferreres Comella

Redrafting Constitutions in Democratic Orders: Theoretical and Comparative Perspectives Edited by Gabriel L. Negretto

From Parchment to Practice: Implementing New Constitutions Edited by Tom Ginsburg and Aziz Z. Huq

The Failure of Popular Constitution Making in Turkey: Regressing Towards Constitutional Autocracy Edited by Felix Petersen and Zeynep Yanaşmayan

A Qualified Hope: The Indian Supreme Court and Progressive Social Change Edited by Gerald N. Rosenberg, Sudhir Krishnaswamy, and Shishir Bail

Reconstructing Rights: Courts, Parties, and Equality Rights in India, South Africa, and the United States Stephan Stohler

Constitutions in Times of Financial Crisis Edited by Tom Ginsburg, Mark D. Rosen, and Georg Vanberg

Hybrid Constitutionalism: The Politics of Constitutional Review in the Chinese Special Administrative Regions Eric C. Ip

Constitution-Making and Transnational Legal Order Edited by Tom Ginsburg, Terence C. Halliday, and Gregory Shaffer

The Invisible Constitution in Comparative Perspective Edited by Rosalind Dixon and Adrienne Stone

The Politico-Legal Dynamics of Judicial Review: A Comparative Analysis Theunis Roux

Constitutional Courts in Asia: A Comparative Perspective Edited by Albert H. Y. Chen and Andrew Harding

Judicial Review in Norway: A Bicentennial Debate Anine Kierulf

Constituent Assemblies Edited by Jon Elster, Roberto Gargarella, Vatsal Naresh, and Bjorn Erik Rasch

The DNA of Constitutional Justice in Latin America: Politics, Governance, and Judicial Design Daniel M. Brinks and Abby Blass

The Adventures of the Constituent Power: Beyond Revolutions? Andrew Arato

Canada in the World: Comparative Perspectives on the Canadian Constitution Edited by Richard Albert and David R. Cameron

Constitutions, Religion and Politics in Asia: Indonesia, Malaysia and Sri Lanka Dian A. H. Shah

Courts and Democracies in Asia Po Jen Yap

Proportionality: New Frontiers, New Challenges Edited by Vicki C. Jackson and Mark Tushnet

Constituents before Assembly: Participation, Deliberation, and Representation in the Crafting of New Constitutions Todd A. Eisenstadt, A. Carl LeVan, and Tofigh Maboudi

Assessing Constitutional Performance Edited by Tom Ginsburg and Aziz Huq

Buddhism, Politics and the Limits of Law: The Pyrrhic Constitutionalism of Sri Lanka Benjamin Schonthal

Engaging with Social Rights: Procedure, Participation and Democracy in South Africa's Second Wave Brian Ray

Constitutional Courts as Mediators: Armed Conflict, Civil-Military Relations, and the Rule of Law in Latin America Julio Ríos-Figueroa

Perils of Judicial Self-Government in Transitional Societies David Kosař

Making We the People: Democratic Constitutional Founding in Postwar Japan and South Korea Chaihark Hahm and Sung Ho Kim

Radical Deprivation on Trial: The Impact of Judicial Activism on Socioeconomic Rights in the Global South César Rodríguez-Garavito and Diana Rodríguez-Franco

Unstable Constitutionalism: Law and Politics in South Asia Edited by Mark Tushnet and Madhav Khosla

Magna Carta and Its Modern Legacy Edited by Robert Hazell and James Melton

Constitutions and Religious Freedom Frank B. Cross

International Courts and the Performance of International Agreements: A General Theory with Evidence from the European Union Clifford J. Carrubba and Matthew J. Gabel

Reputation and Judicial Tactics: A Theory of National and International Courts Shai Dothan

Social Difference and Constitutionalism in Pan-Asia Edited by Susan H. Williams

Constitutionalism in Asia in the Early Twenty-First Century Edited by Albert H. Y. Chen

Constitutions in Authoritarian Regimes Edited by Tom Ginsburg and Alberto Simpser

Presidential Legislation in India: The Law and Practice of Ordinances Shubhankar Dam

Social and Political Foundations of Constitutions Edited by Denis J. Galligan and Mila Versteeg

Consequential Courts: Judicial Roles in Global Perspective Edited by Diana Kapiszewski, Gordon Silverstein, and Robert A. Kagan

Comparative Constitutional Design Edited by Tom Ginsburg

Courts that Matter

ACTIVISTS, JUDGES, AND THE POLITICS OF RIGHTS ENFORCEMENT

SANDRA BOTERO
Universidad del Rosario

CAMBRIDGE
UNIVERSITY PRESS

CAMBRIDGE
UNIVERSITY PRESS

Shaftesbury Road, Cambridge CB2 8EA, United Kingdom

One Liberty Plaza, 20th Floor, New York, NY 10006, USA

477 Williamstown Road, Port Melbourne, VIC 3207, Australia

314–321, 3rd Floor, Plot 3, Splendor Forum, Jasola District Centre, New Delhi – 110025, India

103 Penang Road, #05–06/07, Visioncrest Commercial, Singapore 238467

Cambridge University Press is part of Cambridge University Press & Assessment, a department of the University of Cambridge.

We share the University's mission to contribute to society through the pursuit of education, learning and research at the highest international levels of excellence.

www.cambridge.org
Information on this title: www.cambridge.org/9781009281997

DOI: 10.1017/9781009281973

First published 2024

A catalogue record for this publication is available from the British Library.

A Cataloging-in-Publication data record for this book is available from the Library of Congress

ISBN 978-1-009-28199-7 Hardback

Contents

Figures

Tables

Acknowledgments

This book was made possible by the generosity and support of my family, loved ones, friends, colleagues, interviewees, activists, lawyers, judges, politicians, several institutions, and strangers who went the extra mile. Though all errors and omissions are my own, I am immensely grateful for the many small and big ways in which people, and forces beyond my control – like health scares, international moves, and professional challenges – contributed to making this volume a reality. Writing it was a humbling experience that left me with even more questions, and with the certainty that it is merely the starting point for more conversations.

Courts That Matter started out as my doctoral dissertation at the Department of Political Science, University of Notre Dame. I am grateful to the National Science Foundation (NSF) and the Social Science Research Council (SSRC) for funding the research. I was fortunate to receive a Doctoral Dissertation Research Improvement Grant and an SSRC Mellon International Dissertation Research Fellowship, which allowed me to conduct exactly the kind of fieldwork I had envisioned. The Kellogg Institute for International Studies at Notre Dame was my academic home throughout graduate school: The Kellogg and its amazing staff nourished a vibrant scholarly community and supported me in countless ways. The Center for Asian Studies at Willamette University generously provided a grant to fund a trip to New Delhi, India. The trip was crucial for expanding my horizons and my thinking about the role of courts in rights enforcement beyond Latin America. Thanks to all the people in Colombia, Argentina, and India who patiently or hurriedly put up with my questions, helped me find information, allowed me to observe and learn from their lives and work, and shared their insights and experiences with me. I am especially grateful to Paola Bergallo, Julio Gaitán, and Mario Hernández for opening many doors as I was trying to navigate unfamiliar territories. Anuj Bhuwania, Varun Gauri, and Jinee Lokaneeta were very helpful as I was planning to visit India. I cannot begin to do justice to India or its judiciary in the pages that I dedicate to it here, but as a Latin American, I was astounded by the many parallels and the divergences I glimpsed. Visiting New Delhi, meeting some of its people, and having the opportunity to learn about India touched me deeply.

My dissertation committee – Daniel Brinks, Scott Mainwaring, and Michael Coppedge – provided unwavering support and incisive comments that pushed me beyond my limits. The book took shape slowly over several years and was forged by many exchanges with two scholars who have had a huge influence on my work: Daniel Brinks and Ezequiel Gonzalez-Ocantos. I am grateful to Dan for his generosity and his guidance, and to Ezequiel for his patience and his willingness to help me dig myself out of academic holes. Others provided very useful feedback at different points of the writing process: Thanks to my colleagues at Notre Dame who read different versions, fellow panelists at the Law and Society Association and Latin American Studies Association congresses over the years, constructive reviewers, as well as Juan Diego Prieto, Silvia Otero Bahamón, Nathalia Sandoval, and Benjamín García Holgado.

This book will appear as part of a Cambridge University Press series, inclusion in which I thought I could only dream about. Thanks to the editors, and particularly Ran Hirschl, for welcoming this book. Ran's encouragement and input helped me get unstuck and see my work in a different way at a crucial moment. Matt Gallaway and Jadyn Fauconier-Herry at Cambridge University Press were a pleasure to work with throughout the editorial process. Vicky De Negri saved the day with her expertise and kindness. Thanks to David Goyes for helping me map.

I have crossed paths with dear friends whose example and companionship have challenged, inspired, and sustained me at different points in this journey: Juan Albarracín, Nestor Castañeda, Manuela Fernández, Laura Gamboa, Victor Hernández, Allison Hobgood, Álvaro Hofflinger, Esteban Manteca, Michael Niño, Silvia Otero Bahamón, Nara Pavão, Jason Ruiz, Cayla Skillin-Brauchle, Lucia Tiscornia, and, most definitively, the WOL.

This book and the project from which it emerged developed as I moved several times across the United States and then back home to Bogotá, Colombia. Throughout this voyage, whether near or far, my family was always there. My parents Maria Eugenia and Hector, my sisters Carolina and Andrea, my nieces, and my other close relatives are the light that never goes out. I am deeply grateful to and for Santi, for bringing laughter, love, lentils, and joy into my life – and for his undying belief that I can and I will, even when I fear in my bones I cannot.

1

Introduction

On the morning of October 11, 2012, the Supreme Court of Argentina held a public hearing to follow up on the implementation of its ruling in the *Causa Mendoza* case. The case, which the court took up in 2006, was an ambitious environmental rights ruling ordering the national government, the government of the province of Buenos Aires, and that of the city of Buenos Aires to work together toward the recovery and preservation of the Matanza-Riachuelo River basin. The Matanza-Riachuelo is one of the world's most polluted rivers – 40 miles long, traversing Argentina's most densely populated zone before flowing into the Rio de la Plata in the heart of Buenos Aires.

This public hearing was not a routine fact-finding one geared at informing the court's decision. In fact, the ruling had already been handed down four years ago, but the Court had stayed involved since, and would continue to be. Like similar hearings on this case held before and after 2012, it was part of a larger collaborative effort that engaged the court, government agents, and civil society actors in monitoring progress of the ruling's implementation. In the main hall where the audience was held sat members of the court, government officials, journalists, and court staffers. The area outside it was set up as an alternative public viewing space with over seventy seats and two large video monitors live-streaming the hearing. The area was already at capacity well before the hearing started at 10 a.m. More lawyers, rights activists, NGO staffers, university students, journalists, and citizens – especially inhabitants of some of the neighborhoods closer to the river's mouth, *vecinos* – crowded the adjacent viewing area. Over the course of the next few days, those present at the hearing as well as those following it (outside or through social media) watched as the Supreme Court heard reports from, and asked questions of, federal and local government officials, representatives of private companies, NGOs, and individuals involved with the implementation of *Causa Mendoza*. Based on these interventions and reports from different social and government organizations, the court wanted to ascertain what progress had been made. Anyone following the hearing could not miss the peaceful protests from *vecinos* against some of the measures taken in the context of the implementation of the ruling. They sought to be heard by government officials and the court.

The scene at Palacio de Tribunales that day exemplified two developments: the judicialization of rights enforcement and a tribunal actively following up on compliance with its own decisions. This ruling is part and parcel of a decades-old worldwide trend observable in both young and established democracies whereby courts have become central players and important sites for political battles over the enforcement of rights. In many countries in the Global South, socioeconomic rights are part of democratically enacted legal and constitutional frameworks. Efforts to enforce the right to food, housing, or a clean environment, just to name a few, entail charged political battles about their implementation and about the content of the rights themselves. These battles strike at the heart of democratic quality and involve consequential disputes over power across branches. When deciding on socioeconomic rights, like the Argentine court did in *Causa Mendoza*, courts often face important public policy decisions that pit them against the status quo and can have significant consequences.

Just to name a few examples of similar cases: The Colombian Constitutional court ruled[1] safeguarding the rights to health, water, and food for children of the Wayuu community in the department of La Guajira, asking multiple administrative agencies and the national and local governments to act in coordination to protect this group. The Colombian court, along with the Costa Rican Constitutional Chamber, has jurisprudences in favor of the rights of sexual minorities, including (among many topics) same-sex marriage and decisions requiring access to health and other services for same-sex partners.[2] The Costa Rican court has also ruled protecting aquifers and access to potable water.[3] The Colombian, Indian, and Argentinean tribunals have also ruled favorably for the environmental preservation of rivers and other specially protected areas, which has sometimes meant halting major private and/or governmental development projects or holding governments accountable for redressing complex and long-standing problems. In 2014 the Supreme Court of India – which has an impressive track record as a steward of environmental rights – ordered the national government to create a National Environmental Regulator, with offices in every state, charged with appraising and approving projects for environmental clearances. Climate change has also become judicialized, with tribunals across the Global South increasingly faced with innovative legal challenges that involve governments, private actors, and communities (Rodríguez Garavito 2022).

1 Colombia, Corte Constitucional (2017). T-302 2017. M.P. Aquiles Arrieta.

2 See Albarracín (2022) and López Sánchez (2021).

3 For an overview of the rulings and the judicialization of water disputes in Costa Rica, see Villareal and Wilson (2022).

The hearing I described is also exemplary of a specific development within that broad framework of judicialization: court-promoted monitoring of implementation. Like its counterparts in Colombia, Costa Rica, and India, the Supreme Court of Argentina stayed involved in this and other cases. It did so through the use of a series of institutional tools that I refer to as monitoring mechanisms. Chief among these tools are periodic, multi-actor public hearings (like the one described above) and establishing follow-up committees with the participation of civil society organizations. These committees inform the court on their assessment of implementation and issue periodic information requests to the parties involved, to experts, and to other stakeholders. When embarking on this long process of promoting follow-up, the Supreme Court of Argentina was doing something that challenges traditional notions of what high tribunals do, since we tend to think of them as deciding a case and then stepping back. Through court-promoted monitoring, tribunals attempt to open political spaces for engagement with multiple actors on complex policy issues.

Throughout the Americas, Europe, Africa, and Asia, other courts are facing and deciding major socioeconomic rights cases similar to the ones described above. Are these rulings merely aspirational? Under what conditions can courts in the Global South produce political and social change? More specifically, why do some rulings have higher impact than others? This book tackles these questions, examining the actual results of new court-ordered or court-modified policies as well as other effects of judicial intervention in the aftermath of socioeconomic rights rulings by the Colombian and Argentine highest courts. I highlight the role of two elements in influencing judicial impact: on the one hand, the oversight mechanisms that some high courts deploy to monitor compliance with their structural rulings.[4] And, on the other, the role of organized constituencies in civil society, that is, legally empowered individuals and NGOs doing advocacy work. On their own, both monitoring by the court and civil society engagement can enhance impact. Together, they can produce a particular synergy: the presence of a dense legal constituency that can engage with court-promoted oversight mechanisms can create institutional spaces, which I refer to as collaborative oversight arenas, where the court, elected leaders, private actors, and civil society agents converge to address issues.

I develop this argument through comparative case studies of eight selected structural cases on socioeconomic rights, particularly environmental, health, and social welfare issues. These landmark rulings had the potential to deeply influence public policy, politics, and the lives of many in Colombia and Argentina: Some have been widely studied, which provides us with a wealth of secondary information on

4 Structural rulings are those decisions on public policy of large scope that set forth broad solutions and generally implicate more than one institution in their implementation (Sabel and Simon 2004).

them, and others are less explored. All were decided at least a decade ago, which allows me to track their impact over time. I show that courts are not the silver bullet, rather, they can be coordinating devices that allow for the convergence and the activation of multiple actors. While the primary empirical focus is on these two Latin American countries, the argument can shed light on the experiences of other countries with assertive high courts and a track record of jurisprudence in socio-economic rights. To illustrate this, the book includes shadow case studies of two landmark rulings decided by the Supreme Court of India, the highest court that first deployed oversight mechanisms and that has the most extensive experience with these tools.

1.1 THE ARGUMENT IN BRIEF

This book shows that post-decision politics are crucial, in complex cases, for producing important impacts. I focus on the relevance of two elements in explaining levels of judicial impact in structural cases: monitoring mechanisms and legally empowered civil society organizations. Monitoring mechanisms impose costs on the target(s) of the ruling and they also generate resources so that the court can offset informational and power asymmetries. By requiring reports and information on implementation, court-promoted oversight can promote accountability. Public, institutionalized venues for discussion draw the attention of key related actors to the issue as well the attention of actors beyond those involved originally in the case: the public, other key players, and the media. This monitoring can expose policy and implementation gaps, contributing to what Rodríguez Garavito (2010) calls putting "political pressure" on the targets.

Further, monitoring also helps the court alleviate informational and power asymmetries. Oversight generates public information, which provides the court with expertise – and the authority that comes with it – on specific technical topics. Oversight also produces input to inform the ongoing modification of court-mandated reforms to facilitate compliance and maximize rights effectiveness. These mechanisms offer courts the chance to hear multiple actors and become aware of the broader policy arena as they monitor implementation. Beyond gaining more knowledge of the issue, monitoring also shifts the distribution of power among the relevant actors. The court's presence empowers new players (external oversight agencies, civil society organizations, etc.) by making them part of monitoring venues and giving them a new voice. In so doing, it creates space for the voices of actors that are often excluded from institutional venues.

Importantly, the tools directly under the control of the courts are only part of the story. As previous research on rights litigation shows, courts do not operate in a social or political vacuum. Organized civil society activity can play a significant role in the impact of the ruling before, during, and following the decision (Albisa and Shanor 2017; Epp 1998; Sigal, Rossi, and Morales 2017; Wilson 2009). The question is how? Legal constituencies (the rights advocacy organizations and legal representatives who have a stake in the issue) are crucial in two ways: they are the agents that can exercise follow-up through legal as well as social mobilization, and they are central to the diffusion of rights-based discourse.

On the mobilization side, civil society organizations can work to extend the benefits granted on a given decision to other individuals or groups by filing legal challenges, thus precipitating a judicial cascade of related cases. They also mobilize in other spaces and produce information. Such actions generate media attention and exert pressure on implementing agencies and other governmental powers. On the ideational level, as previous research has shown, legal mobilization by civil society organizations can facilitate the spread of rights rhetoric among activists (McCann 1994), key officials, and other actors. The density of a legal constituency is important to these processes: the denser, the greater its ability to magnify effects and engage with the court. As I discuss in Chapter 2, I characterize the density of the different legal constituencies by looking at the number of active organizations that make up the structure, whether they are connected by preexisting ties (networks), and their funding.

On their own, the presence of court-promoted oversight mechanisms or of legal constituencies can promote some effects. My argument is that together, these two elements can create institutional spaces, which I refer to as collaborative oversight arenas, where the court, elected leaders, private actors, and civil society agents converge to address issues. The participation of external actors in such venues, particularly of legally empowered civil society organizations, is crucial. Where civil society organizations can engage in these institutional spaces we can see greater information flows, and the creation of mechanisms and spaces for accountability, policy updating, and ideational change among bureaucrats and key actors. In short, via the creation of collaborative oversight arenas, courts can become facilitators, focal points, that actors in society can use to coordinate and generate change.

This argument builds on the insights of prior research on judicial impact; some have emphasized the role of tribunals (Rodríguez Garavito and Rodríguez Franco 2010), others that of litigants (Epp 1998) or that of political elites (Rosenberg 2008). I propose an explanation that is aware of the political context but underscores the importance of understanding courts as one of many actors that are all an integral part of ongoing processes of change. Other scholars also study how courts interact with legal advocacy organizations and other branches of government to effect sociopolitical change (Gauri and Brinks 2008; Gloppen 2011). This book contributes to specifying the mechanisms through which judicial intervention produces change. I advance efforts to open up the black box of what happens after litigation (in this case, after a victory in court) by specifying the causal pathways through which court-promoted oversight mechanisms and legal constituencies contribute to impact on their own, and in combination with each other.

1.2 CONTRIBUTIONS

This book makes three main contributions. First, it speaks directly to a long-standing debate that has occupied socio-legal scholars, comparative courts and politics specialists, as well as policymakers and activists worldwide: Can courts effectively advance rights? In line with Rosenberg's (2008) cautious view of the null potential of courts to advance change in the United States, some argue that turning to courts to seek the enforcement of rights is at best ineffectual. For these scholars, judicial intervention can go so far as to exacerbate preexisting inequalities by producing backlash after the decisions or by favoring individualistic, piecemeal, and irrational approaches to public policy (Ferraz 2011; Klarman 2004). Others have a more optimistic assessment of the role for courts in these arenas, claiming that courts can contribute to mobilization (McCann 1994) to spurring negotiations and actions (Cavanagh and Sarat 1980) – and, under certain conditions, to the advancement of the rights in question (Rodríguez Garavito 2010). This book shows that advancing this debate requires thinking about impact in a comprehensive manner and that the answer necessarily involves actors and institutions beyond the judiciary.

I am not alone in emphasizing the importance of a comprehensive understanding of judicial impact beyond strict compliance (see Gloppen 2011; Langford 2021; Rodríguez Garavito and Rodríguez Franco 2015; Rodriguez Peñaranda 2021; Rosenberg, Krishnaswamy, and Bail 2019). As Kapiszewski and Taylor note, impact is broader, neighboring, but distinct from compliance in that it "concerns the effect of court rulings beyond the actions or policy changes that directly result from them" (2013, 5). Efforts to simplify impact often paint partial pictures, as reducing it to rule abidance and policy changes sets aside discursive and symbolic effects that are central to what makes courts powerful: their ability to shift political and social dynamics (Howse and Teitel 2010). With this in mind, I define judicial impact as the changes in the ideational, discursive, legal, organizational, and material realm that are attributable to the court ruling, and the transformation in life outcomes that follow upon these changes. This study shows that observed influence can be varied and often hinges crucially on the ability of the court to work alongside other actors, creating political spaces for discussion, accountability, and change.

Thus, we need to think about impact broadly and we also need to look beyond courts themselves in the production of impact. Courts can be most consequential, broadly speaking, when they act in concert with other actors to create political spaces for ongoing discussion and engagement with regard to rights. Post-decision politics are crucial, in complex cases, for producing important impacts (Botero and Brinks 2023; Langford, Rodríguez Garavito, and Rossi 2017). Seminal work on this subject, like Rosenberg's, tends to assume politics are static – his framework takes for granted that the preferences of political elites will remain unchanged by the processes following judicial victories, for example. Comparative scholars have qualified this view, highlighting the importance of publicity and information after the rulings in fostering accountability and compliance (Gauri, Staton, and Vargas Cullell 2015; Vanberg 2001). My work uncovers the mechanisms that make greater visibility and information work, suggesting that greater impact stems from greater visibility accompanied by more information, resources, and access to the state. It also indicates that the preferences of legal and political elites can be changed through their participation in commonly shared political spaces in the aftermath of the ruling.

Second, by focusing on court-promoted oversight, relatively new and understudied institutions, this research also advances our understanding of the new role for courts in the Global South. Most of our theories assume courts have a fixed set of areas of concern and a fixed set of capabilities. In places like Colombia, Costa Rica, South Africa, and India, courts have been entrusted with new areas of concern, and they have developed (and continue to develop) other capabilities to handle their new responsibilities, in cooperation with civil society and governments. Court-promoted oversight is part of that process, though such tools remain rare among high courts in many of the most studied Global North democracies. I provide an empirical classification scheme for these mechanisms and offer the first systematic small-n comparison of their effects. My research suggests we need to move beyond a view of all courts as holding "neither the purse nor the sword": In the Global South, courts are bringing the purse, the sword, and the sovereign (the people) together to draw attention to long-standing problems and find solutions. In doing so, they do not displace politics, or elected policymakers, they create new political spaces devoted to special problems.

The use of monitoring mechanisms when deciding structural cases at the highest level has implications for how judicial power is constructed and exercised. Theoretically, judicial power has two sides: the capacity for action conferred by institutional design – that is, potential power – and observed influence – or active power (Kapiszewski and Taylor 2013). Studying the impact of judicial rulings, their actual, multifaceted influence, means inquiring into the process by which active power is exercised and enhanced. Court-promoted monitoring is part of a series of tools associated with a dialogical approach to judicial review which tries to foster a different kind of relationship between the judiciary, other branches, and (at times) civil society (Bonilla Maldonado 2013; Gargarella 2014b). Collaborative oversight engages the court, government actors, and civil society in a shared enterprise over a prolonged period of time. In that process, the court works with those involved to craft programs, set deadlines, and produce information. In doing so, these courts are acting as facilitators, without necessarily assuming that they have all the answers. They do not demonize politics or attack the Executive: Even if they do not always get it right, they try to foster exchange in areas that are crucial to public policy.

These courts play what Kureshi (2022) would call a *representation reinforcement role* – creating new avenues for engagement and enhancing existing ones – in contrast to a *representation replacement role*, in which assertive constitutional courts impose their voice as the only truly representative one, thus fueling confrontation between branches. Such conflict is what Huq (2018) refers to as "abrasive contact," a tension between the judiciary and elected branches that has proven instrumental in recent episodes of democratic erosion. The experience of high courts like that of Argentina and Colombia suggests that not all judicial assertiveness must lead to the deterioration of the regime. The way in which these courts exercise judicial power (halfway between passivity in one extreme, and countermajoritarianism in the other) may, in the long run, strengthen democracy and the rule of law. In that sense, the empirical study of monitoring – with its potential, as well as its imperfections – can be particularly useful in the current juncture of democratic backsliding, in which courts are often important players.

Third, and relatedly, the study of the effects of this type of judicial intervention adds an important empirical dimension to a crucial normative debate. Critics often express unease at the idea that a minoritarian non-elected institution decides on and defines the content of and realization of rights, a task usually associated with (and better left to) a representative institution like the legislature (see Tushnet 2008). To Waldron (2005), for example, judicial review on matters of rights tramples on principles like representation and participation and is therefore democratically illegitimate. As others have noted (Brinks and Forbath 2014; Rodríguez Garavito and Rodríguez Franco 2015), this normative discussion benefits greatly from an empirical perspective. As mentioned above, my findings show courts can act as facilitators, catalysts for change, without necessarily imposing their slanted vision or a final answer. Promoting dialogue and cooperation among many and diverse actors, amid institutional weakness, is fraught with difficulties and entails risks (Liebenberg 2014).

Generating and sustaining participative forums for discussion and policy reform exposes the process and the court to political pressures that can derail the original claimants and result in delays that can lead to roadblocks and fatigue, as some cases in this book show. Understanding these dynamics in their full complexity is essential, precisely because courts are being placed in these positions with increasing frequency. Despite the difficulties, what my research suggests is that these courts do not displace democratic politics, or elected policymakers; instead, they can create new political spaces devoted to special problems.

This mode of judicial intervention should alleviate the concerns of those that see judicial decision-making on economic, social, and cultural rights as evidence of a juristocracy bent on advancing the strategic interests of a minoritarian elite (Hirschl 2004) or as faulty enterprise (Gutiérrez Beltrán 2018; Puga 2012). Working with other political and social actors, courts cannot solve all problems or satisfy everyone involved, but they can create change, enhance accountability, and increase responsiveness.

1.3 PLAN AHEAD

I explore these issues in the context of eight rulings (see Table 1.1) handed down by the highest courts in Argentina and Colombia, two tribunals with a history of assertive rights-based jurisprudence. The focus is on major socioeconomic rights cases that address complex public policy questions. This is an area where scholars and practitioners often doubt meaningful change can be made – as such, these cases are great venues to study the politics of impact. The eight rulings cover a range of issues: health, environmental rights, social welfare, and prior consultation. I combine within-case process tracing with cross-case comparisons to enrich the theory-building and the theory-testing exercises. Cross-case comparisons are not risk-free, but when theoretically informed, they can provide rich insights. Each pair of cases (one case from each country) has a different combination of the two elements under study: In the first pair both court-promoted oversight and a dense legal constituency are present, in the second and third pairs only one of them is, and in the fourth pair neither. This case selection strategy, explained in more detail in Chapter 2, allows me to study the particular synergy that court-promoted oversight and dense legal constituencies can produce when together, as well as isolate the effects of monitoring and civil society on their own. Some of these rulings have been widely studied (like *Causa Mendoza*, Verbitsky, and T-760), as they are truly landmark decisions that these two courts have worked with for decades. This allows me to build on rich existing information from a new perspective while comparing these to more understudied rulings (for example, T-231, T-547).

Chapter 2 develops a theory of how court-promoted monitoring and organized legal constituencies in civil society influence impact. Higher levels of impact in particular hinge on the presence of a dense legal constituency that can engage with the institutional spaces that the court creates, crafting "collaborative oversight arenas": spaces in which multiple actors converge in a larger and lengthy process of change. This chapter also introduces the two high courts that are the main focus of this study (the Colombian Constitutional Court and the Supreme Court of Argentina) and the logic that informed the selection of the eight structural rulings I delve into. Chapter 2 looks at the cases with the highest impact of my sample:

TABLE 1.1 *Cases under study and expectations*

	No monitoring	Monitoring
Denser legal constituency	Medium impact [*Causa Verbitsky* and C-383]	Higher impact [*Causa Mendoza* and T-760]
Less dense legal constituency	Lower impact [*Causa Chaco* and T-231]	Medium impact [*Causa Badaro* and T-547]

ruling *T-760*[5] (COL), safeguarding the right to health and calling for a restructuring of the national health system, and *Causa Mendoza*[6] (ARG), safeguarding the right to a clean environment and ordering the government to clean up and preserve the Matanza-Riachuelo River basin. In Chapter 3 I reconstruct and compare the process whereby the actors involved in each of these two rulings crafted a collaborative oversight arena and how their interactions influenced impact. Chapter 4 presents four case studies: two of them have court-promoted monitoring, but no dense legal constituency, and the other two have a dense legal constituency, but no monitoring mechanisms. The aim is to explore in more detail what and how each of the two elements distinctly influences impact. The two cases with legal constituencies are C-383[7] (COL), safeguarding the right to housing through a call to restructure the mortgage credit system in Colombia, and *Causa Verbitsky*[8] (ARG), which sought to safeguard the rights of prisoners in the Buenos Aires Province. In contrast, the two cases with monitoring mechanisms are *T-547*[9] (COL), safeguarding the right to prior consultation in the case of the Puerto Brisa project, and *Causa Badaro*[10] (ARG), safeguarding elderly Argentineans' right to a pension.

In Chapter 5 I compare the (seemingly) negative cases: those where no oversight was deployed and where the legal constituency was not dense. These are *T-231*[11] (COL), safeguarding the right to a healthy environment in Cúcuta by ordering the cleanup of the Bogotá Canal, and *Causa Chaco*,[12] a ruling safeguarding the right to life and health of the Qom Indigenous group, in the Argentinean Chaco. Table 1.1 synthesizes the logic of the comparisons outlined above as well as my initial expectations regarding the impact of each pair of rulings.

Chapter 6 takes the theoretical framework developed in the Latin American context and applies it to two cases decided by the Supreme Court of India: the Right to Food Case and the Delhi Vehicular Pollution Case.[13] Chapter 7 concludes with a comparative overview of the cases, including a discussion of refinements to

5 Colombia, Corte Constitucional (2008, July), "Sentencia T-760," M. P. Cepeda, Manuel José, Bogotá.

6 Argentina, CSJN, M. 1569. XL. "Mendoza, Beatriz Silvia y otros c/ Estado Nacional y otros s/ daños y perjuicios (daños derivados de la contaminación ambiental del Río Matanza – Riachuelo)," 20-6-06; 8-7-08.

7 Colombia, Corte Constitucional (1999, May), "Sentencia C-383," M. P. Beltrán Sierra, Alfredo. Bogotá.

8 Argentina, CSJN, V.856.XXXVIII. "Verbitsky, Horacio s/habeas corpus." 3-6-05.

9 Colombia, Corte Constitucional (2010, July), "Sentencia T-547," M. P. Mendoza Martelo, Gabriel Eduardo. Bogotá.

10 Argentina, CSJN, B.675.XLI. "Badaro, Adolfo Valentín c/ANSeS s/reajustes varios," 8-8-06; 11-26-07.

11 Colombia, Corte Constitucional (1993, June), "Sentencia T-231," M. P. Martinez Caballero, Alejandro. Bogotá.

12 Argentina, CSJN, D.587.XLIII. "Defensor del Pueblo de la Nación c/Estado Nacional y otra (Provincia del Chaco) s/proceso de conocimiento." 9-18-07.

13 India, M.C. Mehta v. Union of India, WP 13029/1985 and India, People's Union for Civil Liberties v. Union of India & Others (PUCL) 2001.

my theory based on the project's findings. In that same chapter, I discuss the book's broader implications: how it showcases the importance of studying impact as collaboration between multiple actors, emphasizing the role of organized civil society and decentering the courts. I also respond to critics of judicial intervention in socioeconomic rights and discuss how and why studying collaborative oversight mechanisms in socioeconomic rights cases is crucial to understanding governance dynamics and the construction of judicial power in the Global South.

2

Coproducing Judicial Impact

When courts tread into social policy areas, particularly rights-based issues, are their rulings merely words on paper? What helps explain different levels of impact? This chapter develops an explanation for the role that court-promoted oversight and civil society actors can play in crafting judicial impact. To do this, I first present a conceptual framework that helps us think about impact as a multidimensional concept. I define judicial impact as the changes in the ideational, discursive, legal, organizational, and material realm that are attributable to the court ruling, and the changes in life outcomes that follow upon these changes. The framework I lay out proposes a way to unify disparate conceptual approaches and has the potential to be applied to the study of a wide range of cases in both substantive and geographical terms. The conceptual discussion is accompanied by examples of specific indicators for my measurement strategy. With that conceptual toolkit in place, I then present the theory.

2.1 CONCEPTUALIZING AND MEASURING JUDICIAL IMPACT

Definitions of judicial impact vary widely. Three different elements are commonly associated with impact in the literature: compliance (whether the actions required by the ruling were carried out), indirect effects (changes in groups and areas beyond the actions directly specified by the ruling, including ideational or symbolic effects), and rights effectiveness (assessments of the ruling's outcomes in terms of actual enjoyment of the right in question for the population of interest). Faced with the complexity of understanding the impact of judicial decisions scholars often choose to focus on one or two of these parts exclusively – yet, any model that simplifies too much yields an incomplete picture. In agreement with others who have worked extensively on the effects of rights-based mobilization (Gauri and Brinks 2008; Gianella-Malca, Gloppen, and Fosse 2013; Landau 2012; Langford 2014b;

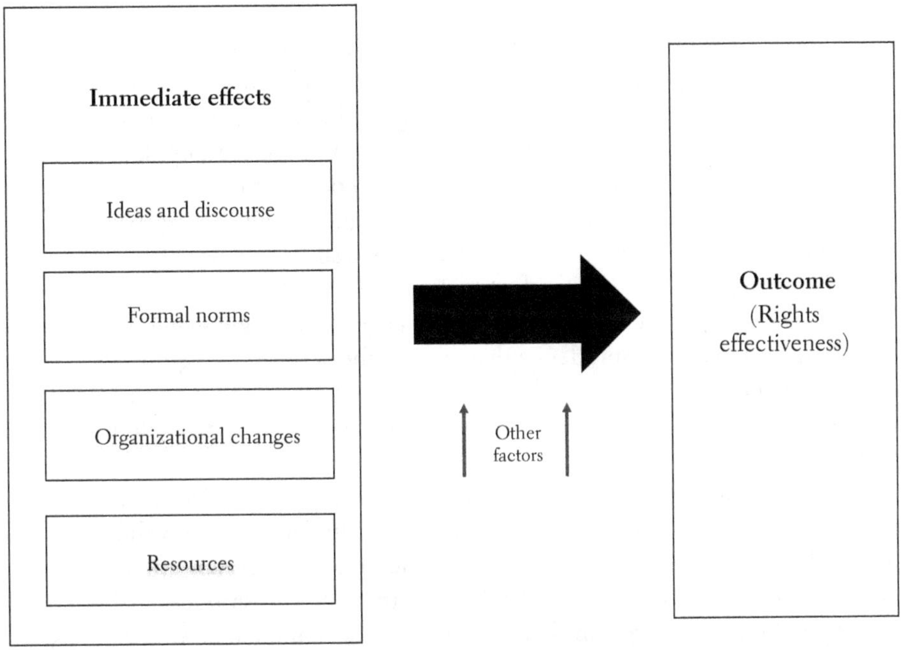

FIGURE 2.1 Conceptual scheme for judicial impact

Merlinsky 2016), my research indicates that we must capture a wider spectrum of effects.

There are two dimensions within impact: *immediate effects* and *outcomes*. Judicial impact is about both the actions taken as a result of a ruling and the changes in ideas and discourse that a ruling may trigger (*immediate effects*) as well as whether these have an effect on the conditions of the target population (*outcomes*). This distinction provides a useful analytical separation between the more proximate effects and the change in terms of rights effectiveness for the population of interest.[1] Within immediate effects are four sub-dimensions that group effects according to the following types: (1) ideas and discourse, (2) formal norms, (3) organizational changes, and (4) resources. Figure 2.1 provides a visualization of the conceptual structure.

Ideational and discursive effects refer to the shared beliefs, normative frameworks, and interpretations about the issue that actors can hold, and how these may change as a result of the ruling. To what extent does the ruling affect the ideas, political discourse, and understanding of the issue among those affected parties related to the case, key decision-makers, and actors beyond those? This category seeks to capture

[1] In specifying two dimensions, my approach builds upon Gloppen (2008, 2011) and Brinks, Gloppen, and Wilson (2012), who focus on stages – although it should be noted that the specific notion of outcomes is absent from their analytical schemes.

effects such as those identified by McCann (1994), who called our attention to the ways in which judicial victories altered women's rights activists' perceptions of the possibility of change and their own understanding of rights entitlement. It also engages with Rodríguez Garavito and Rodríguez Franco's (2015) analysis of the impact of a ruling enforcing the rights of internally displaced populations – they highlight the ways in which judicial intervention modified the ideas of government officials and bureaucrats about rights entitlement and the political relevance of the topic. Interviews with activists and key actors, as well as analyses of relevant news coverage are appropriate ways to identify these types of effects.

Changes to the *formal norms* encompass changes to the legislative and regulatory framework and to the jurisprudence that governs the issue. This requires identifying the relevant changes to the legal framework and relating them to the ruling by looking at records of legislative activities and debates, or through interviews with related actors.

The other kind of formal norms that have interest as part of impact are the judicial pronouncements that build on or expand the ruling under study. How did the ruling change the governing jurisprudence? What other judicial decisions use this ruling as authority to change judge-made law? Note that this jurisprudence should not encompass follow-up litigation that specifically seeks compliance with the original case, unless it is itself creating new law as a result of the original ruling; that type of legal activity is different because it seeks to enforce the ruling itself. Following a term used by Puga (2012), I call these related decisions a "legal cascade"; Nader (2022) refers to them as "irradiating effects," emphasizing that they should be carefully explored in their subnational diversity.

The third sub-dimension, *organizational changes*, captures changes in (or the formation of new) citizen organizations and activist coalitions related to the issue. Although we are likely to observe legal mobilization prior to the ruling itself,[2] a victory in court can promote the larger visibility of the group or coalition, generate incentives for other actors to join in, and result in a qualitatively and quantitatively different type of mobilization after a ruling (McCann 1994). Relevant questions here include: What are the organizations (if any) that mobilized around the issue before and after the ruling? What is their organizational structure broadly speaking and, if there are several of them, how are they connected to each other? What strategies for legal mobilization have they pursued? Interviews with activists are ideal ways to inquire about their tactics, networks, and legal portfolios.

Among the most tangible results of court pronouncements are the financial, human, or informational *resources* that are created or deployed following a court order – these constitute the fourth sub-dimension of immediate effects. Here we should identify the services that were provided, and the resources allocated as a

2 Legal mobilization is defined here as the use of legal norms and resources as a form of political activity by citizens (Zemans 1983).

result of the ruling (or their interruption) and how these changes relate to the ruling. For example, in the case of a ruling that seeks to safeguard access to primary education in a particular city, one can look for evidence of actual allocation of financial resources to primary education programs. Ideally, we should complement this with interview data and/or archival evidence that can link the reallocation of resources with the ruling or concerns spurred by the ruling – in the form of statements by officials in charge, for example.

Aside from material and human resources, rulings can also create and/or make public information on thorny issues and topics that are defined by obscurity and disinformation. Hence, we should also be attentive to information as an important resource that rulings create. This refers not to the evidence that is normally gathered for the strict use of the court during the judicial process, but rather to reports and/or research on the issue that are generated by different actors under the umbrella of the judicial and legal mobilization process. This information can, and usually does, have much wider use. In Chapter 3 I discuss in more detail an example of this dynamic in the case of the *Causa Mendoza* ruling in Argentina. Here, the Supreme Court held government agents and private industries accountable for the environmental recovery and preservation of the Matanza-Riachuelo River Basin. This set in motion the production of large volumes of information on the environmental and human conditions of the area and its inhabitants. This process stands in marked contrast with the previous situation, in which the public was mostly unaware of the problem and its impact on the population.

Together, the four sub-dimensions just reviewed comprise *immediate effects*. The second dimension of impact is the *outcome*, the last and most distant category of effects of a judicial decision. What to include here is necessarily specific to the issue that the ruling under study addresses: In the case of rights-based rulings, the outcome makes specific reference to changes in *rights effectiveness*. Hence, outcomes will, ideally, be assessed using result-type indicators, that is, items that measure the enjoyment or realization of rights. To illustrate, picture a ruling that safeguarded the right to health of the population living with AIDS by guaranteeing access to certain medication. If a researcher were trying to ascertain the effectiveness of this ruling (in terms of its objective to safeguard the right to health) they could look for and discuss data on mortality and morbidity among the relevant population in the years following the ruling. What effectiveness is in this health case is very different from what it looks like in the case of a ruling safeguarding the right to a safe environment for the population alongside a contaminated river. In this second case, the outcome is multidimensional and could include health outcomes for the population, as well as the quality of water and air.

From this conceptual discussion it follows that a measurement strategy for judicial impact entails identifying and assessing what the court mandated and how actors responded. Crucially, however, the researcher must go further into the other dimensions beyond the behavioral outcomes of those compelled by the ruling.

This is a topographical approach to assessing judicial impact, which underscores the importance of an ambitious and careful mapping out of various effects that may well include unintended and negative consequences (Botero and Brinks 2023). Aside from this data collection effort, the researcher needs to make aggregation and scoring choices for the indicators in order to assess impact. When assessing, our job should not be to give a single grade to the ruling (positive impact or negative impact; success or failure) but to fully understand the effects. The scheme I present in this book provides a set of dimensions, or components, that we should be attentive to. Scholars can devise specific scoring and aggregation schemes, if necessary – my measurement strategy is outlined in Appendix A. What is central to this conceptual framework is to assess each of the dimensions on its own – while being mindful of the ways in which they may be related – and to illustrate that this assessment informs the overall conclusion about the effects of the ruling for each of the two stages.

2.1.1 *Distinctive Features of This Conceptualization of Impact*

This conceptual framework builds on traditional conceptions of impact, but goes beyond them, in several ways. First, this two-dimensional structure emphasizes that impact is a process, not a snapshot, one that unfolds over time and cannot be easily reduced to a single static indicator. More specifically, it is akin to what Pierson (2004) calls "slow-moving outcomes" – those processes where meaningful change in the dependent variable occurs over the long term. Its time horizon is not as long-drawn as electoral realignments or demographic changes. Instead, a medium-range time horizon (such as those over which the results of policy reform are assessed) is better suited to fully grasp judicial impact. This means reconstructing the different processes observed in the various stages as they unfold over a given period of time, in a way that is sensitive to the time frame set out by the court, and also, decisively, to the nature of the issue.

Second, and relatedly, in contrast to those who tend to circumscribe impact to compliance, my framework emphasizes the importance of effects beyond policy and regulatory changes. As Kapiszewski and Taylor (2013) note, any existing studies conflate compliance and impact. In his classic book on the effectiveness of judicial intervention on civil rights, abortion, and women's rights in the United States, Rosenberg (2008) works with that kind of understanding. He defines impact as the enactment of social reforms at the national level, in direct response to the court's decisions and affecting large numbers of people. Rosenberg discounts the relevance of ideational effects – whether rulings affect the salience of an issue and/or persuade people and elites to change their positions. For him, these do not matter unless they produce national-level material changes.

My framework goes beyond change conceived only in terms of policy that realizes the letter of the ruling. Effects beyond compliance are meaningful in and of themselves and we observe them even in the absence of compliance with the ruling

(Madlingozi 2014). Additionally, rulings can have more complicated negative effects that could even result in more regressive policies (Klarman 2004; Rodriguez Peñaranda, Jimenez Estevez, and León Peñuela 2021; Rosenberg 2008; but see also Keck 2009). Disregarding any of these can be misleading. We need a framework that can capture the variant directionalities rulings can take. Furthermore, research has shown that there may be connections (feedback loops, reinforcements) between different types of effects. In short, compliance is a part of impact, but it is not *equivalent* to it by itself.

The framework presented here does not circumscribe impact to compliance but neither does it circumscribe impact to symbolic effects and to the constitutive effects of rulings and the law. Instead, I follow work that seeks to build a common ground between conceptualizations that focus on compliance (Langford et al. 2014; Rodriguez Peñaranda, Jimenez Estevez, and León Peñuela 2021; Rosenberg, Krishnaswamy, and Bail 2019) and those, like McCann's (1994), that underscore symbolic or ideational changes exclusively. In his study of women's social struggle for equal remuneration in the workplace, McCann (1994) showed that judicial victories prompted a process that changed activists' understanding of their conditions, increased issue salience, and were used as symbolic resources to promote the cause and fuel organizational and mobilization efforts. My conceptualization assumes that symbolic and ideational effects can be assessed, just as we can assess changes to the legislative framework or to the resources devoted to an issue.

Furthermore, this framework recognizes explicitly (and my analysis shows) that the different dimensions of impact can be connected among themselves. For instance, legal mobilization that comes in the wake of a ruling can expand ideational effects by changing the way other litigants view the issue and moving them to action (McCann 1994); it can create new alliances and give voice and power to activists in new institutional spaces (Dugard 2022). Sometimes decisions to mobilize resources come from ideational changes, sometimes from changes to formal norms. This list is illustrative, but it is in no way finite: Connections between sub-dimensions of immediate effects (that is, between ideational effects, organizational changes, formal norms, and resources) are multiple, recursive, and contingent. The relationships among these sub-dimensions cannot always be specified a priori, and the empirical boundaries between them are not always clear-cut. But the relationships exist and need to be explored.

More broadly, the two stages within impact are connected. Carrying out the changes ordered by the ruling can be linked to changes in the effective enjoyment of the right, or its denial. For example, the *Defensor del Pueblo v. Chaco* (Chaco) decision by the Supreme Court of Argentina (discussed in detail in Chapter 5) sought to protect the rights to life and health of the Qom Indigenous people in the Chaco Province in the face of a severe humanitarian crisis. The court's decision resulted in the devolution of monetary resources and governmental programs to the area, which represented an improvement in some aspects of the basic living conditions of those affected. Aside from that, effects beyond actions taken to comply with the ruling can also be linked to rights effectiveness: For instance, legal mobilization can change the way government officials make policy decisions. This was the case with the *Grootboom* ruling in which the Constitutional Court of South Africa found the national housing policy did not guarantee the right to access housing for the more vulnerable in society. According to Langford and Kahanovitz (2017) the decision "Grootboom-proofed" social policy. They show that leading senior officials at the national and local levels became more attentive to progress in their respective agendas to avoid similar litigation and that they also made policy decisions, such as budgeting, with *Grootboom* guidelines in mind.

2.2 CAUSATION

Exploring connections between the different dimensions of impact brings to the fore a crucial issue to the study of impact: causation. To some, this is indeed the most challenging aspect of studying judicial impact. In bringing causality to the fore, I may appear to run counter to interpretivists, and particularly McCann (1996), who forcefully criticized overly simplistic linear conceptions of causality for offering little insight into the complex contexts and relationships that shape social action and people's understanding of themselves and their social world. However, even McCann (1996), who carefully avoids the use of the word causal, uncovers rich evidence of the ways in which law (as well as rulings as part of law) influences and shapes sociopolitical outcomes within carefully constructed case studies. We benefit from spelling out the causal, and often complex, links between effects. As Goertz (2006) highlights, it is actually common that causal arguments are embedded, but not really explicated, in the concepts that social scientists use to analyze phenomena. I rely on the logic of within-case causal inference using process tracing to claim that there is a common ground on which to study impact, using a comprehensive framework that can accommodate the insights of both interpretivists like McCann and positivists like Rosenberg.

Within-case analysis is ideally poised to unpack the black box of the causal mechanisms through which judicial rulings influence sociopolitical processes. I am not the first to offer an integrative framework (see Brinks, Gloppen, and Wilson 2012; Gloppen 2011; Rodríguez Garavito and Rodríguez Franco 2015; Rodriguez Peñaranda 2021), but I am making explicit the causal debate and the temporal dimension, which can help us overcome some of the difficulties we face in building a common language to talk about judicial impact. Because concepts are at heart theory, being explicit about the structure of our concepts and the causal links helps us to be clear about how our theories work.

Importantly, I do not claim that the effective enjoyment of any right is solely dependent upon judicial intervention. Many other factors can determine the extent to which a right is actually realized for any particular population – judicial intervention in the form of a court ruling is one among many possibilities. This conceptualization simply highlights the pathways through which this particular influence can occur.

Of course, a trade-off of a comprehensive conceptualization is that its complexity can appear overwhelming. However, although the long-term causal implications of rulings tend to be complex and multidimensional and "[u]npacking these causal dynamics can be difficult, (...) the alternative is to accept an overly simple set of causal attributions" (Keck 2009, 156). From that perspective, working with narrow definitions of impact, particularly with definitions of impact that discount ideational effects or organizational changes or that define them too narrowly, leaves out important parts of the story. Taking a deep dive into the different potential effects of a ruling is the only way to fully understand the ways in which it can effect change.

2.3 BEYOND DIRECT AND INDIRECT EFFECTS

It is also worth noting that this conceptualization of impact does not hinge on whether the effects of a ruling are *direct* or *indirect*; rather, it places the emphasis on the realms where we might observe change, or lack of it, in general. Although the distinction I propose between immediate effects and outcomes may not appear intuitive to everyone, I favor it because the most common alternative – to distinguish between direct and indirect effects – can be theoretically confusing and difficult to implement. The direct/indirect distinction rests on the notion that judicial rulings provide specific orders and remedies and that as a result, we may clearly distinguish between actions that are required by the ruling (and of whom) from those that are indirect by-products. This distinction is sometimes difficult to maintain when conducting empirical analysis, since vagueness in judicial decisions is not that uncommon and may be deliberate (Staton and Vanberg 2008). Furthermore, it is a distinction that is rooted in the logic of focusing on compliance with the ruling. Ideational effects and organizational changes are just as possible to trace back to the ruling as policy changes or actions that are specified in the decision.

Additionally, newer trends in the type of remedies handed down by courts deciding socioeconomic rights cases further blur the direct/indirect distinction, as these decisions move away from specifying actions and targets. Domestic courts in India, Africa, and Latin America hand down rulings that make use of a wide variety of remedies falling anywhere between the traditional command and control model all the way to upholding an abstract right while leaving the targets to decide specifically how to address the rights violation (or omission) and implement the decision (Abramovich 2005; Dixon 2007; Tushnet 2008). Drawing sharp lines that distinguish which orders apply specifically to whom is not always feasible, nor does it always provide a useful classification scheme. What the ruling orders is usually a necessary and useful starting point in the discussion, but as laid out above, impact goes beyond these terms. Focusing on broadly defined areas allows us to cast a wider net and makes possible comparisons across different types of rulings, while accommodating the different processes that previous scholarship has outlined.

The conceptual framework I just laid out is the basic assessment tool I use to measure what impact each of the rulings I study in this book had. The following section lays out my argument for what elements influence impact in structural cases, with special emphasis on the role of monitoring mechanisms and legally empowered organizations in civil society.

2.4 EXPLAINING JUDICIAL IMPACT

The literature about judicial impact has two main shortcomings. First, a reductionist view of impact that often paints a partial picture of what is actually a multidimensional phenomenon that unfolds over time. The previous section presented my conceptual approach to judicial impact and outlined the benefits of a systemic framework that captures the multidimensionality of the phenomenon and its temporality, thus addressing the first of these limitations. Second, there is often a failure to take seriously the politics of compliance and judicial impact. When explaining and assessing impact, scholars often focus on a snapshot moment after the decision, which disregards how the processes following rulings may alter the landscape. Together with other more recent work that highlights the importance of politics after the ruling (Cano Blandón 2017; Langford, Rodríguez Garavito, and Rossi 2017), this book helps to tease out the mechanisms that can increase or hinder impact and the process through which it is produced, by multiple actors.

Existing explanations of judicial impact tend to focus on one of three different elements: the court's agency, the role of litigants, or the electoral incentives of elites. Court-centered approaches focus on tribunals as the agents driving change. Such arguments tend to portray the judiciary as either remarkably powerful or largely ineffectual. The more optimistic scholars in this camp see courts as ideally suited to foster deliberation (Rodríguez Garavito 2010). Those at the other end of the spectrum emphasize the non-representativeness of courts, their tendency to focus on the facts of individual cases before them and their insulation. These arguments tend to portray judicial intervention in a more negative light. For them, institutional features ill-equip courts for consequential policymaking (Ferraz 2011) or lead them to make decisions that, in outpacing or contradicting public opinion, generate a counterproductive negative political backlash (Klarman 2004). In choosing to emphasize the elements under the court's purview, these approaches downplay the importance of the coalitions that can build around the court and work with it to magnify effects.[3] Research on rights-based litigation has shown the crucial role that social organizations play in redefining issues, as well as political and legislative agendas.

[3] An exception to this is Klarman's (2004) work.

Litigant-centered explanations do pick up on the importance of civil society actors outside the court. These explanations focus primarily on the role of legally empowered social organizations in securing the decisions, guaranteeing their implementation (see Epp 1998) or promoting other effects. Although civil society actors are a fundamental part of the story because of their role in diffusing effects and mobilizing to follow-up on courts' decisions, arguments that focus exclusively on litigants also paint a partial picture. Actual implementation and impact cannot be secured through the presence of an organized social constituency alone: Their mobilization is not enough to shift the status quo, and although important, it may be muted by other powerful actors. Organized civil society actors are more often than not, by definition, outside or on the fringes of the institutional spaces where decisions are made. Civil society actors need access and leverage to get there (Gonzalez-Ocantos 2016; Sabel and Simon 2004). Also, their work needs to be understood in its institutional and political contexts, which determine the ease of access and the possibilities (Wilson and Rodríguez Cordero 2006). I bridge insights from court-centered and litigant-centered approaches by examining how the deployment of monitoring mechanisms can create political spaces – which I refer to as collaborative oversight arenas – where different actors converge to create change. As I will show, in such settings, civil society organizations, government control agencies, the court, and those who have to implement the decision are involved in oversight of the process for a lengthy period of time.

Finally, politically centered arguments for judicial impact contend that rulings on social policy will be "hollow hopes" unless there is a favorably disposed governmental elite for which implementing the ruling is electorally profitable (Rosenberg 2008). Self-interested political motives and realpolitik are presented as insurmountable obstacles to the realization of rights (Hirschl and Rosevear 2011). On a basic level, elite political support is not a necessary condition across the board. A notable example is the TAC case in South Africa,[4] which was successfully implemented despite the Court's ruling directly defying the government's policy prescription. Furthermore, elites are not monolithic, and bureaucrats or powerful agents in the executive or congress may well benefit from or agree with a court's intervention and act in its support. We need to be aware of ruling actors' political incentives and how these affect the process. However, in overemphasizing their electoral incentives, their logic mistakenly assumes that those are the only incentives that matter and that preferences, or calculations, cannot change.

In other words, most politically centered approaches assume politics are static. Comparative scholars have qualified this view, highlighting the importance of visibility, mobilization, and information after the rulings in fostering accountability

4 In this case, South Africa's Constitutional Court affirmed a lower court decision ordering the government to ensure HIV-positive pregnant women access to drugs preventing mother-to-child transmission.

and compliance (Cano Blandón 2017; Gauri, Staton, and Vargas Cullell 2015; Nader 2022; Vanberg 2001). My work suggests that greater impact stems from greater visibility accompanied by more information, resources, and access to the state; it also indicates that the preferences of legal and political elites can be changed through their participation in commonly shared political spaces in the aftermath of the ruling. This book shows that post-decision politics are crucial, in complex cases, for producing important impacts. My argument is that monitoring mechanisms and the presence of a vibrant and legally empowered legal constituency can both influence these post-decision dynamics. Let us see how.

2.5 THE ARGUMENT

2.5.1 *The Role of Monitoring Mechanisms*

Court-promoted monitoring mechanisms are key to my explanation. As I discuss in more detail in the following pages, deploying monitoring mechanisms allows courts (and other participants in monitoring venues, if they are present) to impose costs on the targets of the rulings and also to offset information and power asymmetries. Oversight mechanisms are relatively new to the toolkits of high courts around the world; as a result, there is much that remains to be explored about their features and how they work.

The lack of monitoring mechanisms was highlighted as problematic by early studies of judicial impact on social policy in the United States which, not surprisingly, flagged courts' inadequacy to serve as forums for consequential decision-making (Horowitz 1977). However, this view grew out of the American experience and is not always accurate for that country (Cavanagh and Sarat 1980), much less in other settings. In the context of increased judicial activism in the sphere of socio-economic rights, high courts in countries like Argentina, Colombia, Costa Rica, and India have turned to deploying novel institutional mechanisms through which they monitor compliance with their rulings. Once the ruling is handed down, these courts may initiate sustained monitoring efforts over time through information requests, public follow-up hearings, and the creation of follow-up commissions involving all parties with a stake in the process: the targets of the decision, government units, and civil society organizations.

The use of monitoring mechanisms by these courts was initially seen by some as a way to overcome states' institutional weaknesses and coordination problems while respecting the separation of powers and providing legitimacy to the judiciary's intervention (Bergallo 2006). One of the earliest empirical studies contends that when courts make use of monitoring mechanisms, they can function as forums for discussion in which, via a dialogic, collective decision-making process, all actors with a stake in the ruling reach consensus and thus build a binding solution (Rodríguez Garavito and Rodríguez Franco 2015). More recently, Cano Blandón (2017), Moog (2019), Nader (2022), and Rosenberg et al. (2019) suggest that monitoring has a positive influence on implementation. Landau's (2012) assessment is more tempered, though he concedes that when compared to individual litigation which tends to favor the middle classes, this kind of ruling can potentially benefit the poor. For others, the use of oversight mechanisms is a trap that legitimizes governmental pronouncements but fails to improve the lives of those it should benefit, leaving the most vulnerable worse off (Baviskar 2012; Puga 2012) and generating little by way of actual change (Gargarella 2014a).

Taken together, these studies shed some light on the potential effects of oversight in structural cases, but they reach apparently contradictory conclusions. These contradictory conclusions are in my view a function of two problems shared by both camps. First, the majority of these are single case studies. As a result, it is difficult to extract comparative lessons that might travel across different contexts, legal and policy issues. Second, confusion is compounded in no small part by the use of different yardsticks when measuring and assessing impact. To my knowledge, this study is the first to conduct a systematic small-n case study comparison across issue areas.

Beyond research design and measurement, however, an additional difficulty with studies of impact is that many tend to assume all monitoring is equal (but see Cano Blandón 2017; Moog 2019). Scholars who research monitoring mechanisms identify their presence based on the text of the rulings and assume from the text that they have been deployed. The literature thus provides a very narrow and empirically unsatisfactory understanding of monitoring mechanisms. An important exception to the dearth of work in this area is Cano Blandón's (2017) work on the implementation of rulings on the right to water by the Colombian Constitutional Court, in which she carefully documents and evaluates the effects of different new and experimental tools that this tribunal makes use of, including monitoring. In reality, courts can draw on a variety of monitoring tools (formal and informal) and the extent to which they make use of them matters. In what follows I will present a more complex conceptualization of monitoring mechanisms, classifying them according to the degree to which they reflect an institutionalization of monitoring. This will allow me to make theoretical distinctions from the deployment of these tools and to evaluate whether they play out when discussing cases.

We can think of different monitoring mechanisms as if they were located along a continuum of degree of institutionalization (see Figure 2.2): On the left-hand extreme is the most basic form of monitoring which is the court requesting to be informed about measures taken to comply with its decision through reports. Requesting that the target of the ruling reports back to the court following certain types of rulings is not uncommon, particularly for writs of protection like amparos and tutelas.[5] Merely requiring a report in a ruling is not a strong indicator of monitoring.

5 Amparo and tutela are roughly equivalent legal mechanisms designed to provide a relatively quick way for citizens or groups of citizens to seek legal redress when they feel that a constitutional right has been violated.

FIGURE 2.2 Court-promoted monitoring

If the report is simply filed away to gather dust, reporting is just a formality that does not trigger the back-and-forth exercise required of active monitoring. Processing reports requires individuals inside the court charged with studying them to follow up with those who produce them.

Moving further to the right of Figure 2.2 we see other instances of monitoring, like public hearings, where the court holds public hearings to request information and progress updates from all parties involved. On the right-hand side, we would also find the appointment of special bureaucrats by the court, individuals whose job is to coordinate and liaison between the tribunal and different external actors – this is roughly the job description of commissioners in India, for example. Their exact placement along this continuum likely depends on the extent of the mandate given to them by the high court, as well as who is appointed (as leadership qualities can make a significant difference).

On the right-most end of the continuum seen in Figure 2.2 is the mechanism that is most complex and requires greater engagement from the court and from all involved: the configuration of what I call a *collaborative oversight arena*. This is a space where civil society organizations, government control agencies, the court, and the targets of the decision participate in the oversight process over an extended period of time. I refer to it as a collaborative oversight arena because it involves all actors interacting in a space that encompasses several monitoring institutions: public follow-up hearings in the court, the periodic production and processing of compliance reports, and a follow-up commission. In this book we will see examples of collaborative oversight arenas in Colombia, Argentina, and India – I say more about their configuration further ahead.

Equipped with a more nuanced sense of what monitoring might look like empirically, we are better positioned to theorize how it works. How does court-promoted oversight work, at its most basic level? Monitoring exerts influence on impact through two mechanisms: It imposes costs on the target(s) of the ruling and generates resources so that the court can offset informational and power asymmetries. First, in terms of imposing costs: By requiring reports and information on implementation, as well as by setting deadlines, and doing so publicly, court-promoted oversight furnishes some incentives for compliance and promotes other effects (Gauri, Staton, and Vargas Cullell 2015). Public, institutionalized venues for discussion extract information from the target(s) and draw the attention of key related actors to the issue – and, also, of actors beyond those involved originally in the case: the public, other key players, and the media. This monitoring can expose policy and implementation gaps, contributing to what Rodríguez Garavito (2010) calls putting "political pressure" on the targets.

Second, monitoring also helps the court alleviate informational and power asymmetries. Oversight generates information, which both provides the court with expertise – and the authority that comes with it – on specific technical topics and produces input to inform the ongoing modification of court-mandated reforms. Through oversight the court can hear multiple actors, including policy experts, and become aware of the broader policy arena as it monitors the development of the ruling. Oversight generates information but it is also about power: granting external actors some power through access but, also, influencing the court's own power in the long run. Judicial intervention can tip the balance in favor of change in a particular issue area, by giving visibility and weight to the issue (Langford 2014a; Sturm 1990) and to specific groups of actors, including claimants, or disadvantaged beneficiaries. At the same time, as Staton (2010) has shown, when judges provide more information and raise the public's awareness about rulings (inevitable in the context of monitoring), this transparency is a way for them to expand – within institutional and political constraints – the boundaries of their own power.

Imposing costs and generating resources to offset asymmetries are sometimes closely intertwined and can be mutually reinforcing. I separate them for analytical clarity, but in reality, we may often see them acting together. In either case, or in both, courts that actively deploy court-promoted monitoring mechanisms are making use of tools and acquiring new resources that shows they are willing (to different degrees) to engage with and receive input from multiple external sources.

The previous discussion summarizes what court-promoted monitoring mechanisms can bring to the table. In specifying the mechanisms through which court-promoted monitoring works, my research builds on and expands the work of Rodríguez Garavito (2010), who provided an essential first look at these institutions (but see Cano Blandón 2017). However, the tools directly under control of the courts are only part of the story. Civil society activity before, during, and following the decision can play a significant role in the impact of the ruling (Albisa and Shanor 2017; Bryerley 2019; Cano Blandón 2017; Epp 1998; Sigal, Rossi, and Morales 2017; Wilson 2011).

2.5.2 *The Role of Legal Constituencies*

I define a legal constituency as the rights advocacy organizations and legal representatives who have a stake in the issue the court decides on. I am concerned with the role that these organizations can play after the rulings have been handed down to influence impact, and, particularly when monitoring mechanisms are present, with their ability to engage with these. Legal constituencies are crucial because they are the agents that can exercise legal follow-up and mobilize around the issue.[6] Legal constituencies, like Epp's (1998) "support structures," are usually made up of a cluster or network of several organizations. Epp (1998) focuses on the role of legal organizations in getting cases before high courts that are not easily accessible and therefore emphasizes the centrality of funding to determine their presence or absence. His logic is that generous funding is necessary to see through long strategic litigation campaigns. However, generous funding is not a necessary condition where high courts are more easily accessible. More specifically, funding is not the only condition that determines whether a group of organizations can furnish some support.

There are numerous ways to assess and evaluate social movement organizations. The literature is too vast to review here, but some key perspectives are: Some scholars focus on resources, others on power, others on their structure, and yet others on the environment in which organizations operate to understand their effects and effectiveness (see McAdam and Scott 2005 for an overview). To characterize legal constituencies, I focus on their *density*, that is, a group of characteristics that influence the extent to which a group of organizations can mobilize in and outside institutional spaces to advocate for a particular issue following a court victory. Density has important consequences: The denser the legal constituency, the greater its ability to magnify effects by itself and engage with the court, if monitoring mechanisms are present.

To assess a legal constituency's density we can look at the number of active organizations working together, whether they have preexisting ties (networks), and their funding situation. My understanding of density thus has elements that the literature on resource mobilization has identified as crucial (organizations' human and material resources) and combines them with a focus on how these organizations interact with each other, their networks – a dimension to which the organizational literature on social movement has paid more attention to (Robertson 2011). Table 2.1 lists the relevant dimensions of legal constituencies, their properties, and provides examples of the indicators used in this project to assess them.

The *number of organizations* that form the structure provides information on the size of the constituency and hints at a constituency that can draw on increasingly varied resources (human as well as financial) to work on the case. Whether there were preexisting *networks* among some of these organizations is of interest for two reasons: To begin with, seasoned, repeat players have important advantages in navigating the judicial system (Galanter 1974). Furthermore, when social organizations operating in a common field are well connected and organized, they can more effectively engage with and negotiate with the state and private actors (Robertson 2011). Finally, I look at *funding* as an indicator of resources.

[6] This notion is closely related to Epp's (1998) support structures (which he defines as "rights-advocacy organizations and rights-advocacy lawyers organizing to exercise deliberate and strategic litigation efforts") but I am interested in capturing a fuller range of variation.

TABLE 2.1 *Characterizing legal constituencies*

Characteristics of rights advocacy organizations	Rationale for inclusion	Indicators
Number of organizations (those litigating, filing amicus "support" briefs, but also those participating in implementation, monitoring venues)	Legal constituencies that are more numerous suggest a wider constituency and the potential to draw on more resources (of different varieties) to advance their efforts.	A basic count of the number of organizations that make up the legal constituency. The cases I study (different rulings in Colombia and Argentina), for example, fall between zero organizations involved and fifteen.
What, if any, is the **network** of relationships between participating organizations?	This is a categorical indicator that indicates whether these organizations had preexisting ties (that is, experience working together) before this joint venture. Seasoned, connected, "repeat" players (Galanter 1974) have important advantages. Networked organizations can better respond to and negotiate with external actors, particularly the state.	Self-reported coordinating meetings or organizations identified through interviews and secondary sources. ("No" indicates a less dense legal constituency. "Yes" indicates a denser legal constituency.)
Funding	This tells us whether NGOs have outside funding (governmental or otherwise) for the legal advocacy activities related to monitoring and implementation.	The existence of funding for the organizations was identified through interviews and secondary sources. (Yes/No.[7])

I put together information on the number of organizations with an interest in the ruling, the preexisting networks between them, and their funding to characterize the **density** of a given legal constituency. A denser, interconnected, and generously funded cluster of organizations is better poised to actively participate in policy discussions, negotiations, and in monitoring implementation of high court decisions. But, even one legal advocacy organization or a small cluster of lawyers can at least use a victory in court to pursue related litigation strategies with other similarly

7 Funding is not a dichotomous variable. I dichotomize this indicator, regardless, because I am interested in a rough indicator of external support, in general: Are resources being funneled to one or some of the organizations that are a part of the legal constituency? When there is a dearth of funding (not uncommon in some cases), it is usually easily identifiable. Nuances and variations are discussed in the case studies, where applicable.

situated groups, create information on the issue, or respond to occasional requests for information from the court on that particular case. A tightly knit network of experienced actors can still make a difference even in the absence of adequate funding – although they can only go so far.

Capturing variation when studying the relevant legally empowered actors in civil society is helpful to better disentangle the close relationship that may exist between these organizations and a legal victory in the first place. It is often the case, particularly when studying structural rulings (although this is true with individual litigation as well), that we are likely to observe legal mobilization prior to the ruling itself. Yes, these rulings do not come out of thin air – there are usually one or two organizations related to the case. However, the fact that there was some level of prior organization does not mean (a) that all types of organization are equal or (b) that we cannot ascertain the extent to which legal intervention (the victory in court and the deployment of oversight mechanisms) may have an effect on the legal constituency itself – what I call *mobilization effects*. The ruling can promote the legal constituency's larger visibility, generate incentives for other actors to join in, and result in a qualitatively and quantitatively different type of mobilization after a ruling (McCann 1996; Bryerley 2019). Careful process tracing allows us to distinguish mobilization before the ruling from what happens afterward.

How can legal constituencies influence impact? Legal constituencies can have an influence on the impact a ruling has through two mechanisms: mobilization and spurring ideational change. Mobilization is an umbrella term that can encompass many different strategies. Legal mobilization, for example, is often one among a broad repertoire of strategies pursued by civil society organizations (Langford 2014a) when trying to advance an issue. Mobilization through the legal system can precipitate a cascade of related cases and decisions. As mentioned in Chapter 1, legal challenges that draw inspiration from a given ruling are distinct from those that seek to guarantee the implementation of the original victory. When I use the term legal cascade in this book, I refer specifically to rulings that seek to widen the limits of the original ruling or extend benefits to new, distinct populations. Aside from working in the legal sphere, legal constituencies can also engage in political mobilizations like awareness-raising activities, lobbying, as well as participation in rallies and events (among others). Political and/or legal advocacy can generate visibility and resources, including significant amounts of information about the issue.

Mobilization by civil society organizations that are part of the legal constituency can play an important role in generating media attention and exerting pressure on implementing agencies and other governmental powers. Ultimately, such action can contribute to greater accountability, that is, making responsible parties answerable for their behavior. Mobilization is, more specifically, part of what Peruzzotti and Smulovitz (2006) call "social accountability." According to the authors, public exposure of actions, or inactions, by social organizations can put the issue in the public agenda thus raising the symbolic costs, possibly forcing action, and even raising actual costs.

A second mechanism through which legal constituencies can increase impact, as previous research has shown, is by facilitating the spread of rights rhetoric among activists themselves (McCann 1994) and among key officials and other relevant actors (Keck 2009). Overall, legally empowered civil society organizations can be crucial to the creation of new understandings of rights that are further enforced through their mobilization efforts (Siegel 2006).

Clearly legal constituencies can play key roles. Discussing their capacities raises the issue of endogeneity: Is it the case that only where there is already a dense legal constituency a court deploys oversight mechanisms because it knows that it has the support of that constituency? Empirically, that is not the case: We observe oversight mechanisms in cases with low-density legal constituencies, like two of the rulings under study in this project (T-547 on prior consultation and *Causa Badaro* on pensions). The research in this book and other work confirms that the two can be related along the lines sketched in previous paragraphs, namely, a victory in court can foster the growth of a particular movement. Theoretically, this issue asks us to consider the motivations driving judges' decision to monitor, which I discuss in more detail later in this chapter.

2.5.3 *Collaborative Oversight Arenas*

On their own, the presence of court-promoted oversight mechanisms or of legal constituencies can promote some effects, as I outlined previously. My argument is that combined, they can configure a collaborative oversight arena and ultimately yield higher impact results. What is the value added that collaborative oversight arenas can produce? And through what mechanisms?

Collaborative oversight arenas can create unique synergies and feedback loops that can magnify the effects monitoring which legal constituencies promote on their own. First, they can further enhance the creation and flow of information. The deployment of court-promoted oversight mechanisms (particularly the use of monitoring mechanisms that entail greater engagement from the court) is often associated with the production of more information on the issue and with information on the attainment of the objectives set out by the court. When there is a dense legal constituency that the court can engage with, it can use this information, combine it with its own, reproduce it, and magnify it to wider audiences. The participation of multiple actors in public venues like these also increases the visibility of the issue in other arenas like the media and among similarly situated actors outside the ruling. Creating a supervised process for compliance generates the conditions for keeping the case in the public eye providing the media information that both highlights the problems created by the violation and hopefully creates pressure for the Executive and bureaucracy to solve them.

Second, the creation of a collaborative oversight arena opens more points of access to the state for external actors concerned, particularly the legal constituency, which can trigger a number of processes. On the one hand, more access to the state facilitates accountability. Mobilization by civil society organizations, on its own, creates political pressure and information. Peruzzotti and Smulovitz (2006) viewed this kind of mobilization as part of social accountability, as I mentioned. A collaborative oversight arena facilitates and magnifies this accountability work as it brings closer institutional and non-institutional accountability agents: oversight agencies and judiciary together with civil society organizations. Some government oversight agencies can also impose their own sanctions (or bring to bear other formal relevant procedures), which can incentivize compliance.

Sustained access to the state and to other parties also gives civil society organizations (of all stripes) new channels to diffuse their work, and to discuss and introduce their own policy ideas and proposals. This creates the opportunity for synergies among different actors. A particularly important kind of synergy is that oversight mechanisms create the opportunity for legal constituencies to provide feedback on the implementation of the ruling and, occasionally, on the policy itself. In the process, at minimum, multiple actors are providing the court with information that will allow it to tweak policy as it is being produced and implemented.

By enhancing access to the court and to the state, collaborative oversight arenas can also shift the distribution of power among the relevant actors. The court comes in as a new actor that all players must reckon with. In turn, its presence empowers new players (external oversight agencies, civil society organizations) by making them part of monitoring venues and giving them a voice and new roles. The court creates spaces where civil society organizations can develop what Andreassen and Crawford (2013), building on Lukes, refer to as "power with." Namely, alternative sources of power (via networking and alliances) that enhance their capacity to meaningfully engage with institutional actors. These spaces can give weight to the actions and voices of actors that are often excluded from institutional venues.

Third, collaborative monitoring can also contribute to the spread of ideational effects both within the actors linked to the ruling as well as to other circles: with actors not directly involved in the ruling but crucial to its implementation and outcome. As for those actors directly involved in the ruling, the meetings, public hearings, and networks that are generated in the context of oversight create institutional spaces in which they come together. These sustained interactions can alter the normative orientations, the taken-for-granted assumptions, values, attitudes, and collectively shared expectations about problems and their solutions, for litigants, their representatives, and for government agents and policymakers (Langford 2014a).

Collaborative oversight arenas can also generate the conditions for sustaining a protracted interactive process that can contribute to the effective diffusion of policy ideas and new cognitive paradigms among governmental actors (Stone 2000). These interactions can help diffuse the rights-based framework among those charged with designing policy and implementation.

Ideational effects of this sort are not inconsequential. When it comes to substantially altering the way things are done in a particular policy area in order to ensure higher levels of rights effectiveness, it is essential to get decision-makers and government officials to consider new policy ideas or to incorporate rights-based considerations in their bureaucratic decision-making and in their cognitive frameworks. Eventually, this can change the very politics of an issue, so that courts are no longer needed to put and keep the issue on the policy agenda. In short, a collaborative oversight arena substantially reshapes the incentive structure facing the targets of a court order, empowers the claimants to monitor compliance, and broadcasts their concerns to the population at large, thus offering a powerful additional tool to social actors seeking to produce social change through litigation.

All in all, collaborative oversight arenas create institutional spaces for the interaction of very diverse actors around multifaceted and complex public policy issues. They can bring together different issue-specific social organizations while also opening up spaces for the interaction of these organizations with state agents that usually function in the context of a fragmented state. In the context of collaborative oversight arenas, diverse actors generate (or at least debate) a common discourse, debate policy ideas and programs. In doing this, the court functions more as a device that facilitates coordination than as the sole agent of change.

None of this is to suggest that collaborative oversight arenas are silver bullets. At the same time that collaborative monitoring opens spaces for higher levels of impact, the creation of these spaces also generates openings for added political pressures and fatigue. Depending on how monitoring is designed, many external actors can potentially gain access to the court. Creating and sustaining participatory oversight processes over long periods of time subjects the court and participants to pressures from outside actors that can easily result in roadblocks, or corruption. More generally, the nature of the process is prone to generating fatigue which can derail the court and the monitoring process from the original claims. Our assessments need to be sensitive to unintended consequences and to the subtleties of these processes as well.

2.6 RESEARCH STRATEGY

This book develops this argument and illustrates it through in-depth case studies of four rulings from Argentina and four from Colombia (see Table 2.2). My aim is theory building and unpacking of the causal mechanisms; to this end, I combine within-case process tracing with a cross-case comparison. This section details the research design and the data I drew on throughout this investigation.

Throughout the book, I rely on process tracing methodology, ideal for including both a temporal dimension and historical narratives into social science analysis

TABLE 2.2 *Main cases under study*

Colombia	Argentina	Oversight?	Legal constituency
Salud or T-760 2008 (Restructuring Health System)	*Mendoza* 2008 (Riachuelo River basin Cleanup)	Yes	Dense
Consulta Previa or T-547 2010 (Right to prior consultation, for the Puerto Brisa project on the Caribbean)	*Badaro* 2006 (Recalculation of Retirement Pensions)	Yes	Low
UPAC or C-383 1999 (Restructuring Mortgage Credit System)	*Verbitsky* 2005 (Rights of prisoners in the Buenos Aires Province)	No	Dense
Cúcuta or T-231 1993 (Bogotá Canal Cleanup, in Cúcuta)	*Chaco* 2003 (Right to health and food in the Chaco Province)	No	Low

(Mahoney and Rueschemeyer 2003). The weight of the causal leverage is, thus, in the within-case analyses. Within each case, I compare the difference in the situations before and after the court's decision and trace the role that oversight and a legal constituency jointly, on their own, or their absence (depending on the case configuration) played in explaining impact. The strength of process tracing is to carefully reconstruct the causal mechanisms and provide rich descriptions over time that can clarify the complex ways in which certain elements may affect an outcome while evaluating alternative explanations (George and Bennett 2005; Mahoney 2012). Although ultimately rights effectiveness does not only hinge on judicial intervention in the form of a court ruling (many factors can determine the extent to which a right is realized for any particular population) process tracing is able to show what difference it did make, even when other factors are at play. Appendix A details the empirical implications of the causal mechanisms I posited.

The eight case studies (see Table 2.2) are nested in a comparative cross-case design that allows me to control for some alternative explanations while putting case-specific findings and observed patterns in comparative perspective. I selected the rulings in order to compare across them, depending on whether both key elements – oversight and a dense legal constituency – were present, only one of them was, or neither. The first pair of case studies had both a dense legal constituency and oversight, that is, a collaborative oversight arena was configured. I reconstruct and compare the process whereby the actors involved in two rulings, *Mendoza* in Argentina and *T-760* in Colombia, crafted these institutional spaces and how their interactions generated higher impact.

Second, I compare across cases where only one of the two elements was present, to isolate the individual causal contribution of the deployment of oversight or of the presence of a dense legal constituency in the absence of the other. These two pairs of cases allow us to observe the unique dynamics generated in rulings with monitoring but no dense civil society engagement (*Consulta Previa* and *Badaro*) and in those with a dense legal constituency but no oversight (*UPAC* and *Verbitsky*). Third, I compare across the (seemingly) negative cases: those where no oversight was deployed and where the legal constituency was not dense (*Cúcuta* and *Chaco*). The added analytical value of the cases without a collaborative oversight arena is to observe what happens in the absence of the synergies that are specific to those spaces.

In the later part of the book, I apply the theoretical framework developed and illustrated in the Latin American context to the analysis of two rulings with collaborative oversight arenas decided by the Supreme Court of India. The cases are the Right to Food Case – which the court monitored between 2001 and 2017 – and the Delhi Vehicular Pollution Case – which the court started monitoring in 1999. These shadow case studies were chosen with two causal criteria in mind:[8] (1) Selecting cases where the causal mechanisms I posited originally could be observed at work over the longest period of time. Because the Indian court has been engaged in the use of oversight tools for longer than any other high court in the world, it is an ideal choice from this perspective, (2) Selecting cases with most similar background conditions and causal configurations as those in the Latin American cases.

Cross-case comparisons are not without challenges: It is difficult to hold all elements outside of primary interest constant and their generalizability has been questioned. Despite these challenges, theoretically informed and clearly justified cross-case comparisons are particularly well suited for theory development. In combination with a robust strategy for within-case causal inference, like process tracing, they can offer invaluable comparative insights (Mahoney 2003). As Slater and Ziblatt (2013, 1322) explain, controlled comparisons cannot perform inferential miracles, but they can "offer direct evidence of limited transferability and the theoretical foundations for wider transferability." Such comparisons can provide important insights if scope conditions, the nature of the causes and the causal mechanisms, and their empirical implications are specified (Mahoney 2003; Slater and Ziblatt 2013). The remainder of this section explains how my research design addresses these concerns and justifies the focus on Colombia and Argentina.

2.6.1 *Why Argentina and Colombia?*

This book focuses on cases decided by two of the most assertive high courts in Latin America between the early 1990s and 2015: the Colombian Constitutional Court (CCC) and the Supreme Court of Argentina (SCA). The former is widely renowned

[8] I follow Gerring and Cojocaru's (2016) guidelines for causal case studies.

and studied for its activist profile and the latter, though less known for rights activism, is an equally fascinating case. Since its inception following the promulgation of a new constitution in 1991, the CCC has protected the rights of Indigenous and other minorities, and it has also played an important role in expanding socioeconomic rights, particularly the right to health (Nunes 2010). At the same time, it has also been willing and able to act as an effective check on the executive (Botero 2018; Uprimny 2003). The SCA had a relatively independent profile in the 1980s (Kapiszewski 2012), was a largely subservient court throughout the better part of the 1990s (Larkins 1998; Verbitsky 1993), and then transitioned into a more assertive tribunal as of the early 2000s, after key reforms under President Nestor Kirchner (Ruibal 2014). Since then, the court has played a salient role with some key decisions regarding human rights, social welfare reform, environmental issues as well as consumer and minority rights. Throughout the period under study, it exhibited a more independent profile *vis-à-vis* the executive than its immediate predecessor.

Focusing on these two courts allows me to control for two possible alternative explanations for judicial impact: institutional design and levels of legitimacy. A purely institutionalist account would suggest that the court with greater institutional authority will be associated with greater on-the-ground influence. As for legitimacy, earlier studies argue that courts that are perceived as more legitimate can generate higher levels of compliance and impact overall (Gibson, Caldeira, and Baird 1998). A brief introduction to the characteristics of both courts can help us understand why, although both arguments would expect higher levels of impact in cases decided by the Colombian tribunal, this expectation is not borne out.

The CCC is the head of a mixed system of judicial review.[9] The court has broad formal review powers and is the tribunal of last appeal in constitutional matters with both concrete a posteriori review and abstract review.[10] Nine justices serve non-renewable, non-staggered eight-year terms.[11] This court is easily accessible and has full control of its docket. The SCA is also the highest constitutional court in its country; additionally, it functions as the last court of appeals for other matters at the federal level. Both constitutions have individual systems for control of constitutionality that can be filed with any court (decentralized) and may reach the highest

[9] Before the new constitution was signed in 1991, a constitutional chamber within the Supreme Court of Justice dealt with such matters. Since 1991 the Colombian judiciary has four distinct apex courts: the Constitutional Court, the Supreme Court of Justice (the highest criminal and civil tribunal), the Council of State (in charge of administrative matters), and the Supreme Council of the Judicature. Because of the broad powers of the CCC and the existence of tutela, in practice, matters from other tribunals may end up there.

[10] Abstract judicial review refers to the powers of a court to review the constitutionality of legislation without a concrete controversy (case) before it. Concrete judicial review refers to the ability to review legislation as it applies to a particular case; a posteriori review further specifies that the review can only happen after the law has been enacted.

[11] Members are elected from lists of three candidates presented to the Senate by the president, the Supreme Court of Justice, and the Council of State, alternatively. After their tenure in the court, justices are banned from accepting any public appointments for one year.

courts: tutela in Colombia and amparo in Argentina. The Supreme Court of Argentina has broad formal review powers (concrete a posteriori) but, unlike the CCC, it has no abstract powers of review. Compared to the Colombian court, access to the SCA is somewhat more limited as cases must be federal and may not be filed directly with the court except under certain circumstances.[12] Yet, the Supreme Court of Argentina is not as difficult to reach as the Mexican court, or as Supreme Court of the United States, both notorious for their strict standing rules. The Argentine justices continue to serve life-long terms – during most of the time period covered by this study, the court had a maximum of seven members.[13]

These two courts have features which make them comparable in their capacity as constitutional tribunals and in their levels of independence during the time of this study – see Figure 2.3 for a graphic visualization of the latter. Yet, differences in terms of the scope of their authority – namely, those institutional features in a court's design that determine its ability to intervene decisively in a broad range of politically significant disputes on behalf of a broad range of actors (Brinks and Blass 2018) – and their legitimacy might suggest that the Colombian court's decisions would have greater impact than those of the Argentine.

Neither of these courts is powerless on paper, but the Colombian court has higher levels of institutional authority as can be seen in Figure 2.3. A measure of judicial authority that ranges from 0 to 1 gives the Colombian court an average of approximately 0.8 and the Argentinean court a 0.6 in the years since the major constitutional overhauls in both countries.[14]

As for institutional legitimacy, the Colombian highest court also appears to have higher levels than those of the Supreme Court of Argentina. We have more survey data on trust in the CCC than on the SCA, but what is available gives us an idea of overall trends. An analysis of LAPOP's survey data on respondents' trust in these courts (available for 2006–2016 for Colombia and for 2008, 2010, 2012, and 2017 for Argentina) shows that, on average, more Argentineans (49 percent) placed themselves somewhere between feeling neutral toward the Supreme Court and not trusting it at all. In contrast, an average of 37 percent Colombian respondents felt neutral toward the constitutional court or do not trust it at all, though the negatives

[12] More specifically known as "competencia originaria" regulated by art. 280 of the *Codigo Procesal.*

[13] In 2006 Congress approved a law that set the number of justices of the court at five, the original composition that had been altered by President Menem's 1990 "ley de ampliación" – a court-packing maneuver that increased the number of justices to a total of nine (ADC 2008). After 2006, any vacancies that opened in the court (due to death, retirement, or impeachment, the only possible removal mechanisms) were not filled. With the death of Enrique Petracchi in 2014 the court returned to its five-judge size.

[14] These scores apply between 1991 and 2010 for Colombia and 1994 and 2010 for Argentina. The starting year corresponds to the promulgation of the new constitution in Colombia and to the year in which a major constitutional reform was passed in Argentina by President Menem. Reforms in both countries significantly expanded constitutional review.

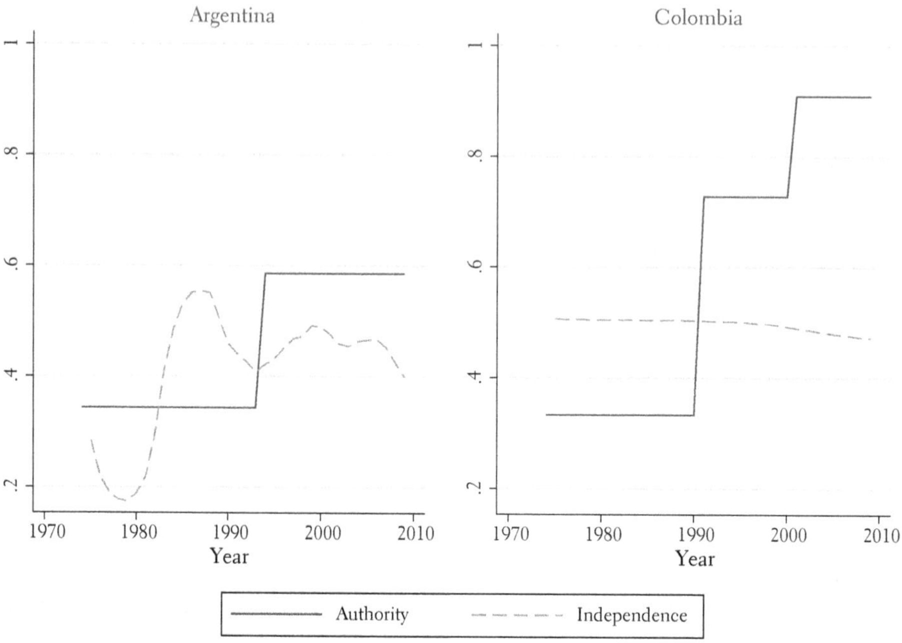

FIGURE 2.3 Authority and independence in the Argentine and Colombian high courts.
Sources: Authority: Brinks and Blass (2018) Independence: Linzer and Staton (2015)

for the Colombian court have risen since 2012 (Botero 2020), putting it closer to Argentine levels in recent years. Historically, however, and in particular during the years under study here, the Colombian court enjoyed a higher degree of legitimacy among its populace than the Argentine court.

Given these characterizations, if we assumed that observed influence follows automatically from institutional design and/or that public support determines impact, then we would expect the Colombian court to have higher levels of impact on average in the cases under study. Mine is a small-n comparison and my cases, by design, were not randomly chosen – yet, it is important to determine what role these two factors play in explaining different levels of impact. The ruling with the highest impact in this book (*Causa Mendoza*) was handed down by the Argentine court, and nothing suggests that all the Colombian rulings have higher levels of impact as a whole when compared to the Argentine ones. These could be one-time exceptions, but neither factor appeared as playing the primary causal role in explaining levels of impact in any of the case studies.

2.6.2 *Focusing on Socioeconomic Rights (Case Selection Criteria)*

Within the universe of cases decided by the Colombian and Argentine high courts, I use landmark socioeconomic rights cases as my window into the study of judicial impact. Because of their scope, these kind of complex public policy decisions are known as structural rulings. Structural injunction cases are very different from individual rights-based cases where, for example, a citizen asks protection of her right to health seeking judicial-ordered access to a medication or a procedure. Structural cases have more in common with cases like constitutional challenges to government legislation or with public interest litigation, more broadly. Although they differ in terms of substance from more purely "political" against the government cases, structural cases are politically charged, important decisions that deeply affect public policy and challenge the status quo. These cases involve different political and social actors (often beyond the government, and including the other branches) in reforming or producing public policy and changing the behavior of multiple actors around contested and complex issues. Because of the strong challenge they pose, they are optimal cases in which to study impact if one is skeptical that courts can produce any.

Structural socioeconomic rights cases are ideal to evaluate impact – but, while they are not that uncommon, they do not exist by the hundreds. It is impossible to find, for example, multiple structural health rights cases that exemplify all relevant selection criteria in Colombia or Argentina. Fortunately, this is not an insurmountable difficulty. I identified issue areas in which both courts were active and chose cases from different areas. While focusing on a one issue area has some obvious benefits, cross-issue area analysis presents other advantages and can be equally enriching. In tracing the mechanisms, I emphasize processes that have comparable features and actors across themes: I am interested in the actions taken by those involved (how the different monitoring tools and venues are used, or what types of mobilization and when legal constituencies engage in, for example), how ideas and rights discourses circulate, and how policy is produced.

I intentionally place the focus on the interactions among the actors involved and the common stages in the post-litigation processes, regardless of issue. At the same time, process tracing facilitates being mindful of the specifics throughout the analysis. Where I identify a difficulty or a particular feature that is associated with the nature of the case, I note it. For instance, a government oversight agency unique to Argentina's institutional set up, the *Defensor de la Tercera Edad*, played a salient role in *Causa Badaro*, a case where the availability of financial resources was crucial. I describe this and its implications at length in Chapter 4.

To select specific rulings, I started by identifying an initial list of potential structural cases on socioeconomic rights for each country through secondary literature on the SCA's and the CCC's jurisprudence, searches in their online databases and newspapers. I sought feedback from country experts on that list. With their help – and with the two selection criteria I will explain next as my guide – I narrowed the list down to the eight cases that are the focus of this inquiry. First, as mentioned earlier, I was looking to have different combinations of presence or absence of legal constituencies and oversight mechanisms. Second, the case selection process was also sensitive to the scope of the challenge that the ruling's implementation posed. Third, I was interested in tracking important cases over a significant period, which meant focusing not on novel, current decisions, but instead concentrating efforts on relatively older rulings (some very well studied, some not at all) aiming to drill down on the post-decision phase.

As discussed before, structural socioeconomic rights cases are hard. However, even among hard cases, there is harder and easier. Scope is itself a potential alternative explanation; under this logic, "easier" cases would most likely have greater impact. Working with paired, cross-country case studies, it is important to minimize this particular bias in the comparison. Because of its relevance, this second selection criteria merits some additional explanation.

2.6.3 *Scope of the Challenge*

To distinguish among cases, we can think of two dimensions along which the scope of the challenge can be classified.[15] First, the *size and degree of geographic dispersion* of the beneficiaries: whether the case deals with a focalized subgroup (a specific minority group or the inhabitants of a small city, for example) versus a more numerous and dispersed subnational or national group. The latter configuration usually poses greater administrative and political difficulties – it is likely to involve more people and entail greater administrative, financial, and even discursive efforts to address. A second dimension is the *aim of the case*: On one end, it may seek to resolve a specific conflict or issue (improve health outcomes for HIV patients) and, on the other extreme, it may have the broader aim of reforming government structures (like changing the national health system to improve health outcomes for all). Both dimensions are jointly mapped out in Figure 2.4.

Figure 2.5 maps out my eight cases according to the two criteria outlined above, classifying them according to the scope of the challenge they pose. A few things are worth noting at this point. First, cases T-231 and *Causa Chaco* (Cúcuta and Chaco in Chapter 4), which I classify as lower impact cases are "easier" challenges. These two rulings are targeted at focalized subgroups, inhabitants of Cúcuta, Colombia, and the Qom inhabitants of *El Impenetrable* in the Argentine Chaco. Additionally, they aim to fix specific issues – the execution of an environmental cleanup program in a river in a small city and the delivery of food and health services to the Qom. To be sure, the original legal claims sought redress for long-standing, complex problems. The environmental conditions alongside the Bogotá Canal in Cúcuta had been a concern for several decades and the Qom have been ignored or ill-served by the Argentine state for even longer. Addressing both issues involved a number of different actors: the mayor and the public services companies in Cúcuta; the provincial government and select national agencies in Chaco. Successfully moving

[15] This classification uses as its starting point a continuum proposed by Cepeda (2011).

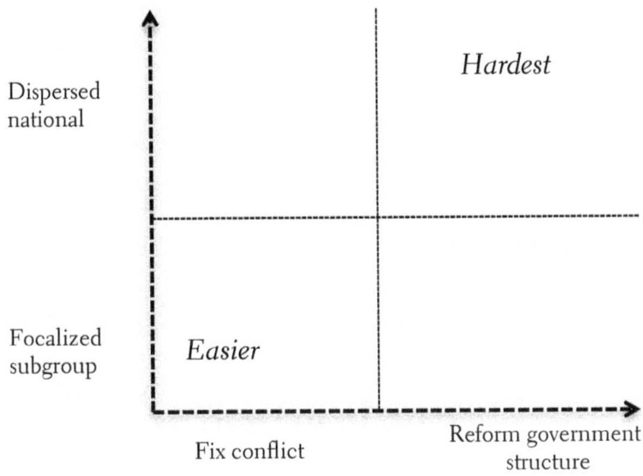

FIGURE 2.4 Scope of challenge

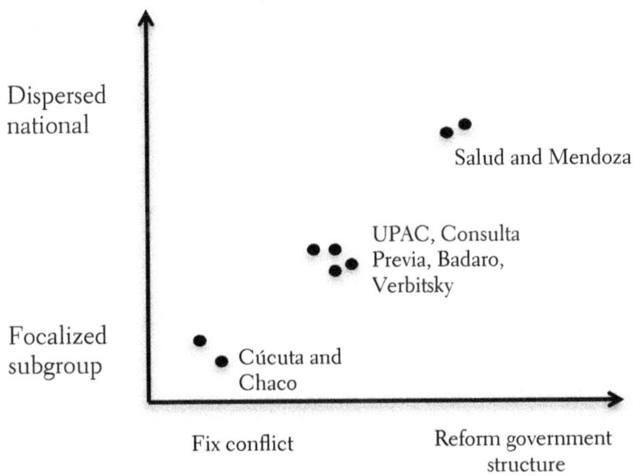

FIGURE 2.5 Scope of challenge for rulings under study

the needle, so to speak, was not expected, much less guaranteed by the time the court entered both scenarios. Yet, even though these two cases entailed significant challenges, the remaining six are even more ambitious.

Consider, for example, how hard modifying the status quo was by the time the Badaro and Consulta Previa rulings (two of the middle-range cases) were handed down. In Badaro, the Argentine court was calling on Congress to reform the national pension system, a change that had significant budgetary implications and ripple effects on multiple private and governmental stakeholders. Opposition from the executive in particular was fierce and had been for consecutive governments. In Consulta Previa (T-547), the Colombian court ordered the execution of a prior consultation process with Indigenous groups. This seemingly procedural request involved at least four different Indigenous groups, three governmental agencies, and a powerful private company. This company had made a strategic, long-term, multi-million-dollar investment to build the port in this area and forcefully rejected undertaking a prior consultation process. Shifting the status quo was not a given in any of these two cases. At the outset, the most likely outcome was quite the opposite: that there would be no reform to the pension system and that the port construction would continue, undisturbed.

Nonetheless, nowhere was the challenge greater than in cases T-760 and *Causa Mendoza* (Salud and *Causa Mendoza* in Figure 2.3), the rulings I classify as having had higher impact. To better illustrate the scope of the challenge they posed, contrast the following with my earlier description of the scope of the "easier" cases, Chaco and Cúcuta. Compared to these two, both Salud (T-760) and *Causa Mendoza* target larger, more spread out, and more heterogenous populations: Colombian nationals in T-760 and millions of inhabitants along the Matanza-Riachuelo River basin, Argentina's most densely populated area. Both Salud and *Causa Mendoza* aimed to reform entire governmental structures working with different administrative and private entities at different levels: In T-760, the objective was to ignite meaningful change in the Colombian national health system involving its units, several regulatory agencies, and different private health providers. In the case of *Causa Mendoza*, the court's attempt to clean up and restore the Matanza-Riachuelo River basin involved the provincial government, the mayor's office in Buenos Aires, and multiple local provincial governments, including their respective environmental subunits. Altering the status quo in both scenarios was an enterprise of national and subnational scope that required the participation of numerous agencies and actors with diverse and competing interests.

The preceding discussion makes clear that all cases under study pose significant challenges and, at the same time, that not all challenges are equivalent. Socioeconomic rights cases are often thought of as easy, a "window dressing matter." If socioeconomic rights cases were slam-dunks overall, we would see full compliance and high impact across the board, in all rulings. This is not the case. However, this should not lead us to conclude that they are impossible feats that cannot ever be solved: If judicial intervention were a dead end, an analysis of their aftermath would show nothing. As this book shows and as other research indicates, that view is not accurate either.

Thinking carefully about the scope of the challenge also highlights that an easier challenge does not assure greater impact. If easier challenges drove greater levels of judicial impact, we would see the "easier" rulings in this book having overall higher levels of impact – this is not the case. In fact, the opposite relation holds: the hardest cases are those that have higher impact. The scope of the challenge needs to be kept in mind, but it is not the underlying explanation. This book uncovers how the politics of compliance, and in particular, monitoring mechanisms and civil society engagement, may contribute to understanding different degrees of impact.

The scope of the challenge that rulings entail raises another possible alternative explanation: Could it be that judges are "cherry-picking," that is, choosing to monitor cases in which they know such an intervention will make a difference? While providing a definitive answer to why courts choose to deploy monitoring mechanisms is beyond the confines of this book, here I can discuss some insights from my own and others' research that shed light on this matter.

2.6.4 *Why Monitor?*

Why do judges choose to monitor the implementation of certain cases? This is an important question that requires a separate study to be answered in full. Though I cannot answer in full, I will briefly describe when the Argentine and Colombian high courts began using them and explain the ideas that guide my thinking about the choice to monitor. Monitoring mechanisms for structural rulings in socioeconomic rights cases were first deployed by the Supreme Court of India. Indian high court judges started using them in the late 1990s, in the context of an expansion of the Supreme Court's influence and the appearance of other procedural and substantive legal innovations, including public interest litigation (PIL, a legal mechanism that facilitated litigation on behalf of public interest, see Chapter 6 for an overview). These tools (special public audiences, expert committees, collaborative monitoring) were deployed with special intensity in the area of environmental rights, to which the Supreme Court of India was particularly attentive to(Sahu 2008). Environmental rulings by the Supreme Court of India became famous worldwide. Though the Argentine court had already made use of public audiences (not necessarily in the context of collaborative monitoring as I understand it, but as a procedural innovation in different types of cases, see Benedetti and Sáenz 2016) some of my interviewees in Argentina recalled that the environmental decisions hailing from India inspired the approach of their own federal tribunal in the Matanza-Riachuelo case. By the early 2000s both the Argentine and Colombian high courts were engaged in monitoring ventures in socioeconomic rights cases.

In the early years of the twenty-first century, Colombia and Argentina in particular (but also Latin America more broadly) were fertile ground for the diffusion of innovative legal arguments and tools in no small part due to the deep changes in the region's legal cultures, which began to move away from legal formalism and toward neoconstitutionalism – also known as interpretivism or social constitutionalism. According to Gargarella (2014b), the use of audiences and the adoption of tools associated with collaborative monitoring are key markers of this new constitutionalist approach. In general terms, this new, less formalistic, more interpretivist legal culture is associated with favoring more subjective judgments with regard to the principles that judges can apply in the enforcement of rights, a move away from textualist techniques and a greater willingness to problematize the content and modification of rights and rules (Ansolabehere, Botero, and Gonzalez-Ocantos

2022). Changes to legal cultures explain the existence of judges and legal operators strongly committed to enforcing and expanding rights, including also having a more friendly disposition toward experimenting with alternative arguments, procedures, and remedies.

A changing legal culture helps explain why some Colombian and Argentine judges might have been exposed to and willing to try monitoring. In addition, it is useful to consider that turning to monitoring might also make sense for strategic considerations. The fact that some justices build oversight mechanisms into their decisions speaks not only of the legal culture in which they are imbued, but also suggests a concern with the institution and the consequences and implementation of rulings that lies beyond the explanatory power of any single traditional model of judicial decision-making. This book is guided by the notion that a qualified version of the strategic model of judicial decision-making (Epstein and Knight 2013) is most useful for understanding the behavior of high court justices. These judges are surely cognizant of the external constraints imposed by other political institutions, but it is important to remember that strategic behavior is not limited exclusively to bargaining or retreating (Gillman 1999). Courts accumulate political goodwill and legitimacy over time (Gibson, Caldeira, and Baird 1998) and there is reason to believe that such capital is associated in no small part with the impact of that court's rulings (Epstein, Knight, and Shvetsova 2001). Indeed, legitimacy and power can be influenced by the court, within political and institutional boundaries, through different factors like increasing information and awareness about rulings (Staton 2010), or catering to certain constituencies (Gibson, Caldeira, and Baird 1998), among other options.[16] Monitoring, which increases awareness and information about rulings, while engaging other actors in that process, might appear beneficial to the judges.

Benedetti and Sáenz's (2016) study of public audiences in the Supreme Court of Argentina indicates that this tribunal's initial push toward going public through audiences and involving external actors was very much related to an interest in increasing visibility and legitimacy via openness after an institutional crisis. With regard to Colombia, the following excerpt from an interview with a former judge of the Constitutional Court provides some support to the idea that judges first considered monitoring mechanisms as a useful tool in their quest to further institutional legitimacy and power, and illustrates well the comments I heard in other interviews with magistrates and their assistants:

> [When we first set up a follow-up commission and monitoring mechanisms] we sought to avoid the absence of results and with it, that the court would squander its

[16] Those other options include vagueness in rulings (Staton and Vanberg 2008), court-like behavior (Hibbing and Theiss-Morse 2002), or due to the framing of its arguments (Forero Alba and Rodriguez Raga 2022).

> [political] capital. It was very important to channel support [for the Court] and guarantee its legitimacy. (...) having a commission means support, legitimacy and strength.[17]

In short, the evidence that we have from these tribunals suggests that the choice to monitor is complex, probably shaped by cultural, institutional, and strategic considerations. The book tracks the effects of this enterprise, for a sample of hallmark structural socioeconomic rights cases, seeking to better understand post-ruling dynamics.

2.6.5 *Data Sources*

This book is based on a combination of sources: archival material,[18] 130 semi-structured interviews, published and unpublished secondary sources, and participant observation in meetings and public hearings. I conducted sixteen months of fieldwork in Colombia and Argentina between February 2012 and July 2014 in the cities of Bogotá, Cúcuta, Buenos Aires, and La Plata. Additionally, I spent two months in the summer of 2016 in New Delhi, India. Interviewees included scholars, human rights activists, lawyers, litigants, government officials, current and former justices, high court clerks, NGO members, experts, and members of the follow-up commissions in both countries. Interviewees were promised anonymity for this project – I do not provide extensive personal or institutional affiliation details unless I was authorized to do so.

I observed more than seventeen meetings of the Follow-up Commission in the T-760 case and sat in on several Congressional debates. I also attended public hearings on oversight on the cases I was studying both in the Colombian Constitutional Court (in Bogotá, on April 2012) and in the Supreme Court of Argentina (in Buenos Aires, throughout October and November 2012). Additionally, I built a database of newspaper coverage of all the decisions under study for several publications in both Latin American countries.[19]

[17] Interview with former Constitutional Court Justice Bogotá, August 14, 2012. This and all translations from Spanish are the author's.

[18] I conducted archival research in the Colombian Ministry of Environment, the Colombian Constitutional Court, the Tribunal Supremo in Cúcuta (Colombia), Congreso Nacional in Buenos Aires, the Biblioteca Nacional (in Buenos Aires and Bogotá), and the Tribunal Supremo de Buenos Aires in La Plata, Argentina.

[19] El Tiempo and El Espectador in Colombia. Página/12, La Nación and Clarín in Argentina (as well as *Diario Norte*, a local newspaper from El Chaco for the Defensor del Pueblo/Chaco case).

3

Collaborative Oversight Arenas

3.1 INTRODUCTION

This book argues that court-promoted monitoring mechanisms and legally empowered civil society organizations can help craft higher levels of impact in structural rulings. This chapter presents comparative case studies of two such rulings: Argentina's *Causa Mendoza* – an environmental ruling – and Colombia's T-760 – a ruling safeguarding the right to health. Both have dense legal constituencies and court-promoted oversight mechanisms. I reconstruct the ways in which court-promoted monitoring of the rulings' implementation imposed costs on the targets (through formal mechanisms, as well as political pressure) and how it generated resources to offset the informational asymmetries that often plague courts, like lack of technical expertise. I show that civil society organizations that made part of the legal constituency in both rulings contributed to generating information about the issues, and about compliance with the rulings in the context of monitoring. Both the Argentine and the Colombian courts drew on this input to monitor and to update some of their decisions about policy. The collaborative oversight arenas created spaces in which different participants could exercise accountability for unfulfilled commitments from the government and private agents and, more specifically, for the implementation of different aspects of the ruling. Additionally, the creation of spaces for sustained interaction around some of these issues offered the chance for the diffusion of policy ideas and a rights-based framework, while giving civil society actors access to the state.

The first case I discuss is a ruling handed down by the Supreme Court of Argentina ordering government officials at different levels to work toward the environmental protection and recovery of the Matanza-Riachuelo River basin. The Matanza-Riachuelo River basin is situated in the southern area of the Greater Buenos Aires; more than six million people live along its length. The severe environmental degradation of the river is caused by the spillage of industrial and untreated sewage waste into it, as well as by hundreds of open-air dumps (Napoli 2009). This bleak panorama is aggravated by the multitude of administrative jurisdictions that converge and occasionally overlap along the river – fourteen municipalities, the national and provincial governments as well as the City of Buenos Aires. This administrative complexity leads to a breakdown of the system – a historic lack of attention to urban planning, and a near-total absence of governmental attention to the river's deterioration or its social and environmental consequences.

In 2004 a group of residents of Villa Inflamable (one of the neighborhoods in the vicinity of the Dock Sud petrochemical port on the river) and health workers from a public hospital filed a legal complaint for environmental damages with the Supreme Court of Argentina. The Court took the case and swung into action in mid-2006, requesting information from the defendants (government and industries) and asking the government to devise a cleanup plan for the river basin. Between mid-2006 and mid-2008 – when the court first ruled – as well as afterward, it monitored compliance. The ruling, known as *Causa Mendoza*, called attention to six areas: public information, industrial contamination, open-air dump cleanups, river margin cleanups, infrastructure, and the creation of an emergency health plan. For each of these, it outlined some actions and general objectives that should be pursued, leaving choices about the specifics of implementation to the authorities.[1]

The second case that I discuss is a right to health ruling handed down by Colombia's Constitutional Court in 2008. This ruling, T-760, sought to provide a more structural solution to the mounting challenges facing the national health system by ordering the government to undertake important reforms. Colombia's health care system was praised for its technocratic profile and nearly universal coverage as well as criticized for its inequality (Gianella-Malca, Gloppen, and Fosse 2013). The system, put in place in 1993 after a drastic institutional reform, aims for full coverage and is heavily funded by the state, though management and service delivery is largely in the hands of private third parties. Critics argue that "the consequences of this model have been a consolidation of resources in the hands of the insurance companies, the widening of social inequalities, and the abandonment of public health" (Hernández Álvarez and Torres Tovar 2010).

In the early twenty-first century, the lack of regulation of private service and insurance providers and some of the negative consequences of the reform implemented in 1993 evolved into a deep crisis in the health sector. Private and public hospitals went bankrupt or faced huge liquidity problems due to corruption and backlogged payments. As of 2012, more than 4 billion pesos were owed by service providers and governmental entities to Colombian hospitals, half of it was past-due-portfolio (ACHC 2012). Citizens routinely faced difficulties in accessing health services because of bureaucratic barriers and denial of services, treatments, or

1 At the time of writing, the case remained open with regard to collective reparations for past environmental damage.

procedures. Colombians frequently turn to the legal system for redress – as a result, this country is one of the most dramatic cases of the judicialization of health in the Latin American region (Rodríguez Garavito 2012; Yamin and Gloppen 2011).[2]

In T-760 the Colombian court brought together twenty-three individual health tutelas and handed down a ruling that established health as a fundamental right, asking different levels of government (Ministry of Health, national government, health regulatory agencies, and providers) to work together to reform the health care system and guarantee citizens' right to health. The court charted broad objectives and laid out a timeline for actions in the following areas: reforms to the health coverage plans, safeguarding the right to information, improving governmental control and regulatory capacity over the system, streamlining the flow of financial resources, and diminishing the need for recourse to the judiciary to access health services while seeking to preserve the system's financial sustainability. Like its Argentine counterpart in *Causa Mendoza*, it left the specifics of how to implement the ruling largely to the government.

Both rulings faced enormous challenges and both had significant impact on the issues they sought to address. *Causa Mendoza* was not merely words on paper: It spurred the creation of a new regulatory structure, the allocation of new resources for cleanup efforts, for an industrial reconversion program, and for water and sewage networks as well as the passing of new environmental regulations. Existing resources were also reallocated to support programs in local environmental agencies. Critically, the ruling put the environmental conditions of the river basin front and center in the local and the national political arena, making it a policy priority. Finally, it enhanced the capacities of the civil society organizations tasked with oversight, giving them access to institutional forums they lacked before and adding to their resources. Ultimately, these processes contributed to significant improvements in sewage coverage and access to water throughout the river basin, though contamination in the river persists and the challenge continues.

T-760 also had an important impact: Here too we can trace the effects of the court's intervention on the legal and regulatory framework in the form of new institutions, updates to the national basic coverage plans, and changes to the financial regulatory structure. Among other things, the ruling elevated health to the rank of a fundamental right and this had a huge imprint in the framing of public policy, on legal mobilization, and on public discussions. The ruling came amidst a larger crisis in the national health system, which contributed to the introduction of a health reform bill in 2013 by President Santos. It would be inaccurate to claim that the court's intervention explains the implosion of the system, but it would be an

[2] To illustrate the scope, note that according to the Defensoría del Pueblo (Ombudsman's Office) more than 140,000 health claims (tutelas) were filed in 2008 alone, countrywide. That was roughly 40 percent of the total number of tutelas filed that year (345,780, according to the Constitutional Court).

oversight to conclude that the process that led to this juncture was entirely divorced from the court's intervention. The court provided a forum in which certain civil society actors and government control agencies were able to hold the government and other agents in the health system – particularly insurance companies – accountable. In enabling greater transparency and answerability, the court thus played a key accountability function (Gloppen, Gargarella, and Skaar 2004). Ultimately, these immediate effects helped bring about improvements in access to health for millions of Colombians.

This chapter shows how and to what extent collaborative monitoring contributed to enhancing immediate effects and ultimately rights effectiveness in both instances. Though there were positive synergies in certain areas, the rulings did not offer magical solutions. Addressing centuries of institutional abandonment and environmental degradation in the most densely populated area of Argentina is a long-term project, as is guaranteeing full access and enjoyment of the right to health for all Colombians. In that sense, much remains to be done in both cases. I start tracing in 2008 for both cases, and follow events and effects until 2016, with some nods to later events.

The chapter proceeds as follows: Each case study begins with a more detailed description of the impact of the court's ruling followed by a characterization of the monitoring tools used and of the legal constituency present. The case studies then go into details about the ways in which collaborative monitoring helped generate significant impact in both cases. The final section compares the two rulings and highlights key insights.

3.2 ENVIRONMENTAL RIGHTS: *CAUSA MENDOZA* (ARGENTINA)

3.2.1 *Impact*

In the case of *Causa Mendoza*, looking at impact from a systemic perspective provides clear evidence of significant impact. My assessment, as well as other studies (Bergallo 2014; Merlinsky 2016; Nader 2022; Ryan and Napoli 2017) disconfirms those who suggest that the ruling has left the status quo largely undisturbed, or that the policy changes underway are merely window dressing with little to no consequences for the environment and the inhabitants of the Riachuelo River basin (Gargarella 2014a; Puga 2012). *Causa Mendoza* triggered a broad and diverse set of changes across the different dimensions outlined earlier. As the discussion below will show, there is variation in the reach of changes within dimensions. Overall, I classify it as high on the immediate effects dimension and low on the outcome dimension. Table 3.1 presents an overview of changes across subdimensions.

Given the vast complexity of the problem the case addressed, comprehensively covering the advances, gaps, and setbacks in all the areas is a task beyond the scope

TABLE 3.1 *Summary of impact for* Causa Mendoza

Immediate effects	
Ideational: The court's intervention helped put the contamination of the Matanza-Riachuelo River in the national political agenda, and with it, environmental issues.	High
Formal Norms: - AYSA (sewage and water utility company) revises its master plan for sewage construction and water networks for the city of Buenos Aires and the following municipalities: Avellaneda, Lanús, Lomas de Zamora, Almirante Brown, Esteban Echeverría, Ezeiza, La Matanza, and Morón. - Drafting of a plan and directives for the management of solid residues (GIRSU) for the entire river basin. - Drafting Clean-Up Master Plans (PISA) for the River Basin - Regulations for Contaminating Agents - Creation of ACUMAR (Autoridad de la Cuenca Matanza-Riachuelo) on July 2007 - Regulations for Water Use and Quality Aims - Legal cascade of related rulings	High
Organizational Changes: - New networks among environmental and human rights NGOs around policy and social processes in the Matanza-Riachuelo basin. Greater political leverage and access. - Used as precedent in ongoing attempts to generate similar structural environmental rulings (i.e.: Rio Reconquista).	Med
Resources: - Industrial Reconversion Program - Cleanup of River and Open-Air Dumps - Cleanup of the River Margins (Camino de Sirga) - Monetary resources to municipalities for environmental programs through ACUMAR - Creation of *Mapa Sociodemográfico* - Survey of Risk Factors - Census of Industries - Periodic monitoring of water, groundwater, and air quality.	High
Overall immediate effects	High
Outcomes Extension of sewage networks and access to drinking water. Water quality and effectiveness of industrial contamination control.	Low

of this chapter. I pay particular attention to control of industrial contamination and the extension of sewage and drinking water networks to illustrate the more detailed reconstruction of the process that can be done. Due to space constraints, I cannot discuss health and housing effects in full detail, and hence will only touch briefly upon them.

3.2.1.1 Immediate Effects

Changes to formal norms following the Supreme Court's ruling were particularly noteworthy. Whereas earlier the river basin lacked a common governance framework and structure, the Supreme Court ruling set into motion the creation of institutions and regulations that have begun to give substance and weight to the presence of the state in its socio-environmental management. The most noteworthy and important institutional change was the creation in July 2007 by the Congress of the Matanza-Riachuelo River basin authority, ACUMAR (*Autoridad de la Cuenca Matanza-Riachuelo*), a governmental institution created by an order of the court, with significant government funding and dedicated exclusively to executing the cleanup plan and ruling. As Gutiérrez and Merlinsky (2011) and Nader (2022) suggest, and my discussions with experts and government officials in different municipalities confirmed, ACUMAR came to function as the much-needed mechanism for inter-jurisdictional coordination of environmental policy in the river basin.[3] The directors of environmental offices in different provincial municipalities highlighted, in particular, that participating in ACUMAR's Municipal Council and accessing funds through it greatly increased the incidence and the capacity of their units.[4]

Beyond new institutions, the ruling prompted new environmental regulations, the allocation of new resources for cleanup efforts, for an industrial reconversion program, and for water and sewage networks. Soon after the court's first pronouncement in 2006, and almost in parallel with the creation of ACUMAR, the first draft of the master cleanup plan for the Matanza-Riachuelo River basin was produced. The ruling also prompted the creation of regulations to govern the use and aims of the river's water quality and of the type and amounts of substances that industries can dispose of in the river. Merlinsky (2016) argues that as ACUMAR settled and institutionalized in the years following its creation, its growing importance and that of the regulation it has created, or is in charge of enforcing, have themselves shifted the discussion toward one of implementation of public policy.

For example, in 2012, following a collaborative process that incorporated input from the different municipalities, a common plan for the management of solid residues for the entire basin (known as GIRSU) was drafted and put into operation. In an area where 30 percent of the trash produced on a daily basis was disposed of illegally (Napoli and García Espil 2011), the handling of solid residues was one of

3 Interview with subsecretary of environment A, Buenos Aires Province, February 14, 2013; Interview with subsecretary of environment B, Buenos Aires Province, February 8, 2013; Interview with subsecretary of environment D, Buenos Aires Province, March 8, 2013; Interview Member of Cuerpo Colegiado. Buenos Aires, December 3, 2012.

4 Interview with subsecretary of environment A, Buenos Aires Province, February 14, 2013; Interview with subsecretary of environment B, Buenos Aires Province, February 8, 2013; Interview with subsecretary of environment D, Buenos Aires Province, March 8, 2013.

the biggest challenges. According to ACUMAR's report in 2013, 40 percent of illegal open-air dumps had been cleaned up by late 2013. By end of 2016, when this study closes, 92% of the open-air dumps originally identified had been closed, and a new base line was to be established in 2017 (ACUMAR 2022). The head of one of the municipal environmental agencies in the province stated: "[T]he additional 24 million pesos [that my municipality received from ACUMAR] allowed me to hire 216 people [trash collectors, for cleanup]. Those are 600 tons of trash that will not be disposed of in the Riachuelo."[5] In that sense, the GIRSU and the creation of twelve waste processing sites in different municipalities, known as *eco puntos*, were an important step forward. However, waste disposal and in particular open-air dumps continued to be a problem: Only one year later, a report by the Defensor del Pueblo cautioned that between 60 and 70 percent of the illegal dump sites monitored by ACUMAR remained active in different municipalities (DNP 2014).

Resources were also funneled to monitoring water quality and building drinking water networks and sewers. AYSA, the company in charge of waterworks and sewage disposal in most of the metropolitan area, reformulated the priorities and plan to extend water and sewage networks for the city of Buenos Aires and municipalities in the lower- and mid-river basin (CELS 2009). The auditor-general (Auditoría General de la Nación 2016) confirmed that 41 percent of total disbursements to ACUMAR between 2011 and 2015 corresponded to the line item for sewage and drinking water.[6] Financed by international donors, massive projects got underway, not without delays. Since half of the population in the river basin (by ACUMAR's own figures) did not have sewage service by 2016 (FARN et al. 2017), that the projects took off the ground was significant, though much remained to be done.

The ruling charged ACUMAR with playing a role in yet another domain: controlling and preventing industrial contamination by constructing a census of the industries and inspecting them. As a result, in 2011 ACUMAR finalized the first-ever census of industrial establishments identifying a total of 21,939. The number of environmental inspections conducted monthly by ACUMAR rose since mid-2008, when there were no inspections conducted, to 514 inspections recorded in December 2011. If, upon inspection, a given industry was classified as contaminating, it was required to present and carry out a "reconversion plan," laying out what steps it would take to reduce the contamination it produced.

Those numbers indicate a positive trend in terms of immediate effects, but they tell us little about actual control over industrial contamination or its results. We can dig deeper and look at the behavior of the industries that were identified as being contaminating agents by ACUMAR's inspectors. Did they submit a plan for reconverting to more environmentally friendly practices, and did they reconvert? By early 2012, four years after inspections began in mid-2008 and six years after the ruling,

5 Interview with subsecretary of environment A, Buenos Aires Province, February 14, 2013.

6 9,082,726 of 21,919,071 Argentine pesos (Auditoría General de la Nación 2016, 13).

the majority of contaminating industries (71 percent of the 780 total) had submitted an environmental reconversion plan within the time frame required by ACUMAR. Twenty-five percent had yet to submit a plan, 3 percent reported having finished executing their plan, but had not been evaluated yet while 1 percent had been certified as having successfully reconverted.[7] By 2016, 45 percent of the industries had reconverted (Cuerpo Colegiado 2016), though no information was available about emission levels after the reconversion. The inspection process as it began was far from perfect. Note, however, that the Argentine government began to exercise some measure of environmental control over the behavior of industries in the river basin where none had ever been exercised before.

The ruling also served as a starting point that encouraged similar litigation, and some successful judicial pronouncements, elsewhere in Argentina. Nader's (2022) study carefully tracks the existence of seven distinct legal challenges seeking to activate rights-based judicial intervention to preserve the basin of the Salí Dulce River in Tucumán. He shows that the legal challenges (some lodged at the Tucumán highest court, others at the Supreme Court of Argentina), directly drew on the *Causa Mendoza* model in their efforts to hold private businesses and local governments accountable for contaminating practices and conservation efforts.

Causa Mendoza also spurred the creation and circulation of information; the bulk of what we know today about the environmental conditions of the river basin, including how far there is to go, is based on data that was created because of the Court's decision. Before 2006, not even a basic census of the industries in the area existed and neither did any reliable environmental indicators or diagnostics of contamination-related health problems. Since the ruling was handed down, not only did the industrial census take place and the periodic monitoring of water, groundwater, and air quality start. Furthermore, at the behest of the Supreme Court's intervention, a socio-demographic map of the river basin was charted, accompanied by a survey of socio-environmental risk factors.

Another dimension in which the effects of the ruling were particularly noteworthy, even before changes to formal norms or resources had emerged, was the ideational level. Activists, government officials, and environmental experts' views coincide in highlighting the fact that the court's intervention put the Matanza-Riachuelo and environmental topics, more generally, in front and center of the national political agenda.[8] The secretary of the environment at one of the fourteen municipalities

7 Author's calculations based on an index of industrial reconversion designed by QPR, *Que Pasa Riachuelo* (an NGO coalition working on Matanza-Riachuelo issues) based on ACUMAR data for 2013.

8 Interview with member of the Cuerpo Colegiado, Buenos Aires November 27, 2012; Interview with member of the Cuerpo Colegiado, Buenos Aires November 28, 2012; Interview with subsecretary of environment A, Buenos Aires Province, February 14, 2013; Interview with subsecretary of environment B, Buenos Aires Province, February 8, 2013; Interview with subsecretary of environment D, Buenos Aires Province, March 8, 2013; Interview with expert on public law litigation, Buenos Aires, March 12, 2013.

explained this well: "[The ruling] gave hierarchical importance to environmental issues on a national and social level. . . . [this is crucial because] if it is not in the public agenda, no one cares about it."[9] The river's pollution had been a problem since the late nineteenth century, but one that had been persistently and consistently ignored by authorities. In her own assessment, Merlinsky (2016) also highlights the importance of the ruling to shifting perceptions and discussions around environmental and housing policy in the river basin, reconfiguring municipal priorities. For his part, Nader (2022) also underscores how the ruling empowered inhabitants to further seek redress and mobilize after the ruling gave visibility to their plight and allocated responsibilities to specific governmental agencies, including the new ACUMAR.

This type of effect was purposefully sought by the court: When asked if in deciding on this issue the court was "making [unnecessary] noise," Chief Justice Lorenzetti summed up his view of the importance of the court's intervention in the following words: "Yes [we, the court, are stirring the debate] and it is a good thing. Our role is to stir the debate. (. . .) Our duty is to preserve the rights of the citizens. Society must discuss how it will address its problems, and there you apply all the majoritarian criteria, Parliaments, elections. (. . .) What is key to democratic dialogue is that high courts introduce topics into the public agenda."[10]

In terms of organizational changes, the ruling further enhanced an organizational process around environmental concerns that was already underway in the basin. It did so by generating opportunities for sustained interaction within an institutional setting, providing information and giving the organizations and new networks access to public policy spaces. Local groups, NGOs, a few professionalized environmental and human rights NGOs already existed in the river basin (Merlinsky 2009) long before the court intervened. These organizations had been working together prior to the court's intervention to raise awareness of the environmental conditions of the river.[11] In the wake of the ruling, some of these civil society organizations found themselves working closely in a new institutional venue created by the court to monitor the ruling – the monitoring commission or Cuerpo Colegiado. I will discuss the work of the Cuerpo Colegiado in more detail further ahead. What is important to note at this stage is that the monitoring experience also influenced their capacities. My interviews with different members of this joint organization show that their monthly monitoring meetings and related activities not only focused on the implementation of the ruling, but that they went beyond into furthering the work of each of their organizations and generating new joint ventures.[12] These activities

[9] Interview with subsecretary of environment D, Buenos Aires Province, March 8, 2013.

[10] Pg/12. "La función de la Corte es poner ruido." June 25, 2006.

[11] Interview with member of the Cuerpo Colegiado, Buenos Aires November 27, 2012; Interview with member of the Cuerpo Colegiado, Buenos Aires December 3, 2012; Interview with member of the Cuerpo Colegiado, Buenos Aires December 18, 2012.

[12] Interview with member of the Cuerpo Colegiado, Buenos Aires November 27, 2012; Interview with member of the Cuerpo Colegiado, Buenos Aires December 3, 2012; Interview with

include, for instance, analysis of the monthly water and air data, and using industrial contamination data for a crowd-sourced monitoring platform developed and maintained with the local communities (*¿Qué Pasa Riachuelo?*).

3.2.1.2 Outcome

Nearly two decades after the ruling there are those who discount the existence and/or the importance of the effects I just outlined. To discuss the *outcome* of the ruling in terms of rights effectiveness I will focus on a few indicators that pertain directly to some of the *immediate effects* I already discussed: first, access to clean water and extension of sewage networks along the river basin and, second, the river's water quality.

Earlier I mentioned the advances in terms of resources dedicated to extending sewers (or sewage treatment) and drinking water to the river basin – an effort directly related not only to health and quality of life but also to the river's pollution. One million people gained access to drinking water as a result of the changes and plans that AYSA implemented since ACUMAR was put into place (FARN 2014). As of 2017, by ACUMAR's own count, sewage projects in all municipalities were underway. Though much work lay ahead, construction had begun on infrastructure projects that experts emphasize (Fundación Metropolitana 2018) were absolutely crucial as untreated sewage was one of the main sources of contamination.

When we turn to the concrete results of efforts to implement control of industrial contamination and water quality in the river, the picture becomes bleaker, while requiring more nuance. The sheer volume of data reporting on air and water quality along the course of the Matanza-Riachuelo increased. Based on data made available by ACUMAR from the different stations monitoring superficial water quality along the river, Greenpeace (2013) produced a report which concludes that there was no clear tendency toward improvement in the water quality between 2008 and 2012. In agreement with earlier statements made by the Cuerpo Colegiado, the report suggests that ACUMAR's thresholds with regard to the amount and type of substances that could be dumped into the river were too lenient and needed to be raised for substantial improvement to follow. Three years later, it appeared that the situation in terms of oxygen levels in the water had not improved.[13] In terms of concrete results for water quality, there was little progress. In any case, it stands out that this is a process where different types of effects can become interwoven: At minimum, the decision created an informational feedback loop that can improve policy and perhaps lead to stricter standards.

member of the Cuerpo Colegiado, Buenos Aires December 18, 2012; Interview with member of the Cuerpo Colegiado, Buenos Aires, November 18, 2012.

[13] "Riachuelo: La Corte Suprema desnudó los escasos resultados del plan para sanearlo." La Nación. Diciembre 1, 2016.

Before concluding, a few words should be said about health – and relatedly, housing – topics that I cannot discuss in detail due to space constraints. Of the areas in which the Court focused on its ruling, health is probably the one where effects are lowest, progress is slowest, and monitoring is most challenging. Studies conducted in the early 2000s by the Japanese Cooperation Agency were the first to provide conclusive evidence of the dire effects of contamination on the air quality and on the infant population in the area of Villa Inflamable (see Merlinsky 2009 pp. 184–185). Beyond that, there were no baseline studies that assessed the contamination-related maladies for the population of the river basin at large.

Following the ruling, but with some delay, ACUMAR began conducting baseline studies. The larger issue with health, however, is that the health problems that the ruling would seek to alleviate are partly a result of long-standing contamination and thus, in the medium and long term, they depend not only on the improvement of air and water quality but, more generally, on structural changes to the development and planning model in the river basin. To improve living and health conditions, but also as part of the efforts to clean up the river margins, ACUMAR undertook projects to relocate thousands of people away from industrial areas and off the river margins. This relocation process, discussed in the next section, is very important but has experienced significant delays and difficulties. From its inception it was controversial, oftentimes poorly executed by the local authorities (ACIJ and Junta Vecinal de Villa Inflamable 2012) and has been delayed. By 2017, the ruling's follow-up commission reported that only 37 percent of the total number of families had been relocated, though construction efforts had begun anew (FARN et al. 2017).

There is improvement in access to drinking water and sewage coverage. Should the ruling be seen as having low or no impact, since contamination persists – or in light of other shortcomings? Such an assessment would be inaccurate and misleading, for several reasons. To begin with, it would discount the progress that has been made in different areas. In general terms, as one interviewee put it: "It is a fact that there is a before and an after the Court. More has gotten done in the last four years than in the previous two hundred."[14] Moreover, as I show in the discussion above, policy changes, organizational changes, and the creation of new information about environmental and health conditions in the area generated concrete changes in the environmental politics and in the living and environmental conditions of the affected population, although the latter are uneven and come more slowly. Time is a tricky but necessary component in this evaluation. Saying that we are at an early stage in the process is not an excuse, but rather a reality check: The cleanup of England's river Thames (a similar endeavor in scope and complexity) took over fifty years (Attrill 1998). One of the greatest challenges for the Matanza-Riachuelo lies in maintaining these efforts over time.

[14] Interview with environmental expert and activist. Buenos Aires, November 27, 2012.

3.2.2 *The Collaborative Oversight Arena in* Causa Mendoza

Recall that collaborative oversight arenas are configured when court-promoted monitoring is in place and a dense legal constituency exists that can participate in and engage with these institutional spaces. Over the years, the Supreme Court of Argentina relied on a combination of different mechanisms to monitor compliance with *Causa Mendoza*. Within the court, one of the clerks, or *secretarios letrados*, was charged with following-up with this ruling. He coordinated a team of 10–15 individuals that came together from different *secretarías* (units) of the court and met regularly for this purpose. The court initially delegated the day-to-day oversight on a lower court judge in the municipality of Quilmes, later, on two other lower court judges.[15] It also created an external follow-up commission, called the Cuerpo Colegiado, where the Defensor del Pueblo de la Nación (national ombudsman) and different NGOs participated. Following its ruling, the Supreme Court held four follow-up hearings in which all the parties involved in follow-up presented reports, updates, and answered questions.[16] Public hearings as well as the periodic information requests to different actors (in the form of *autos*) were handled by the designated clerk and his team. Going back to my discussion in Chapter 2 of the continuum of oversight mechanism a court could deploy, this web of institutional tools configured a highly institutionalized type of monitoring.

The monitoring structure put in place by the Argentine court met with a dense legal constituency that was able to engage with and populate these institutional spaces. It is worth noting that local organizations had a history of working on this issue and with each other. Prior to the ruling, a larger group of NGOs and the Defensor del Pueblo de la Nación had been involved in efforts to mobilize and call attention to the environmental crisis in the Matanza-Riachuelo River basin (Merlinsky 2009). When the court ruled, there were already a number of organizations that had a history of advocacy and activism on environmental and human rights issues in general and in the Matanza-Riachuelo River basin specifically. Of these, six organizations were invited to participate in the follow-up commission. Their preexisting networks and experience made coordination easier. This Cuerpo Colegiado became the main contact point between the court and external civil society actors. The characteristics of *Causa Mendoza*'s legal constituency are summarized in Table 3.2.

[15] In 2012, this judge was separated from the process by the Supreme Court following corruption accusations. The Court reconfigured the oversight system delegating day-to-day follow-up in two municipal tribunals: Some competencies were distributed to Sergio Torres (*Juzgado Nacional en lo Criminal y Correccional Federal No. 12*) and Jorge Rodríguez (*Juzgado Federal en lo Criminal y Correccional No. 2, Morón*). My analysis stops shortly after this announcement, which marks a new phase in the process. Nader (2022) covers the role of these three judges in greater detail.

[16] Three information gathering public audiences were held before the ruling was handed down in 2008. Four follow-up audiences were held between 2006 and 2016. The 2016 one lies outside the scope of my study: It is expertly dissected by Barrera and Sáenz (2020).

TABLE 3.2 *Characteristics of the legal constituency for* Causa Mendoza

Rights Advocacy Organizations (those litigating, filing amicus "support" briefs, but also those participating in implementation, monitoring venues)	Asociación Ciudadana por los Derechos Humanos, la Asociación de Vecinos "La Boca," Centro de Estudios Legales y Sociales (CELS), Fundación Ambiente y Recursos Naturales (FARN), Greenpeace, ACIJ, Defensor del Pueblo, Defensoría de la Nación, Defensoría de la CABA.
Was there a preexisting network between participating organizations (previous joint work experience on the topic or closely related issues)?	Yes. The Espacio Matanza-Riachuelo was a network of associations working on these issues.[17]
Funding (do the organizations have funding resources for their legal advocacy or mobilization work?)	Yes. Not specifically for monitoring, but some of the organizations (specially the more established ones) had resources that they could channel to related activities.

3.2.3 *Explaining* Causa Mendoza's *Impact*

Collaborative oversight is essential to understanding *Causa Mendoza*'s impact. In this section I will show how this web of institutionalized monitoring spaces and the actors that converged in them helped enhance the ruling's impact.

For the first two years after the ruling, compliance with the most basic requirements set out by the court was minimal.[18] The year 2010 marked a turning point when the follow-up structure put in place by the court started imposing reputational and financial costs on the entities responsible for cleaning up and preserving the river basin: That year, the Quilmes judge fined the head of ACUMAR for noncompliance. My interviews with environmental experts, rights advocates, and government officers coincided in highlighting the ability of the Quilmes judge to, as one interviewee described it, "clear bottlenecks."[19] Nowhere was this more obvious than in getting ACUMAR off the ground. The public follow-up hearings, the

[17] Participating NGOs were: FARN, Greenpeace, Asociación de Vecinos de la Boca, CELS, Fundación Metropolitana, Poder Ciudadano, and Fundación Ciudad. (Interview with member of the Cuerpo Colegiado, Buenos Aires December 18, 2012). In 2003 some of these organizations partnered with governmental oversight agencies and a university to produce a report aimed at highlighting the environmental crisis in the river basin (Defensor del Pueblo de la Nación et al. 2003).

[18] Napoli and Javier Garcia (2011) and CELS (2009, pp. 333–358).

[19] Interview with member B of the Cuerpo Colegiado, Buenos Aires, December 3, 2012; Interview with member C of the Cuerpo Colegiado, Buenos Aires, December 18, 2012; Interview with member D of the Cuerpo Colegiado, November 28, 2012; Interview with member A of the Cuerpo Colegiado; Interview with subsecretary of environment B, Buenos Aires Province, February 14, 2013.

requests for progress reports, and pressure from the court for the agency to present an action plan succeeded in spurring it into action.[20]

A collaborative oversight arena can also provide the court with information about what is happening on the ground, as well as technical expertise that can refine monitoring decisions. Both processes are crucial to alleviating informational asymmetries and power asymmetries. The Supreme Court and the Quilmes judge relied on reports and feedback from the Cuerpo Colegiado to inform their monitoring decisions and update policy. For instance, the Cuerpo Colegiado and the University of Buenos Aires were asked to weigh in on the first draft of the master cleanup plan for the Matanza-Riachuelo. University experts were critical,[21] and in subsequent follow-up hearings, the Cuerpo Colegiado continued to voice concerns at newer versions. ACUMAR had to respond to these criticisms by updating the plan on various occasions. It was at the request and insistence of the follow-up commission that the plan was updated again in 2015.

Since late 2008, the Cuerpo Colegiado was also asked to comment on the different reports produced by ACUMAR and especially, on the air and water quality reports that were produced every three months in the new measurement stations set up throughout the basin. Their continued insistence on the need for different and better indicators to monitor process, progress, and results for ACUMAR led the institution to change some of its practices and indicators. The Cuerpo Colegiado was insistent in its reports and in judicial audiences with their demands for tighter standards. The process resulted in changes from ACUMAR to the regulations for the type and amounts of substances that industries could dispose of in the river. Members of the Cuerpo Colegiado saw the participation in the process and these changes as positive, but still insufficient.[22] This example illustrates how input from the follow-up commission in the context of oversight can have some influence on policy. Relatedly, it also underscores that participation in the collaborative oversight arena creates access points to the state.

Information was produced in the context of monitoring flows via written reports, but also through and at the yearly follow-up hearings organized by the Supreme Court with participation from all the parties involved. Different clerks who worked with *Causa Mendoza* inside the court described the hearings and the information that the court received before and after them as crucial for arriving at a sense of what was really going on and, for certain topics, necessary for processing

20 Interview with member C of the Cuerpo Colegiado. Buenos Aires, December 18, 2012.

21 Interview with member of the Universidad de Buenos Aires team. Buenos Aires, November 10, 2012.

22 Interview with member of the Cuerpo Colegiado, Buenos Aires December 3, 2012; Interview with member of the Cuerpo Colegiado, Buenos Aires November 27, 2012. In its 2013 report, "*Estudio Especial. Sistema de Indicadores Informe Anual 2013 ACUMAR,*" the Auditoría General de la Nación underscored this very issue highlighting ACUMAR's reticence to use results indicators. See also an extensive interview in Fundación Metropolitana (2018) with several experts and activists, including Andrés Napoli from the FARN, discussing this very issue.

information on an issue in which the court had no technical expertise. One clerk described the input and reports from the Cuerpo Colegiado as "helpful to the court in evaluating its own objectives ... [and beyond that] a useful [social] thermometer."[23] A senior clerk, who supervised the team within the court, highlighted the following:

> [The Cuerpo Colegiado] made important contributions to this monitoring process in terms of [providing] information. Particularly in sensitive topics like housing, trash, and public health. [...] Decrypting the information we receive can sometimes be extremely hard.[24]

The flow of information from external actors into the oversight process can also generate a feedback loop and enhance accountability. In other words, this is not just about the court receiving written reports that are evaluated based on criteria set in stone. The interaction among different actors makes possible a continuous and more participatory monitoring process that is akin to the experimentalist remedies examined by Sabel and Simon (2004). In both cases, permanent updating and revision is required. In addition, courts can open up a process of experimentation and work with actors to define the terms of compliance, rather than force adherence to a pre-established set of fixed criteria.

A good example through which one can see this process at work is the case of the relocation of thousands of families along the river basin. Cleaning the river's towpath (35 meters on both sides) required the relocation of thousands of families from their current homes to new neighborhoods. In some cases (e.g., the neighborhoods Villa 21 and 24), the relocations were also envisioned as necessary to improving the living and health conditions of families that inhabited contaminated areas. The implementation of relocations presented serious obstacles, providing an excellent example of an instance in which monitoring opened the possibility for the court to update policy as it was implemented. It is also a process in which the importance of the role played by civil society actors in bridging the gap between the court (and other instances of government) and those affected is very clear. Let us look at that process in more detail.

In 2011, the first relocations brought with them complaints from the community – some of whom reached out to legal aid organizations. Their lawyers recounted to me serious problems: Procedures were conducted through arbitrary means – without proper notification, without consulting the inhabitants, and, occasionally, people being moved into living quarters that were not even suitable for habitation.[25] Pressure

[23] Interview with secretario letrado 35, Buenos Aires, March 13, 2013.

[24] Interview with secretario letrado 32, Buenos Aires, March 13, 2013.

[25] Interview with lawyer Defensoría de la Ciudad Autónoma de Buenos Aires, Buenos Aires, February 4, 2013; Interview with lawyer ACIJ, Buenos Aires, November 23, 2012; Interview with lawyer Defensoría de la Nación, February 7, 2013. See also ACIJ's "Villa Inflamable: Donde Comenzó El Caso 'Mendoza' Los Derechos Siguen Esperando" (Buenos Aires, 2012).

from these organizations resulted in the Quilmes judge issuing a resolution in February 2011 in which he signaled there was a problem with relocations and a need for authorities to be mindful of the social consequences. Over the next two years, a protocol on how to conduct relocations was discussed, and some of the municipalities set up venues in which inhabitants could be informed of and participate in the relocation decisions (*Mesas de Trabajo*). Not all of the municipalities had these, or if they did, not all of them were successful or taken seriously by the local administrations. Discontent continued, with strong criticisms leveled against the role of ACUMAR. Further mobilization resulted in reaching out to the Cuerpo Colegiado and a meeting with one of the justices before the yearly follow-up hearing held in the Supreme Court in late 2012. At this hearing, Cuerpo Colegiado brought up the problems, and members of the community were present to forcefully voice their concerns.

In direct response to these moves, a few months later in December, the Supreme Court issued a resolution that was seen as an important and positive step forward by all the lawyers that I interviewed who had worked closely with people subject to relocations. In essence, as a result of the information that the court received, the Court changed the way the relocations were being conducted, putting in place safeguards for the inhabitants. The Court defined standards for the participation of the neighbors in the legal process, something which they did not have before, as they lacked legal standing. It also established minimum standards that new homes had to meet before people were asked to move into them. These standards were the initial building blocks that culminated in 2017 in ACUMAR issuing a protocol for relocation and re-urbanization. As Ryan et al. highlight (2017), the process clearly illustrates the incremental evolution of judicial requests that shifted to demand and generate more space for the participation of *vecinos* in the process.

In the case of relocations as in other instances, through their reports to the court and in hearings, civil society organizations and other independent government agencies influenced the oversight process and the decisions that the court and other actors made as they monitored implementation. Aside from what I just described, Ryan and Napoli (2017) also document the key role of the Cuerpo Colegiado in influencing policy regulating water discharge. Civil society organizations provided information to the court, enhancing its technical capacity but, more generally, widening its view. This is an illustration of the feedback loop to the court and the type of tweaking and updating of implementation that can happen as a result of contact with and responsiveness to the broader social context. At the same time, as Ryan and Napoli (2017) highlight, it showcases how members of the legal constituency have more access points to the state, and can increase their influence.

Aside from promoting the flow of information, accountability, and increased possibilities for feedback and updating, a collaborative oversight arena can also magnify ideational effects. As was mentioned earlier, activists, government officials, and environmental experts coincided in highlighting the fact that the court's ruling had a significant immediate effect in this sense: It put the Matanza-Riachuelo and environmental topics, more generally, in front and center of the national political agenda.[26] In a similar vein, the ruling was described as a precedent that would shape future decisions by lawyers and bureaucrats with no direct stake in it. It put environmental issues on their radar, as exemplified by those of a high-ranking lawyer and public official who volunteered: "*Causa Mendoza* put environmental rights at the center [of politics at the national level]."[27]

These ideational changes had local ramifications. At the bureaucratic provincial level, the newfound hierarchy and resources given to environmental units and the existence of ACUMAR resulted in the creation and entrenchment of a layer of government officials conversant in and working for environmental rights, with resources. All the secretaries of environment that I interviewed saw their positions and proposals empowered, if not newly created, in the context of continued oversight of the ruling. What the entrenchment of the environmental rights discourse and professionals in the area can mean is well captured by the statements of Beatriz Mendoza, a health professional in Avellaneda who was among those who filed the original claim: "There have been tremendous gains in the many years I have been working on this topic ... before, when you talked to people about contamination, people laughed at you and did not believe what you were saying."[28] In short, the continued process of monitoring that followed the ruling helped environmental rights discourse make inroads.

The court's intervention gave political importance to the issue among key actors; its sustained and collective monitoring increased its visibility beyond the litigants and those who were already mobilizing around the issue. An indicator of this is news coverage of the Matanza-Riachuelo. Figure 3.1 graphs the number of monthly news pieces that three main national newspapers in Argentina (*El Clarín*, *Página 12*, and *La Nación*) ran on environmental issues pertaining to the river starting in 2004, two years before the court took the case. Coverage of the Riachuelo basin was very low in the two years prior to the ruling, reaching a total of eighteen and six yearly pieces in 2004 and 2005, respectively. Starting in mid-2006, when the court took the case, news coverage of the river increased dramatically to a total of 205 that year alone and showed a sustained upward trend. Interestingly, if one maps some of the key events that followed the court's initial foray into the Matanza-Riachuelo River basin issue –

[26] Interview with secretary of environment C, Buenos Aires Province, March 8, 2013; Interview with subsecretary of environment B, Buenos Aires Province, February 14, 2013; Interview with member D of the Cuerpo Colegiado; Interview with member A of the Cuerpo Colegiado; Interview with former director of legal services and human rights NGO, March 12, 2013.

[27] Interview with former director of legal services and human rights NGO, Buenos Aires, March 12, 2013.

[28] Beatriz Mendoza in interview with Fundación Metropolitana, July 2012. On file with the author.

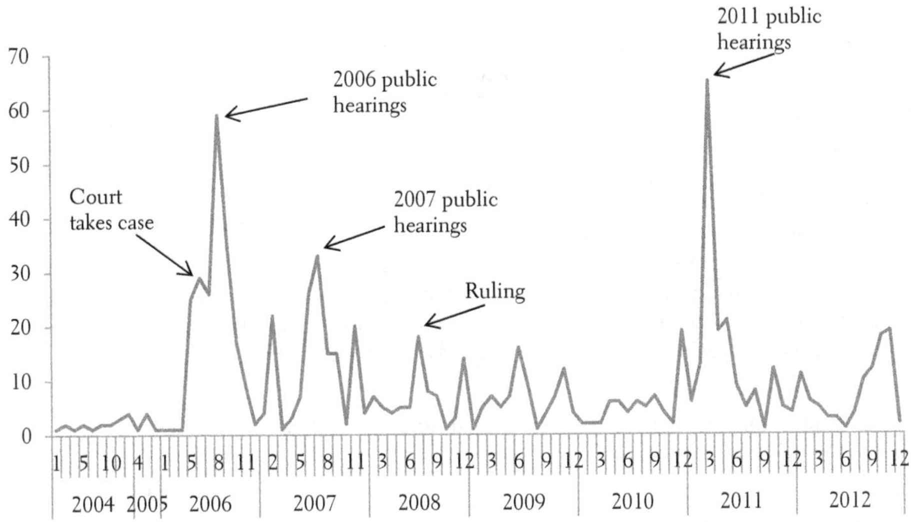

FIGURE 3.1 Monthly printed news coverage of El Riachuelo

events that are directly associated with the decision to exercise follow up over time – we see that other peaks in the news cycle correspond to initiatives like the holding of yearly public follow-up hearings. This suggests that the sustained and increased media attention to the topic may well be related to the court's own sustained engagement with the issue.

3.3 RIGHT TO HEALTH: T-760 (COLOMBIA)

3.3.1 *Impact*

I now turn to my second case study, the 2008 T-760 ruling in which the Colombian Constitutional Court ordered the government to overhaul the national health system. Somewhat similar to *Causa Mendoza*, a systemic assessment of impact shows uneven effects across categories. As the discussion illustrates, the ruling had significant and high impact in terms of changes to the formal norms especially with regard to the updates to the coverage plans and the equalization of benefits for all users. Both measures had as a result greater access to the system and the access of more users to more services, so ultimately rights effectiveness also improved. However, the status quo remained unchanged in several other areas (for a summary see Table 3.3). Overall, I classify it as a Medium on Immediate Effects and Medium on Outcomes.

As in the previous case, a detailed and fully comprehensive account of the developments in all areas is impossible. The following discussion pays particular attention to updates to health coverage plans, the unification of the benefit plans

TABLE 3.3 *Summary of impact for T-760*

Immediate effects	
Formal norms: - Creation of the Health Regulation Committee (CRES) - Law 1438 (reforms to the system) - Updating the health coverage plans - Unify health coverage plans (June 2012) - Different measures to improve the flow of financial resources in the system. (For example, modify procedure for charging from FOSYGA: in this context, reformulating the role of Technical Scientific Committees.) - Thousands of tutelas based on health as a fundamental right.	High
Organizational changes: - New institutional venue for fostering networks among health activists. Access to policy discussions.	Medium
Resources: - Instituted direct payment to hospitals from the government (bypassing subnational units and EPS). - The contents and process of definition of the health coverage plans were made public. - Research on corruption in the health sector by governmental agencies and NGOs is disseminated, and triggers investigations from governmental oversight agencies (Fiscalía and Contraloría).	Low
Ideational: - Health as a fundamental right - Raises awareness about crisis in sector	High
Immediate effects overall	Medium/High
Outcomes Access to health care	Medium

(first for children and then for the population at large), and measures seeking to improve the financial flow of resources within the system.

3.3.1.1 Immediate Effects

I first review some of the key changes to the legal and regulatory framework where the government acted on matters that it had long neglected. A good place to start is the most easily identifiable formal change brought on by the ruling: the creation of the health regulatory and oversight agency, CRES (*Comisión Reguladora de Salud*, in Spanish). Although the creation of the CRES had been ordered by law in 2007, its members had not been appointed by the Ministry of Health. A former CRES officer with a long trajectory in the public health sector characterized this omission as evident lack of political will, pointing out that the actual creation of the CRES one year after T-760 is directly attributable to the court's ruling.[29] The CRES was a missing piece in the institutional framework since it was responsible for updating the health coverage plans and was designed to be the regulatory principal for the private insurance companies that provide health services (*Empresas Promotoras de Salud*, or EPS for their acronym in Spanish). Along with the Ministry of Health, it was the party responsible for implementing many of the changes requested by the Court. Several of my interviewees described commissioners who lacked the necessary technical expertise as well as having a strained relationship with the Ministry of Health and other government agencies.[30] In this context, it is not surprising that despite the court's nod, which pushed the government to create it, the CRES was actually short-lived. The president terminated it in December 2012, and with that, all regulating functions went back to the Ministry.

Nevertheless, while the CRES was operational, it fell on the agency and the Ministry of Health to reform the health coverage plans – that is, the list of medicines included, as well as the services and illnesses covered. The court had requested changes in two directions. First, it ordered that the plans be updated. Second, it ordered dismantling the regulatory structure according to which those with higher incomes were entitled to better coverage.[31] Both things were geared toward enforcing the original intent of the 1993 health bill that all those affiliated to the system should enjoy equal coverage.

The government's failure until that point to regularly update the plans was the cause of grave problems in access to health services and medicines and with that, of the exponential growth of tutelas as a mechanism to secure said medicines and services. Since the early 1990s when the coverage plans were first drafted, demographic, social, technological, and epidemiological changes had impacted the dynamics and the financial needs of the national health system. However, the coverage plans had only seen minimum modifications, thus the gap between the changing reality and the outdated plans kept widening. The Court gave the government a February 2009 deadline to update the contents of the coverage plans in line with epidemiological development and extant jurisprudence. From then on, the government was to update the court yearly, make its methodology public, justify its

29 Interview with former CRES officer, May 1, 2012.

30 Interview with former officials at Ministry of Health. Bogotá. March 30, 2012. Interview with former CRES officer, Bogotá, May 1, 2012.

31 For purposes of the Colombian health system, the population is classified into two subsets: Those who earn more than two minimum monthly wages and can contribute to their premium and those who lack this capacity. Colombians receive differentiated health benefits depending on their location on this two-tiered structure and the government pays a higher premium to insurance companies for the users who contribute to their own premium. These differences in the affiliation schemes and coverage plans were originally viewed as temporary by the designers of the 1993 health reform. The plans should have been unified by 2001, which did not occur.

choices, and provide effective and direct participation from users and the scientific community as part of the process.

This was undoubtedly the area where the court's ruling made the most striking impact, though compliance was not as swift as the court's initial schedule aimed for. The government first updated the plan partially with a four-month delay. A full update was announced two years later, in 2011. Given that the coverage plans had not been updated between 1994 and 2011, the update alone was undoubtedly a really important step forward. Afterwards, the coverage plans were updated every two years. In line with the 2015 reform to the health sector (*Ley Estatutaria* 1751 de 2015), the Ministry of Health moved toward a different way of thinking about coverage: not by producing a list of fixed technologies and drugs that were covered but, instead, by defining a list of exclusions. These changes were part of an ongoing national and international debate that health systems all over the world need to tackle as populations age and finite resources are further strained. What matters for our purposes is highlighting that the court's intervention was a key factor in breaking the deadlock with regard to updating the coverage plans.

The process through which the first update took place, however, fell short of the standards laid out by the court in light of two requirements: First, the update process was questioned by some from a technical standpoint, in particular with relation to the lack of transparency and the robustness of the decision rules for including or excluding medicines (Rossi, Umbacía, and Sanchez 2012). Second, others raised questions about the participatory aspect of the process, which was deemed as limited in scope and duration. Early on, Giannella et al. (2009) noted problems with effective access to information about forums for participation and to the public consultations organized by the Ministry along with limited availability of information about the principles and methodology that were used to guide the reforms. According to Vaca (2015), a renowned expert in pharmacology, vetting the updates with the different stakeholders in the system and circulating information about the choices so that the decisions are legitimate continued to be challenging. In any case, the periodic frequency of the updates and continued efforts to refine strategies that can help guarantee the financial sustainability of the system were improvements.

Another area in which the ruling called for action was in the unification of coverage plans into a single universal plan. This unification sought to end the provision of differentiated services depending on the user's income. Though the response here was also delayed, as the initial deadline for unification was not met by the government, the goal was ultimately met. In 2012, the government announced the full unification, claiming it would result in over eleven million Colombians, who were beneficiaries in plans with a more limited coverage, to benefit from access to services in the more comprehensive one.[32] Note, however,

[32] El Tiempo. "Colombianos tendrán el mismo plan de salud desde el primero de Julio" May 17, 2012.

that in monitoring compliance with its ruling, the court itself found the measures lacking, particularly because funding differences depending on income level persisted. The premium the government paid to insurance companies for lower-income individuals was less, which generated a gap in financing.

Yet another objective of the ruling was to streamline the flow of financial resources within the system. Fifty percent of the tutelas in 2008 corresponded to citizens seeking access to treatments and medicines that had been denied by the insurance companies but were included in the coverage plans (Defensoría del Pueblo 2010). The court provided some new guidelines to evaluate these requests and ordered the government take measures to guarantee that health providers would be paid for these services, through reimbursements from the FOSYGA (Fondo de Seguridad Social y Garantía del Sistema General de Seguridad), a government fund.[33] Another part of the efforts to streamline the flow of financial resources was the decision to make direct payments to hospitals, bypassing the insurance companies, thus avoiding the intermediation process in which monies were being illicitly diverted. Direct payments provided cash flow to struggling health service providers for the subsidized regime nationwide. The effects of this measure were positive, and in mid-2013 the National Hospitals Association was requesting that direct payments be more widely extended.

However, efforts to streamline reimbursements also had a detrimental consequence. When the Court set up the system such that FOSYGA was the payer of last resort for denied services, regardless of circumstances, this generated perverse incentives for insurance companies to not pay for services but instead request reimbursements from the government. Between 2008 and 2010, the number of reimbursements from insurance companies to FOSYGA increased by 60 percent, approximately 2.5 billion dollars. These were services that (a) the companies should have been providing in most cases and/or (b) medicines that were in many cases grossly overpriced. Analyses of the aftermath of this particular aspect of the ruling (see for example, Parra Vera and Yamin 2013) as well as several of my interviewees[34] agree that this constituted a particularly negative by-product of the court's intervention. Addressing this negative externality added an additional layer of complication to the already gargantuan task of cleaning up the finances of the Colombian health system.[35]

In terms of ideational effects, there seems to be consensus among the actors in the health sector I interviewed – that the T-760's explicit recognition of the right to health as fundamental was of critical relevance. Until then, the right to health was not

[33] FOSYGA was initially set up to cover costs for people who could not afford to pay affiliation to a health provider (EPS).

[34] Interview with former director of one of Colombia's largest associations of health care specialists. Bogotá, July 3, 2012; Interview with public health expert. Medellin, February 17, 2012; Interview with public health expert. Bogotá, March 13, 2012.

[35] In late 2017 a new entity was set up to manage public health funds: the National Social Security Administrative Unit or ADRES (*Administradora de Recursos del Sistema General de Seguridad Social en Salud*). The ADRES replaced FOSYGA.

constitutional. Such shifts are those that scholars who focus on symbolic effects argue have the potential to alter the framework in which people claim their rights and also the way policy is designed. In this case, the continued wave of subsequent legal claims for the right to health became a powerful transmission belt that diffused the rights-based framework – every health tutela filed since is framed in this manner. Additionally, T-760 had an important ideational effect in changing the discourse of bureaucrats and the governmental sector, and hence on the terms of the policy debate. This point is also emphasized by Parra Vera and Yamin (2013), who show that after T-760 the political discussion shifted from being chiefly technical to being about rights and democracy.

In this ruling the Court emphasized that measures taken and discussions should be based on the logic of health as a fundamental right and should seek to guarantee its effective enjoyment. Activists, bureaucrats, and health experts I interviewed agreed that the ruling altered the terms of the debate dramatically as it is now about "the right to health" and "rights effectiveness" and not merely "access to services" or "coverage." One of the court clerks who coordinated the follow-up chamber summarized the process as follows: "I think that something unique happened with T-760. The moment that the court recognized the right to health as a fundamental one, that logic clashed with the previous one, which understood the right to health as a social one, as the delivery of a service. Two systems collided."[36]

A former officer of the Ministry of Health described the ensuing shift in the following terms: "It is now normal to hear a full-fledged bureaucrat like the Minister of Health speaking in terms of the objective being rights effectiveness, something unheard of until recently."[37] This had very concrete consequences. For example, at a macro policy level, two of the major reforms to the health regulatory framework that happened after the T-760 ruling – Ley 1438 of 2011 and Ley 2715 of 2015 – both referred to the ruling and developed policy within the logic of health as a fundamental right. At a more micro level, we can look at the example of the EPS quality ranking that the Ministry of Health was required by the Court to produce. In late 2013, the Minister of Health explained that he was asked by the court to rework the ranking in terms of rights effectiveness, to help users of the system make informed choices about their health provider in terms of outcomes: "The Court has told us to emphasize more the effective enjoyment of the right, emphasize complaints, correct the variables slightly. We are working on this. . . ."[38] Subsequent versions of the ranking effectively moved in that direction.[39]

36 Interview with former magistrado auxiliar. Bogotá. March 11, 2013.

37 Interview with expert in public health, former official at the Ministry of Health. Bogotá. March 30, 2012.

38 Alejandro Gaviria, Health Minister, in a statement to Caracol Radio. November 20, 2013. www.caracol.com.co/noticias/actualidad/minsalud-entregaria-este-ano-ranking-de-eps-con-mas-quejas/20131119/nota/2019480.aspx

39 See for example: Matajira Gaitan, Escobar Morales and Barney Iglesias (2016); Matajira Gaitan, Barney Iglesias, Bonnet Molina and Escobar Morales (2017); Matajira Gaitan, Barney Iglesias, Bonnet Molina and Escobar Morales (2018).

3.3.1.2 Outcome

What are the results in terms of outcomes of some of the immediate effects mentioned earlier? Updates to the health coverage plans, their unification and other efforts sought to improve the extent to which Colombians could effectively enjoy the right to health. To partially get at this, I will discuss three indirect indicators based on recent studies: first, access to new health technologies as a result of updates to the coverage plans, second, access to health services in the form of appointment availability, and finally, the number of tutelas filed annually (more on the specifics of health tutelas as an indicator below). I do not discuss actual health, since health outcomes hinge on many elements outside judicial intervention. Access is an extremely blunt instrument, but it is a close manifestation of the right. The assumption that undergirds this choice is that unless there is bad medicine, more access should translate into better health, and therefore, that rights effectiveness would increase.

On access, the evidence is mixed, but it suggests improvements. First, I will discuss the effects of the update to the coverage plans on access to medications. Looking at demand for new health technologies before and after the updates, a team of experts concluded that the update represented increased access to medications, as measured through the greater use of new technologies (Romero-Prada et al. 2014). The analysis focused on assessing percentage changes in the national demand for the new medications included in the update before and after it happened. It compared medicines against the new technologies that were replacing them and identified if there was a growth in the channel through which the new medicines were dispensed (personal expense versus coverage by the system). Greater demand and greater flow of the new medications through the system – that is, covered by insurance – suggested greater access. The authors show that 75 percent of the new medications included in the update had greater circulation – 50 percent of them increased their flow in the system by at least twice as much. This is noteworthy, especially if we keep in mind that many of the new medications included in the update were those that had been identified as commonly being requested through tutelas and ultimately paid for with FOSYGA funds.

Second, I want to present the main conclusions of the independent study that the *Departamento Nacional de Planeación* (Department of National Planning) undertook to evaluate the impact of the unification of health coverage plans. Recall that before the T-760 ruling, there existed two different coverage plans under the national health system: A subsidized plan (RS) that was heavily funded by the government and where coverage was reduced and a contributive plan, in which individual contributions to the premium played a bigger role and patients had better coverage. The study showed that the number of appointments in the subsidized regime increased dramatically after the unification. That is, patients with RS coverage had access to more appointments and the trend suggested that prior differences in access to health services between the two systems were smaller. The study also identified some areas that could be subject to improvement: in particular, persistent differences between the two types of patients in terms of timeliness and quality of service. The researchers argued that these differences could have two explanations: On the one hand, service providers had not modified their extant protocols after the unification was announced, or on the other hand it could be due to the continued burden that processing and paperwork placed on some patients (Romero-Prada et al. 2014, 246). In any case, the evaluation forcefully concluded that despite the difficulties, increased and increasingly equal access to health professionals was an outcome of the unification reforms. This unification was made possible by the court's intervention.

Finally, if we look at the overall figures on health tutelas in Colombia, the evidence suggests that access remains an issue. First, a word about tutelas as an indicator of access to health. Tutelas can be filed by any citizen, without a lawyer, before any judge, when they feel a constitutional right has been violated. Since the tutela was created in 1991, its use increased exponentially as it is an easy, accessible, and expedient legal mechanism to enforce fundamental rights. In the late 1990s, tutelas became a primary means for citizens to get access to medications, health services, or procedures that were excluded from the coverage plan (outdated until the court intervened, as we saw) or being refused by the EPS. The number of health tutelas had also been increasing steadily (see Figure 3.2), and it was in response to the growing judicialization of health that T-760 was handed down in 2008. The number of tutelas is commonly used as an indicator of problems with access to health, to the point that the Ombudsman monitors the numbers yearly, analyzing changes in the trends through public reports.[40]

Figure 3.2 shows that following 2008 when the T-760 came out, the number of health tutelas filed in Colombia decreased. However, the data also shows that starting in 2010, the number of health-related tutelas began rising again. We should keep in mind that the number of tutelas filed yearly has grown steadily. To fully understand the trends given in Figure 3.2, it is useful to think about them in a broader context. Figure 3.3 compares the growth rate of tutelas in general with health tutelas in particular between 2000 and 2016. Historically, the growth rate of health tutelas was higher than that of tutelas in general, except for some years after T-760 (2009, 2010, 2013, 2014, and 2016). The changes implemented by T-760 thus put a break on some aspects of the judicialization of access to health in Colombia, but it did not pause the recourse to the judicial system entirely. Despite some improvements, this data suggests that serious problems with access persist.[41]

[40] See, for example, Defensoría del Pueblo (2010, 2011, 2012).

[41] Gianella-Malca, Gloppen and Fosse (2013) reach a similar conclusion in their analyses of the decision's effects on children in Bogotá.

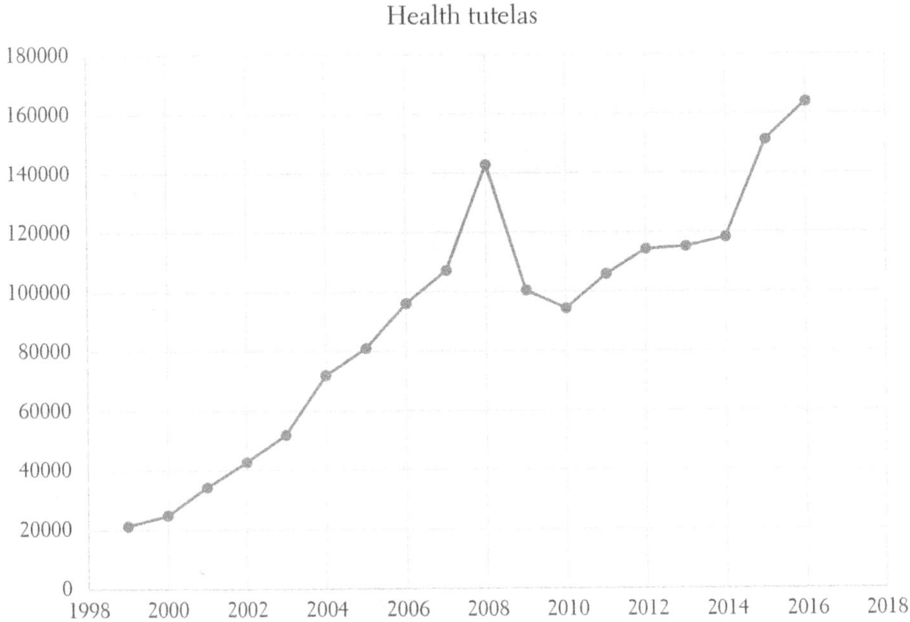

FIGURE 3.2 Total number of health tutelas in Colombia.
Source: Defensoría del Pueblo (2016)

3.3.2 *Collaborative Oversight Arenas for T-760*

After T-760 ruling was handed down, the Colombian Constitutional Court like the Supreme Court of Argentina relied on a combination of institutional tools to monitor compliance which configured a collaborative oversight arena. A special unit within the court was charged exclusively with following up with this case; this Sala de Seguimiento was headed by a *magistrado auxiliar* (clerk)[42] who coordinated a staff of six. Like its counterpart in Argentina, the court held public hearings (July 2011 and May 2012[43]) where different parties presented reports and answered questions. The Colombian court also used *autos* (formal communications) as the main mechanism to communicate with external actors and require information from them.

In addition, the Constitutional Court created two external follow-up commissions: *Así Vamos en Salud* in 2009 and the CSR (*Comisión de Seguimiento a la T-760 y Reforma al Sistema de Salud, CSR*) in late 2010. Of the two, the latter

42 For comparability, I will refer to Argentina's secretarios letrados and Colombia's magistrados auxiliares as clerks.

43 One additional follow-up hearing was conducted in December 2018, but that one falls outside the time frame of this study.

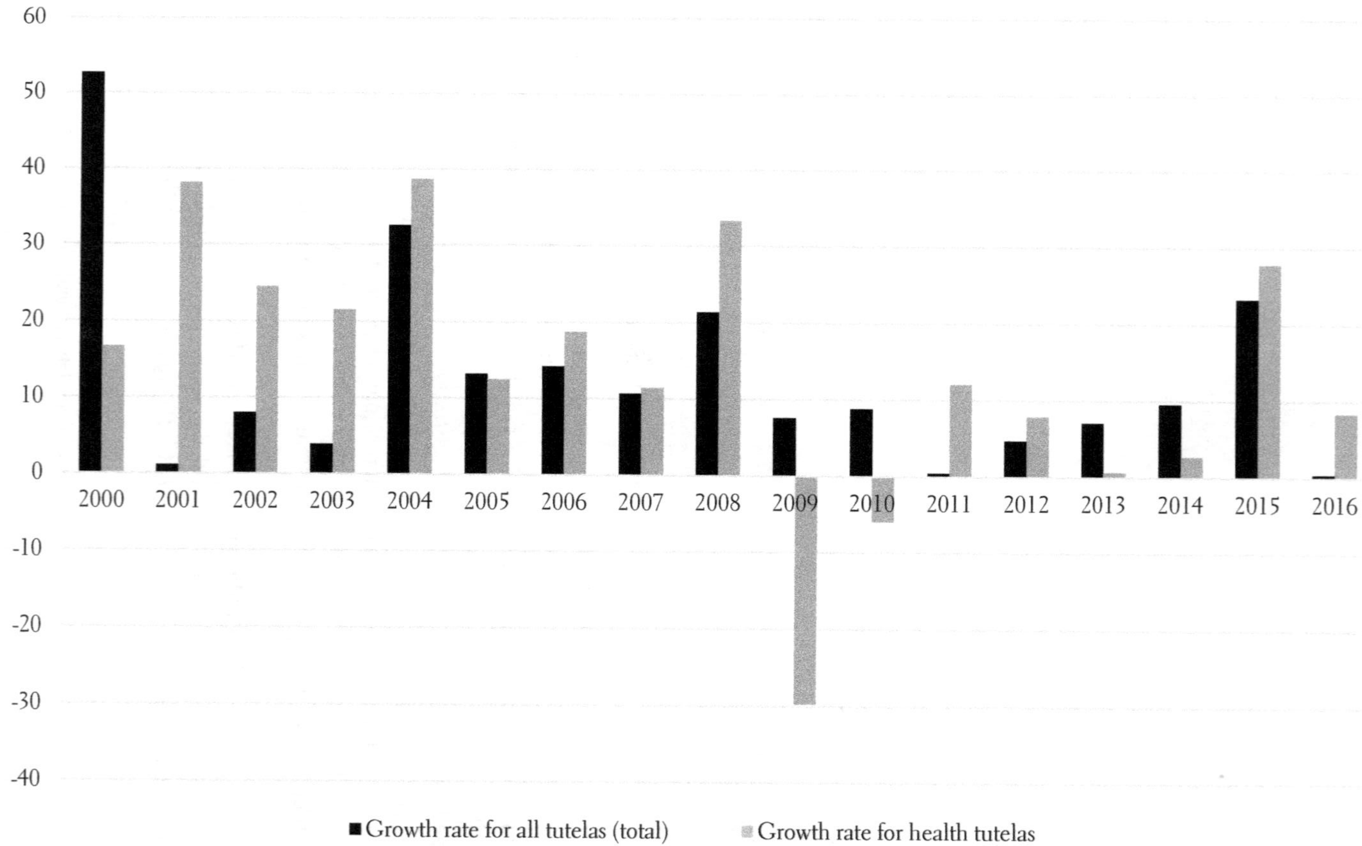

FIGURE 3.3 Growth rate for all tutelas and for health tutelas

TABLE 3.4 *Legal constituency for T-760*

Rights Advocacy Organizations (those litigating, filing amicus "support" briefs, but also those participating in implementation, monitoring venues)	Viva la Ciudadanía, Facultad de Medicina UN, U. Santo Tomás, Asociación de Usuarios de Alto Riesgo, Facultad de Salud Pública Universidad de Antioquia, IFARMA, Universidad Javeriana, MNSS. Así Vamos en Salud.
Was there a preexisting network between participating organizations (previous joint work experience on the topic or closely related issues)?	Yes, most of the participants in the CSR are "repeat players" from social and political mobilization efforts around health in the two recent decades.
Funding (do the organizations have funding resources for their legal advocacy or mobilization work?)	Yes. Not specifically for monitoring, but some of the organizations have resources that they can channel to related activities.

remained active longer, until 2014/2015, and will be the focus of this analysis.[44] Aside from the commissions, the Colombian court also met with civil society experts, control agencies, and different actors in the system. At one point, the court created a team of Constitutional Advisers (*Peritos Constitucionales*) to provide it with technical assistance on specific matters. Aside from the informative meetings that this court occasionally held with different actors (which were mainly the same actors that participated in other oversight venues), the mechanisms the two courts drew on were similar and served roughly the same purpose.

Several civil society organizations working on health-related issues configured a dense legal constituency that was able to meaningfully engage with and participate in the monitoring process. Table 3.4 presents the key features of this legal constituency. Like in the *Causa Mendoza* case, where environmental organizations working on the Matanza-Riachuelo predated the ruling, Colombia also had a tradition of social and legal mobilization around public health (Torres Tovar 2011). The organizations were numerous, and their focus varied: They ranged from large umbrella organizations, to medium-sized organizations representing doctors, to smaller groups bringing together patients who suffer a specific rare disease.[45] Their presence, numbers, and trajectory are evidence of the existence of a pool of

44 Así Vamos en Salud functioned more as a technical advisory body and engaged less with the political spaces monitoring created.

45 From the grassroots collective action perspective, the one organization that brings together health professionals, academics, grassroots activists, and users with a clearly national perspective is the MNSSS (*Movimiento Nacional por la Salud y la Seguridad Social*). The MNSSS was created in 2001 on the occasion of the first National Health Congress, in which more than 2,000 activists gathered: "A common diagnostic of the main problems of the health system in Colombia allowed for the establishment of a political agenda to promote social mobilization in favor of health and social security, seeking to promote and create constitutional and legal changes with respect to life and health." (Torres Tovar 2011. Author's translation)

civil society activists and concerned individuals that were already at work and mobilizing around the national health system before T-760 was handed down.

Which organizations were a part of the CSR follow-up commission for T-760? When the CSR was first set up, twenty-one organizations signed its first press release.[46] Looking at the log of participants in the biweekly meetings the commission held through the first half of 2012, its active core was made up of roughly eight NGOs and civil society organizations who were the most consistent and active participants in these meetings. In terms of its core membership, the CSR was more fluid and permeable than its Argentinean counterpart, whose composition was more stable (recall its six NGO members were determined and fixed by the court).

The follow-up commissions that played key roles in the two cases that are the focus of this chapter (the CSR in the T-760 ruling and the Cuerpo Colegiado in the *Causa Mendoza* case) are dense, although the Argentine one was somewhat denser. First, the active core of external actors involved in the Argentine Cuerpo Colegiado included a government oversight agency, the Defensor del Pueblo. In contrast, the Colombian Ombudsman was also involved in the oversight process, but not as a permanent member of the CSR. At the same time, there was less funding available for monitoring purposes in the Colombian case. The difference between the two processes is particularly evident with regard to the institutional resources that the Defensor del Pueblo brought to the oversight process in Argentina in the form of dedicated staff members, meeting space, etc. Aside from these differences in density, the different civil society organizations that made up the legal constituency were extremely heterogenous in the Colombian case, and also diverse in their interpretations of the appropriate course of action, as we will see in the upcoming section.

3.3.3 *Explaining Impact in T-760*

Quickly after the ruling was handed down in late 2008, the court saw itself flooded with reports and information from the government and the health insurance

[46] The CSR's first press release in late 2010 states the following organizations participate in it: Academia Nacional de Medicina, Asociación Colombiana de Sociedades Científicas, Asociación Colombiana de Facultades de Medicina, ASCOFAME , Asociación de Pacientes de Alto Costo, ASSALUD, ASSOSALUD, Corporación Viva la Ciudadanía, Grupo Guillermo Fergusson, Movimiento Nacional por la Salud y la Seguridad Social, Universidad de Antioquia: Facultad de Derecho y Ciencias Políticas, y Facultad Nacional de Salud Pública, Universidad Javeriana: Dirección de Postgrados en Salud y Seguridad Social, Instituto de Bioética, Decanatura de Medicina y Decanatura de Enfermería; Universidad Nacional: Departamento de Salud Pública, Centro de Historia de la Medicina, Departamento de Salud Colectiva de Facultad de Odontología, Instituto de Desarrollo Humano, Discapacidades y Diversidades y el Observatorio sobre Infancia. Universidad Santo Tomás: Facultad de Economía Unión Temporal Universidad de Antioquia-Universidad Nacional, Campaña Colombiana contra las Minas, Anmucic, Mesa Mujer y Economía, and Campaña Colombiana contra las Minas. This list changed over.

companies, but compliance, here, like in *Causa Mendoza*, was also delayed. As part of its monitoring efforts, the Colombian court, like the Argentine, requested input and information from other external actors (civil society organizations and government control agencies) through *autos* or through hearings. As I will show, the information the court received from the different actors in the context of the collaborative oversight arena was crucial for it to reduce informational asymmetries and it fed into its monitoring and policy decisions.

For example, in monitoring the government's obligation to update the coverage plans, the court asked for input from horizontal accountability agencies like the Ombudsman (*Defensor del Pueblo*) and the General Comptroller (*Contraloría*) as well as follow-up commissions. In June 2010 the Defensoría and Contraloría noted that the participatory component of the update was methodologically problematic. In February 2011, civil society organizations as well as the follow-up commission, CSR, confirmed in their reports to the court many of the problems already highlighted by control organisms. The CSR specifically requested that the court organize a public hearing to assess whether and how health plans were being updated.

In a move that perfectly illustrates the court working with information from the legal constituency, the CCC organized a hearing in July 2001 in response to these requests. The hearing generated a wealth of information with regard to progress with updating the coverage plans. Crucially, it also imposed political costs on the government and exerted pressure by forcing officials to make public statements about their timeline for taking actions, their progress, and to justify delays. This event brought together the Ministry of Health, the CRES, the Ministry of Economics, different EPSs, government oversight institutions (*Procuraduría, Controloría, Defensoría*), civil society organizations, and the officially recognized follow-up commissions to present results and to evaluate the degree of compliance in the area of reforms to health coverage plans. Follow-up commissions, civil society groups, and governmental control agencies were uniformly critical of the actions undertaken by the government in the context of T-760 thus far. Although some level of formal compliance was acknowledged, these groups seemed to agree in pointing out grave problems with the implementation process.

Among the most problematic areas were prevailing barriers to access, continued evidence of illegal conduct, and misuse of public funds, as well as difficulties in assessing compliance in any comprehensive way given the lack of information that pervaded the system. Most existing indicators monitoring the flow of financial resources within the system were produced and controlled by the EPS. To governmental control agencies, this dependency on service providers for all information raised many questions. Although the government insisted in the hearing that the plans would be updated by the end of the year, the title of *El Tiempo's* editorial the day after the hearing summarized an important takeaway from the hearing: "Mediocre balance [in terms of compliance]." This headline adequately echoes what several actors who participated in it also expressed in interviews with me.

Several of my interviewees who belonged to civil society organizations noted that the lack of specific actions from the court following this first hearing reduced the bite of its monitoring, despite the media coverage it generated and the media attention it brought to the topic.[47] Yet, even in light of these shortcomings, the hearing and the court's continued oversight were often referred to by governmental interviewees as central in keeping pressure on government agencies, despite the long-term, and often "frustrating," nature of the implementation process in the eyes of some parties. A health sector officer stated: "[W]ithout the court's oversight, very little would have gotten done."[48] An officer from the Ombudsman's Office explained in more detail: "The fact that the court reserved for itself the verification of compliance with its own orders has implied greater attention from public authorities than would otherwise have been the case (...) The fact that the court adapted its own structure and took on follow-up as a central concern guarantees that the authorities will remain on the lookout until there is light at the end of the tunnel. (...) At least we observe progress."[49]

This bleak panorama in terms of compliance spurred a process already underway inside the court to improve its own capacity to assess compliance on specialized and technical matters. In this instance we can observe how information from external actors, including the legal constituency, was brought before the court or generated in the context of oversight venues to inform the court's decisions on compliance. In the six months following the 2011 hearing, the court called on civil society experts as well as representatives from the EPS to form four groups of advisors known as *Peritos Constitucionales* (constitutional experts). These groups would meet on a regular basis to provide feedback on a set of criteria for assessing compliance that the court wanted to design and to discuss compliance with the ruling. With the help of these groups, the special follow-up unit within the court produced an initial series of indicators (Corte Constitucional de Colombia, n.d.) which were used as evaluation tools in subsequent *autos*.

Here, as in *Causa Mendoza*, the court's interaction with external actors (through hearings, meetings, and reports) was important for it to get an in-depth picture of the implementation and process the information it was receiving. Three Constitutional Court clerks who at different points in time worked in the chamber charged with monitoring the ruling all agreed that the input from civil society and external actors was crucial in helping the court overcome informational asymmetries:

[47] Interview with health activist, Bogotá, March 13, 2012; Interview with former CRES officer, Bogotá, May 1, 2012; Interview with member of the CSR, Bogotá, April 16, 2012; Interview with member of the CSR, Bogotá, April 12, 2012. Interview with member of Federación Colombiana de Medicina. March 7, 2012. Interview with health rights activist Bogotá May 15, 2012.

[48] Interview with former CRES officer, May 1, 2012

[49] Interview with Defensoría del Pueblo officer. May 18, 2012.

> The Court receives an ocean of information and reports. (...) it goes to the experts for help in digesting this information. (...) Precisely to even out the technical expertise is that we call upon experts.[50]
>
> Monitoring mechanisms provide information. The court draws on these for technical expertise.[51]
>
> [Throughout this whole process] the discussion level changed. The information asymmetry began to break down. The court and the lawyers are not supposed to know about these topics.[52]

The discussion above shows that, like the Supreme Court of Argentina, the CCC used the information produced in the context of oversight to monitor progress. In Chapter 2, I proposed that a collaborative oversight arena could also go further and allow the court to build on external input to tweak policy. To illustrate this point, let us revisit the process to unify coverage plans.

Shortly after the first public hearing, in September 2009, the CRES publicly announced the unification of coverage plans for all minors, defining these as children under the age of thirteen. In response, the court declared the government's actions constituted only partial compliance since, according to the constitution, everyone under the age of eighteen is considered a minor. Consequently, the court ordered the CRES extend the unification to that age group and called upon the *Instituto Colombiano de Bienestar Familiar* (Colombian Family Welfare Institute) to monitor compliance with that order. In February 2010, one of the biggest insurance providers (EPS), *SaludTotal*, filed a partial compliance brief before the court alleging that although the coverage plans had been unified so that all children would receive the treatments and services included in the contributive coverage plan, the corresponding fee had not been updated. In practice, this meant that the government wanted more services (those in the contributive coverage plan) to be provided with the same resources (as calculated in the subsidized fee, which is lower in value).

Throughout 2010 the court received more reports from other EPS agreeing that the capitation fee as calculated was not enough to cover the costs of the unification. In March 2011, at the request of the court, both follow-up commissions and other external actors (an Indigenous EPS and ACEMI, the national EPS association) filed follow-up reports highlighting continued lack of clarity in the definition of services to be provided under the coverage plans and persistent difficulties in access to services for minors. In March 2012, the court issued *Auto 065 de 2012*, in which, drawing on the reports and assessments of external actors, the court asked the CRES to provide evidence that the UPC (Unidad de pago por capitación, or capitation fee) as it was calculated then was enough to finance the unification while guaranteeing

50 Interview with former magistrado auxiliar. Bogotá, June 19, 2012.

51 Ibid., April 19, 2012.

52 Ibid., July 18, 2012.

the financial sustainability of the system. It also ordered the Colombian Family Welfare Institute (ICBF) to continue monitoring compliance in light of continued complaints with regard to access to services for children. The group of *Peritos Constitucionales* had devised assessment categories which differentiated between "formal compliance," "material compliance" and "reasonableness in the transit from formal to material compliance;"[53] the court used this framework to remind the Family Welfare Institute and the CRES that the mere issuing of administrative decisions was not enough:

> . . .keeping in mind that there have been several complaints with regards to the lack of material compliance with the twenty-first order (namely, that children in the subsidized regime are not receiving unified health services due to denial of these from the EPS-S [service/insurance providers]) this chamber considers that it is not possible to claim that compliance with said mandate is limited to issuing policies that increase the coverage for minors in the subsidized regime.[54]

This clearly illustrates how, in a manner very similar to that of the Argentine court in the case of relocations, with information and support from external groups, the court modified policy as it developed in the context of oversight mechanisms.

By engaging in collaborative monitoring, the court also created institutional spaces that facilitated accountability by empowering and amplifying the work of external watchdogs: civil society actors and government-controlled agencies. This is clear in the case of the second hearing, held in May 2012, during which the court focused on financial issues within the health system. In this scenario the Comptroller General and the *Superintendencia de Comercio* (and to a lesser degree the *Procuraduría* and the attorney general) reported on the investigations under their charge looking into corruption and resource malfeasance investigations by insurance providers. Civil society organizations like the *Federación Médica Colombiana* had the chance to call attention to their own research showing that the troubling spike in *recobros por medicamentos* was partly fueled by lack of regulations on medicines and the intentional actions of insurance providers seeking to jack up prices. The investigations made public by the superintendent were especially shocking: After fourteen months of looking into ACEMI, the organization that represents insurance providers, they found it guilty of colluding to inflate the price of insurance and to hide and falsify information on medicine costs.[55]

[53] In Spanish: "cumplimiento formal, cumplimiento material y razonabilidad en el tránsito del cumplimiento formal al material." (Corte Constitucional de Colombia n.d., p. 16)

[54] Sala Especial de Seguimiento a la Sentencia T-760, Corte Constitucional de Colombia. Auto 065/12. March 3, 2012. Author's translation. (All the *Autos de seguimiento* issued by the court in the context of its oversight of this decision are available online in the court's website: www.corteconstitutional.gov.co/.)

[55] The *Superintendencia de Comercio* (Business Oversight Agency) presented in the 2012 public follow-up hearing of the results of an investigation which proved that the EPS association ACEMI had undertaken restrictive commercial practices: colluding to define criteria for the

The hearing brought public and government attention to these issues creating a platform that magnified and gave weight to the accusations. In the words of an expert on public law litigation and the T-760 in particular, "the court's entrance made visible the abuses of insurance providers. The process of the implementing and monitoring T-760 empowered control organisms (. . .) This problem was of such magnitude and the court is the first institution that opens a door [to discuss it] . . . given the problem, that was no small thing."[56] The speed and effectiveness of the investigative organisms varied, however, and, in some cases, were not divorced from larger political calculations. Carlos Palacino, the president of Colombia's biggest health insurance provider SaludCoop – who had already been forced to step down in 2011 amidst a scandal of corruption and fraud – was found guilty by the general comptroller of embezzlement. In a similar vein, shortly after the hearing, the superintendent fined ACEMI members. In 2014 the government took over SaludCoop, eventually shutting it down, and the attorney general (AG) started a criminal investigation against Palacino. However, it took until 2016, and the appointment of a new attorney general, for charges to be pressed and a new health fraud investigative unit to be created within the AG's office. The new attorney general charged Palacino of misusing public funds. In essence, the Fiscalia's investigation confirmed what civil society organizations had highlighted during the CCC hearing in 2012: That governmental resources transferred to SaludCoop which should have gone toward covering health services were diverted to finance the company's investments in Colombia and abroad. Palacino was jailed in early 2018.[57]

The limits and delays with the reach of some of the investigations highlight the broader political challenges in fighting corruption. For example, news reports attributed the delays with the investigations within the AG's office before 2016 to ties between the then attorney general Eduardo Montealegre and Palacino, as Montealegre had previously represented Saludcoop. When a new AG was appointed, looking into corruption in the health sector became a priority. Despite these limitations – which underscore the extent to which these processes are not divorced from their context – it is no small feat that the oversight process endorsed by the court was a scenario in which civil society organizations and government-controlled agencies were able to hold agents of the health system accountable for their actions, particularly for the lack of regulation and rampant corruption. As the legal investigations advanced and became known to a wider public, it became increasingly clear that the problem with the health system was not insufficient funding, but corruption.

denial of services outside those defined by the government and coordinating to provide altered information to the Ministry of Health. (Report on file with the author.)

56 Interview with public litigation expert. Bogotá. August 15, 2012.

57 "Expresidente del grupo Saludcoop, a responder por millonario peculado." El Tiempo. July 6, 2018.

Deploying a collaborative oversight arena can also generate bidirectional synergies in the sense that while external actors provide the court with information and technical clout, these actors are also drawn to the court and use their participation to gain access to key political spaces, and to coordinate to diffuse their own policy ideas and generate change. From this perspective, some of the court's oversight mechanisms can serve as institutional spaces for actors in the legal constituency to use as a political megaphone.

Many civil society actors deeply value the court's involvement in the national health debate. They perceive other institutions in the Colombian political system (namely, the Executive and Congress) as very difficult to permeate, corrupt, and/or fully committed to preserving the existing system. Several activists I interviewed considered that the court was either the only avenue open to high-level political institutions or they at least thought of it as a crucial ally. In recognizing coalitions of actors in the legal constituency as its interlocutors, the court has the potential to promote the work of organizations that may go on to build the political dynamic. In this sense, the experience of the CSR as a formally recognized follow-up commission is interesting.

As we have seen, the CSR contributed to the assessment of compliance with the ruling by filing reports, responding to *autos* and participating in hearings and meetings with the court. My observation of CSR meetings in 2013 afforded me a window into their activities and agenda, which often went beyond monitoring, just as the activities of the follow-up commission in *Causa Mendoza* sometimes went beyond. The different organizations that made up the CSR follow-up commission used the recognition that was afforded to them by the court to have access to other institutional state venues: to dialogue with members of Congress, to participate in academic debates, and to connect with other health-related organizations seeking to promote alliances and concrete policy initiatives. This was an interesting organizational change that sprung from the context of monitoring. The ruling offered an opportunity for institutional mobilization and recognition that, like in the case of *Causa Mendoza*, gave actors in civil society who were already working on health-related issues before T-760 a chance to participate and have some incidence in public policy and debates.

From early on, the CSR committed itself not only to monitoring the T-760 but it also chose to adopt a second objective in seeking to promote political mobilization around a reform of the health system (CSR 2010). As such, the CSR was not a technical oversight body, which was the profile of the earlier civil society follow-up commission, *Así Vamos en Salud*, but had a more openly activist profile. The political profile that the CSR chose was no doubt related to the track record and experience of its core members, seasoned health activists, and/or scholars, including some human rights activists. With these profiles in mind, the early decision to give the follow-up commission a broader mission and agenda is not surprising. The CSR was instrumental in the court calling for the first public hearing in July 2011 – as we saw – and in meetings with the court, it provided suggestions as to the list of participants for both that hearing and the one held in May 2012.[58] In both instances, the CSR made it a point to use its intervention not only to evaluate compliance, but also to denounce the flaws and corruption in what they viewed as a failed system. In pursuing their parallel and linked objective of promoting a larger reform of the health system's entire structure, the commission drafted projects for two major health bills (a *Ley Estatutaria* and *Ley Ordinaria*) while promoting meetings and alliances with other players. In short, they actively tried to use their standing as a follow-up commission to coordinate efforts and promote large-scale political change.

This more openly political profile was not something that all of the organizations that participated in the CSR agreed on. My observation of the CSR meetings suggested that the core members of the CSR shared this particular objective and worked toward it. But outside that small nucleus, it was harder to engage other civil society organizations in a sustained manner around this agenda. The differences were rooted in the extreme diversity of interests of the many participating organizations. The organizations were numerous, and they included everything from patient associations, organizations advocating for specific kind of patients (cancer, rare diseases, etc.), doctors' organizations, research-oriented NGOs, and research groups within universities to human rights organizations. While in *Causa Mendoza* a smaller group of organizations with dedicated resources could coordinate efforts more easily, in the case of T-760 this task was harder. The lack of consensus among all participants over the perspective guiding these political efforts and the greater number of organizations involved made broader, all-encompassing endeavors more difficult.

3.4 ALTERNATIVE EXPLANATIONS

Rights effectiveness does not only hinge on judicial intervention. In that sense, my argument does not claim that collaborative oversight arenas are solely responsible for meaningful changes – other elements can and do contribute to the realization of rights. My aim is to specify and uncover the mechanisms that link collaborative oversight arenas and impact. As this chapter showed, the joint presence of court-promoted monitoring mechanisms and dense legal constituencies made possible synergies that account for some unique processes: For example, the creation of large volumes of information regarding implementation by those tasked with complying with the order but also by oversight agencies and civil society organizations. In the absence of the court's monitoring, we would simply not observe the requests for

[58] Interview with members of the CSR February 25, 2012 and April 12, 2012, Bogotá. See also: Sala Especial de Seguimiento a la T-760, Corte Constitucional de Colombia. Auto 110/11. May 27, 2011.

reports and information in the first place, nor would we see the use of that information to follow up with the targets of the ruling.

Still, we should ask: Could other factors outside of the configuration of a collaborative oversight arena better account for some of the changes observed? Chapter 2 outlined some general alternative explanations that the research design allowed me to discard. Other possible alternative explanations are better discussed in the context of specific cases. Two elements could explain whether rulings have a significant impact: On the one hand, a favorable political environment, which includes the presence of political elites for whom compliance was electorally profitable. On the other hand, there could be changes in the economic performance of the country that meant the possibility of allocating greater resources to this particular issue. I discuss these possibilities for *Causa Mendoza* and T-760 in turn, showing that neither political calculations nor economic buoyancy can account for the impact we observe in both cases.

In the case of *Causa Mendoza*, there were no friendly powerful political allies who took up the environmental defense of the river because doing so would have been electorally profitable for them in national political scenarios. Indeed, the cleanup and maintenance of the Matanza-Riachuelo had not been a priority for any national, provincial, or metropolitan government in the previous decades, nor was the court's intervention in 2006 welcomed. Some mid- and lower-level government officials in municipal offices (like the environmental secretaries I interviewed) saw the developments triggered by the court's intervention in positive light and latched on to the opportunities offered by them – but they did so ex post-facto, as I documented earlier. They were low-ranking officers in a complex web of multiple administrative jurisdictions where different political parties as well as factions of the *Partido Justicialista* were in furious competition. Their work at the municipal level, though important, cannot possibly explain the kind of changes I described above.

Some might argue that broader changes in the configuration of political forces in Argentina could have made the opposition to the ruling *Partido Justicialista* take charge of key posts and decide to push forward the environmental agenda. This was highly unlikely: Extreme intra- and inter-party political competition in the Buenos Aires Province made coordination difficult. To illustrate, let us review how key political appointments were staffed in the years under study. The same party, the Kirchnerista *Frente para la Victoria*, was in power at the national level since the court held its first public hearing in 2006 until 2015, which is the focus of this analysis. The provincial government was, since 1987 and until late 2015, in the hands of the *Partido Justicialista*, the main branch of Peronism from which Kirchnerismo splintered. Daniel Scioli, governor for the duration of this analysis, was at odds with the Kirchnerista faction that controlled the national executive. The metropolitan administration on the other hand was in the hands of the left-leaning coalition FREPASO until 2007 and then went to Mauricio Macri's center-right PRO. Although few political actors at low, mid, or high echelons publicly opposed cleanup efforts, there is plenty of evidence of resistance and refusals to coordinate political efforts. The reality is that even after 2015, when Macri's PRO came to control the national, provincial, and Buenos Aires city governments, the Cuerpo Colegiado noted bitterly that the hopes some observers had that the political fragmentation could be overcome because of this did not appear to be bearing fruit (FARN et al. 2017). The fact is that electoral partisan calculation alone cannot explain change in this case: Things started to happen once the court's collaborative oversight arena began work, giving visibility to the issue and publicly scrutinizing the actions of elected and appointed officials as well as those of the industries.

The effects I described are not the result of a newfound abundance of economic resources either. Although Argentina's economy was recovering following the 2001 crisis, after 2009 it saw below-average rates of economic growth. Indeed, financial resources for the cleanup were a contentious issue and once again point to the difficulty of the challenge entailed in cleaning up the Matanza-Riachuelo. In the 2012 public hearings, for example, one of the key points of discussion was the refusal by the provincial and municipal governments to fulfill their share of the financial contributions that funded ACUMAR. Thus, it cannot be said that the backing of key high-level political figures or an influx of new financial resources provide a satisfactory explanation.

Can the presence of politically friendly elites explain the changes we observe in the wake of T-760? The reforms that T-760 sought faced a slightly more amicable political environment than *Causa Mendoza* in that the Colombian national government signaled its willingness to introduce bills that would reform the health sector. The presidency was occupied by the same individual and party throughout the period under study, Juan Manuel Santos and his *Partido de la U*. Lack of overt resistance from the executive does not guarantee impact in cases that seek to enforce rights, however. My assessment not only emphasizes whether national-level reforms were passed or not (as does Rosemberg's, for example), but goes beyond. From this perspective, looking at other actors becomes particularly relevant. Resistance to the orientation of the reforms ordered by the Constitutional Court from the Ministry of Health and the CRES, but mostly from the private insurance agents, imposed a formidable barrier that was (partially) cracked only through the sustained public engagement of the court with other external oversight agents, government officials, and civil society organizations. Monitoring was central to this process. As I already discussed, the heart of the matter is the government's lack of regulatory capacity and rampant corruption in the health sector, which diverted available moneys away from their proper use. The issue here, therefore, was not (simply) making new resources available: It was about harnessing political will, changing the views of officials in the health sector, and holding wrongdoers and government officials accountable. The scope of the challenge here was immense, and is ongoing. Yet the collaborative oversight arena made important contributions in the correct direction.

3.5 CONCLUSIONS

The use of monitoring mechanisms in T-760 and *Causa Mendoza* cases allowed courts to impose costs on targets by making use of different tactics including fines, political pressure, and public exposure. In both cases the courts treaded into extremely complex policy areas, to deal with issues of high technical complexity that involved numerous diverse actors. Monitoring over time generated resources for the tribunals to offset information asymmetries. Collaborative oversight, in particular, gave the courts more information from the government, but also from civil society organizations. With the information on implementation and gaps came greater clout and the ability to make more informed monitoring decisions and tweak policy as it was being implemented. In the context of sustained oversight, the collaborative oversight arena allowed courts and other participants to enhance the court's accountability function while also generating institutional spaces that provided access points to the state for other actors.

In the context of oversight, the courts sought information and opened themselves to external ideas. When participating in these venues, scholars, members of the follow-up commissions, activists, and experts not only diffused policy ideas, but also influenced some of the policy tweaking process and increased the courts' technical capacities. Beyond providing information to the courts, several of those who participated in these venues agreed that such efforts to reach out were also very important in the sense that the tribunals "listened" to a wide variety of views (some of them very critical of the implementation process), regarding how best to assess progress and compliance with the decision itself.[59]

In crafting collaborative oversight arenas, both the Argentine and the Colombian courts embarked on processes that are in no small part experimental. The novelty of the efforts was a common theme throughout my interviews with court staffers and experts as they described the processes they had taken part in. Analyzing how monitoring unfolds and how it influences impact highlights two things: On the one hand, the importance of the role of the justices and legal constituencies and, on the other, the negative externalities that may come from crafting collaborative oversight arenas.

My argument is that both a dense web of civil society organizations and court-promoted monitoring are necessary for greater impact. The reconstruction of the unique synergies that collaborative oversight arenas can generate has important implications for the comparative study of rights enforcement. In his study of rights revolutions in Canada, India, Britain, and the United States, Charles Epp (1998) emphasizes the importance of support structures in explaining growing judicial protection for civil rights and liberties. From his perspective, the leadership of

[59] Interview with a public health expert who participated as a Perito Constitucional. Bogotá. May 4, 2012.

activist justices is an incomplete explanation for the onset and maintenance of rights revolutions; indeed, support structures in civil society are a necessary precondition since they must first place the cases before the court and they can provide more cases and political support afterward. Although I agree with Epp that a look at organized actors in civil society is essential (and indeed my own explanation emphasizes their contribution to impact), my study of the deployment of court-promoted monitoring mechanisms sheds new light on the role of legal constituencies and, once again, brings the leadership of justices to the fore.

According to Epp, support structures require a particular configuration of organizational capacity (the presence of lawyers and funding) to be effective. Indeed, inter-organizational coordination is crucial to sustain long-term strategic litigation efforts so that cases can eventually reach the Supreme Court. My evidence shows that the role of legal constituencies is crucial in the aftermath and implementation of the rulings not only by encouraging follow-up litigation, but also through the influence they are able to exert in the context of sustained oversight. It is this effort at guaranteeing compliance that requires the most coordination – outside the United States, where higher courts are more easily accessible, getting cases before the tribunals is not necessarily an equally demanding endeavor. Moreover, the coordination effort that brings together legally empowered organizations in civil society to work toward legal mobilization is facilitated in no small part by the court. It is the court itself that creates institutional spaces where different actors converge. In the creation of those spaces and beyond, the role of the justices is crucial. Constructing and maintaining arenas for oversight on public policy issues requires courts, and justices, who are favorably disposed to facilitating complex participatory processes on public policy following rights-based perspectives.

Both *Causa Mendoza* and T-760 are rulings that tackle large, complex policy issues where private and public actors with vested interests converge. Although the evidence suggests processes that for the most part contribute to enhancing impact, monitoring over time can also be a double-edged sword. In the process of monitoring the courts open themselves up to interaction with other actors, becoming more permeable. In engaging with other social and political actors the collaboration brings to the fore the potential of the larger political scenario but also its pitfalls. Vague talk of undue influences from different actors in both courts surfaced in some interviews, suggesting the occurrence of calls and pressures from politicians, government officials, or private actors on judges and clerks. Nothing suggests that the pressures were so extensive that they fully paralyzed either process, but the comments were all indicative of the political and economic tensions that both interventions triggered.

In the Mendoza case, for example, the Quilmes judge who had been charged by the Supreme Court to handle the everyday follow-up and paperwork was removed from this position after accusations that his family members had benefited from hefty contracts in the context of cleanup efforts in the river. When the monitoring process was compromised, the Supreme Court reacted quickly and asked the General Auditor to investigate, removing the judge, and making sure that the monitoring process was not compromised. In a political environment where such accusations are common and not often taken seriously, such a response is actually an exception.

Another challenge that begins to surface with in both cases is the time-consuming nature of monitoring. Sustaining these efforts over time requires resources and sustained attention. At the time of writing, both cases were still ongoing, with observers claiming that full compliance with either ruling was far away. This raises an important question: How far and for how long should the court keep these cases open and monitor? There is no easy answer, but in Chapter 6, I explore some alternatives and their implications through two cases decided by the Supreme Court of India, the tribunal that has been engaged in monitoring for the longest period anywhere in the world.

4

Assessing the Effects of Monitoring Mechanisms and Legal Constituencies

4.1 INTRODUCTION

This chapter presents four case studies of landmark rulings on socioeconomic rights. Each pair of case studies seeks to uncover the influence that one of two elements can have on judicial impact: court-promoted monitoring mechanisms and the presence of legal constituencies. Whereas Chapter 3 explored their combined effects – when they come together to configure collaborative oversight arenas – here the paired comparisons allow us to explore their contributions separately.

To begin with, in the first paired comparison I discuss two structural cases that have dense legal constituencies but no court-promoted oversight mechanisms: First, *Causa Verbitsky* in Argentina, a decision in which the court safeguarded the rights of inmates in the Buenos Aires Province. Second, C-383 1999 in Colombia, a decision in which the court safeguarded the right to housing of Colombian mortgage debtors. In Chapter 2, I suggested that the presence of dense legal constituencies should result in judicial cascades – that is, the filing of cases and then judicial decisions extending similar benefits to other similarly situated actors. Additionally, we should also observe that the legal constituencies continue to mobilize after the legal victory (legal and political mobilization), and in so doing, create more information and keep the issue relevant.

As this chapter shows, these cases with dense legal constituencies have higher impact in dimensions associated with mobilization by the legal constituency: a cascade of related rulings that seek to build on the gains of the initial decision; organizational changes can be observed within civil society organizations; we also observe certain types of ideational changes that result from the organization's work to diffuse a rights-based perspective. In these cases, the absence of court-promoted oversight mechanisms means that there were no opportunities for sustained interaction of the different actors involved in the discussion (court, target(s), potential beneficiaries), no information feedback loop toward the court, and that there was no evidence of continued updating on the part of the court.

The second paired comparison looks at two structural cases in which monitoring mechanisms were put in place but where there were low density legal constituencies. The first case in this pair is *Causa Badaro* in Argentina, a decision in which the court protected the right to pension of Argentine seniors earning above 1,000 Argentine pesos. The second case is T-547 2010 in Colombia, a decision in which the court protected the right to prior consultation of the Indigenous people of the Sierra Nevada de Santa Marta. In Chapter 2 I posited that monitoring would be associated with longer engagement over time on the issue from the court, and greater ability to impose political costs on targets, generating higher levels of impact in formal norms and resources. Additionally, we should also observe the court using the information generated through monitoring by external agents to inform its decisions.

The two cases with oversight mechanisms but with low density legal constituencies (*Badaro* and T-547) have a different profile than the pair I first introduced (*Verbitsky* and C-383). In the first two cases, (*Badaro* and T-547), the courts were able to intervene in the matter repeatedly over time, drawing attention to the issue, pressuring the targets of the ruling, and thus having an impact in terms of pushing some changes in formal norms and resources. However, the lack of a high density legal constituency in both makes the flow of external information into the court more restricted when compared to cases like *Verbitsky* and C-383, or even *Causa Mendoza* and T-760 (discussed in Chapter 3). This is not to suggest that no information flows into the court at all, but rather to highlight what kind of information makes it to the tribunal. A key difference is that in the rulings where there is no dense legal constituency, usually the main source of information after the ruling are the targets, who are in charge of implementation: This tends to keep out other sources and other possibilities for external mobilization.

For each of the four cases I present an assessment of impact, characterize the legal constituency as well as the monitoring scheme to then reconstruct the processes following the notification of the decisions. In comparison with the previous two cases discussed in Chapter 3, the impact of these four rulings is more in the middle range. They share overall medium levels, but they show some variation as we disaggregate and look at the different dimensions within immediate effects. Impact reaches into different areas depending in part on whether there are monitoring mechanisms in place or a dense legal constituency.

4.2 CASES WITH DENSE LEGAL CONSTITUENCIES AND NO MONITORING MECHANISMS

As I explained in Chapter 2, legal constituencies can play crucial roles in the aftermath of structural rulings. They work to extend the benefits granted on a given decision to other individuals or groups and can precipitate a judicial cascade of related cases and decisions. Mobilization after the ruling, including litigation and the production of information, can play an important role in generating media attention and exerting pressure on implementing agencies and other governmental actors. Moreover, as previous research has shown, legal mobilization can facilitate the spread of rights rhetoric among activists themselves and among other relevant players. Overall, legally empowered civil society organizations can be crucial to the creation of new understandings of rights that are further enforced through their mobilization efforts (Siegel 2006).

In what follows, I show that in both *Causa Verbitsky* in Argentina and the ruling on the mortgage controversy in Colombia (C-383), a dense cluster of legal advocacy organizations continued mobilizing around the issue after the rulings were handed down, raising awareness, and using the victory as precedent and entry point toward efforts to further these rights to other populations. Both interventions produced ideational changes, but these changes touched on a particular set of actors and policy spheres, depending on the different constituencies that the relevant NGOs were related to.

4.2.1 *Rights of Prisoners in Buenos Aires Province:* Causa Verbitsky *(Argentina)*

In May 2005 the Supreme Court of Argentina ruled favorably on a writ of collective protection, *amparo colectivo*,[1] filed by the human rights NGO CELS on behalf of the inmates under the Buenos Aires Province penitentiary system. CELS argued that those detained were subject to inhumane conditions. At that time, 45 percent of all detainees in Argentina were held under this provincial system. Overcrowding and dire living conditions in prisons and police stations in this province were a concern since the mid-1990s. CELS, along with other NGOs like *Comité contra la Tortura* (CCT) had been denouncing the situation and in some cases working with detainees and public defenders to file complaints. In 2004 CELS reported that several of the major detention centers held more than twice the number of detainees they were designed for. Moreover, they denounced that prison overcrowding had led to the use of police stations, which were meant to be transitory detention sites, as permanent detention sites (CELS 2004). The overreliance of judicial operators on custodial measures explained growing incarceration rates and the fact that only 11 percent of those detained had stood trial (CELS 2004). The growing overpopulation of prisons and police stations was linked to increasing levels of violence and human rights violations, including torture (Comité contra la Tortura 2007, 42–57).

In response to the claim filed by CELS, known as *Causa Verbitsky*, the Supreme Court ordered the highest provincial court and lower judges to review existing

[1] An *amparo colectivo* is distinctive from an *amparo* in that it is a type of case where an organization can file a suit seeking the protection of right(s) on behalf of a group of citizens other than its own members.

custodial measures and report periodically on detention conditions. It also requested that the legislative and executive powers of the province update the criminal legislation to uphold constitutional and international standards – more specifically, the minimum rules for the treatment of inmates drafted by the United Nations and existing national legislation. Additionally, the detention of minors and sick individuals in police stations should cease in sixty days.

The Supreme Court also ordered the Provincial Supreme Court (hereafter, PSC) to act so as to prevent the potential deterioration of detention conditions. The Supreme Court required the provincial executive to inform judges of the detention conditions of prisoners under their charge, so that judges could use this information to order alternative measures if they deemed them necessary. Finally, it requested that the provincial executive organize a working group – known as *Mesa de Diálogo* – to discuss these issues, and to include CELS in it, as well as other nongovernmental organizations. The Mesa's chief task was to discuss policy solutions rather than evaluate whether conditions actually improved or not. As such, it was more of a policy development group than a monitoring group.

4.2.1.1 *Verbitsky*'s Impact

What impact did the *Verbitsky* ruling have? I classify it as having medium immediate effects and low outcome. Table 4.1 summarizes the assessment across the different dimensions of impact.

4.2.1.1.1 IMMEDIATE EFFECTS As far as formal norms, the ruling had several effects. First, a reform to the criminal code was approved in March 2006 (Law 13,449), stipulating that preemptive incarceration should be an exceptional measure, only to be used when other less restrictive ones were not available.[2] Note, however, that this reform did not become the permanent status quo. First in 2008 and then again in late 2012, Governor Scioli pushed for reforms that returned to a more draconian framework. In short, though initially the provincial government complied and made changes to the formal norms in the direction requested, those changes were neither permanent nor comprehensive. In response to the punitive measures, civil society organizations used *Verbitsky* to push back, asking the PSC to declare the reform unconstitutional since it eliminated basic pretrial release guarantees. In early 2013 the PSC agreed with them and temporarily blocked the implementation of the new framework.[3]

[2] Further reforms to the criminal legal framework which used *Verbitsky* as a reference point were Law 14296 and Law 14128.

[3] "Corte a la mano dura en la Provincia," Página 12, February 28, 2013. Note that the criminal code of the Buenos Aires Province had been reformed nine times before Scioli's 2012 reform and went on to undergo more than ten modifications afterward.

TABLE 4.1 *Summary of impact dimensions for* Causa Verbitsky

Dimension	Indicators	Assessment
Immediate effects		
Formal norms	- Creation of the Undersecretary of Human Rights within the Provincial Supreme Court - Law 13449 (2006) - New Protocol for Judicial Visits to Detention Centers - First *amparo colectivo* ruled favorably in Argentina. Opened the floodgate for rights-based collective claims and served as precedent for similar claims at the national level.	Medium
Resources	- Plan for building expansion (*Plan Edilicio*) - Creation of the Undersecretary of Human Rights. This office became a focal point for gathering data on rights abuses, new protocols for visits to detention centers and related activities.	- Low/medium
Organizational changes	- Political access of NGOs to key policy discussion spaces.	Low
Ideas/discourse	- Slow, but important progress within the provincial judiciary and its judges. Limited or non-existent beyond.	Medium
Immediate effects overall		Medium
Outcomes (rights effectiveness)	- Detentions in police stations decreased and then ceased. Yet, dire detention conditions remained a problem.	Low

Other important effects within formal norms were the creation of the Office for the Undersecretary of Human Rights inside the PSC and the cascade of cases and rulings that followed *Verbitsky*, expanding on it. In discussions with activists, government officials, and public defenders in the Buenos Aires Province, several interviewees noted the importance of the undersecretary, created in 2010. This office was charged with gathering data on and working to improve the living conditions of detainees across the provincial detention system. Although it was not perceived as perfect, it was described by members of the CELS team as a source of information, a space for dialogue, and a window into decision spaces in the provincial judicial system.[4] The following remarks from a CELS lawyer who worked with this case and on issues related to the detention system for over a decade capture the logic well:

> The undersecretary created an important space. For example, in San Martin a teenage [prisoner] died last January from a beating. The Defensoría, which now has

4 Interview with former CELS lawyer. Buenos Aires. November 15, 2012; see also CELS (2009) and Garber, Pol, and Martínez (2012).

a presence in this prison as a result of cases that were progeny of *Verbitsky*, alerted the Undersecretary. We also brought the ICHR's attention to the issue – and now the Undersecretary has created a monitoring group for this situation. (...) Also, it was the Undersecretary who was responsible for the Acordada 3415 [new protocol regulating judicial visits to detention centers].

The new protocol that this interviewee refers to was another noteworthy change in terms of formal norms. Judicial visits to detention centers matter because in the Argentine system, the sentencing judge maintains jurisdiction over prisoners while they are under the system. Seeking to improve detention conditions, one of the things the ruling was attentive to was the role of judges and the information they had about the living conditions of inmates under their charge. As I will discuss in more detail below, the initiative for the creation of this protocol lay largely in the hands of the legal constituency, but the Undersecretary was an interlocutor within the government for this discussion. As a lawyer in the Office of the Undersecretary explained, "if there are no common criteria [to evaluate detention conditions] things are naturalized. Certain situations [which qualify as torture according to international standards] are tolerated [in detention centers]. We needed clear criteria for judges' visits and their observing to advance."[5] The protocol was a first step. Still, according to the Comité contra la Tortura (2012), more work was needed for judicial visits to be independent as well as more tools for monitoring, through which judges would commit to improving the living conditions of those detained. Although judges were increasingly calling attention to certain problems and to the role of the administration in them, the frequency, effectiveness, and methodology could still change.

Verbitsky had a huge impact in triggering a judicial cascade within the province and nationally. This case was the first collective writ of *amparo* that was accepted and had a favorable ruling in Argentina. It was referred to by many of my lawyer interviewees as a turning point in terms of having set the ground rules for this type of collective claims and opening the floodgates that inaugurated an avalanche of rights-based collective actions throughout the nation, on diverse topics.[6] Moreover, it was used by other NGOs and government oversight agencies as a precedent to present, and win, similar collective claims in detention centers across the nation.[7]

5 Interview with member of the Undersecretary for Human Rights. La Plata. June 24, 2013.

6 Interview with former CELS lawyer. Buenos Aires. November 15, 2012; Interview with former Supreme Court clerk. Buenos Aires. February 28, 2013; Interview with expert on public law litigation, Buenos Aires, March 12, 2013.

7 For example, Secretaria Penal No. 1, Juzgado Federal No. 2 de Corrientes "Jorge A. Medina I/ Habeas Corpus Colectivo"; Cámara Nacional de Casación Penal, Sala III "García Méndez, Emilio y Musa, Laura Cristina s/recurso de casación"; Juzgado de Ejecución Penal No. 2 de La Plata, "Habeas Corpus (Colectivo) s/Agravamiento de las condiciones de detención en Cárcel N° 1 de Lisandro Olmos"; Sala Segunda, Cámara de Apelación y Garantías en lo Penal Mar del Plata, "Defensoría General Departamental s/ Habeas Corpus correctivo."

In the aftermath of the *Verbitsky* ruling and of the wave of collective claims that sought to make similar safeguards extensive to other detainees, the ruling had a non-negligible ideational impact among legal operators. Legal cultures are difficult to permeate and change. The Argentine judicial system, and Buenos Aires' in particular, have been described as favoring a "mano dura" approach and being less than attentive to the human rights claims of the detainees. Many consider this the biggest obstacle to any meaningful improvement in the effective enforcement of detainees' rights.[8] In their ongoing efforts to monitor detention conditions, CELS and the CCT highlighted the extreme difficulties in getting judges to more actively oversee the conditions of the detained and to disrupt the trend to use preemptive incarceration as their first choice (CELS 2007).

In this sense, *Verbitsky* helped crack a hard wall: Public defenders, justices, and others so inclined found in the ruling a powerful lever that they could use to defend and promote a judicial system that provided more basic guarantees and rights to detainees. At the same time, the ruling was a signal that even those not inclined, or not able, to take a more rights-oriented stand, could not afford to ignore these issues permanently.[9] One staffer of the PSC put it in the following terms: "Before *Verbitsky* there was a lot of resistance. (…) There still is, I am not delusional, but things have improved. (…) The new protocol for judges to conduct visits to detention centers is designed in such a way that it establishes common criteria and brings to light situations that can no longer be ignored. (…) Little by little awareness is created. Members of the judicial system warm up to the idea that they have a responsibility for detention conditions. (…)."[10]

As for resources, the main effect was the creation and execution of a plan for infrastructure expansion – *Plan Edilicio* – which sought to alleviate some of the overcrowding through building new detention sites and remodeling existing ones, in order to increase the capacity of the system by roughly 4,200 inmates. The execution of this plan prompted the first effort in the province to take stock of the capacity and actual occupation of all the units in the provincial detention system, a move that was welcome by civil society organizations. The plan was announced in 2008; in 2011, the Ministry of Justice of the Buenos Aires Province reported that 828 new spots had been created as part of the *Casas por cárceles* program, 576 spots were added in new detention buildings in 7 facilities in the province, and 468 new spots in other sites (Ministerio de Justicia 2010) for a total of 1,872 inmates.[11] However, to the extent overcrowding remained a problem, it also remained a politically contentious issue.

8 Interview with former Defensor of Santa Fe Province. Buenos Aires, December 17, 2012; Interview with CELS lawyer. Buenos Aires. November 11, 2012; Interview with member of Comité contra la Tortura. La Plata; March 25, 2012.

9 Interview with former CELS lawyer. Buenos Aires. November 15, 2012.

10 Interview with member of the Undersecretary for Human Rights. La Plata. June 24, 2013.

11 In its 2011 report, the Ministry conflated the figures for new spots and refurnished ones, making it difficult to distinguish between the two.

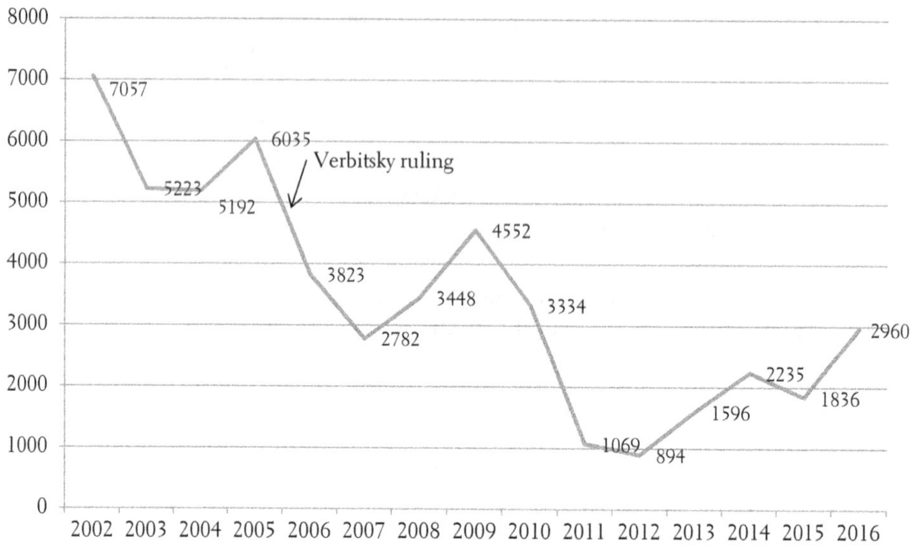

FIGURE 4.1 Detainees in police stations (Buenos Aires Province).
Source: (Comité por la Memoria 2018)

Activists maintain that capacity is lower than official figures indicate, and that overcrowding is higher than any figure the government provides. In short, although there were investments in detention sites, it is clear that upholding international standards for the living conditions of those detained – what the court ruled – was not achieved. Hence, I classify impact in that dimension as low at best.

4.2.1.1.2 OUTCOME One of the central requests of the original *amparo* was that the use of police stations as permanent detention sites should cease. Following the ruling, the number of detainees in police stations, which had been steadily rising, began to drop, as can be seen in Figure 4.1. The reduction could also be attributed to a declining crime rate, but interviews with experts, activists, and NGO members suggest that the trend we observe in this graph for police stations was indeed associated with compliance with the ruling in two ways: first, the results of putting in place a less draconian legal framework and, second, the decision to stop holding people in police stations and instead move them to permanent detention sites.[12] This downward trend was sustained over time and it is one of the few areas on which the assessment of both the government (Ministerio de Justicia 2010) and that of members of the legal constituency[13] coincide. The trend after *Verbitsky* was only

[12] Interview with Secretary of Criminal Justice, Buenos Aires Province. La Plata. March 21, 2012; Interview with former CELS lawyer. Buenos Aires. November 15, 2012; Interview with member of the Undersecretary for Human Rights. La Plata. June 24, 2013.

[13] Interview with CELS lawyer. Buenos Aires. November 11, 2012.

interrupted by a spike in 2008 and 2009 which was associated with the changes to the criminal code implemented by Governor Scioli and described earlier.

While there was considerable reduction in the overcrowding of police stations, detention conditions remained a problem throughout the province for the duration of the time period covered by this study (CELS 2012; Fillipini, n.d.). Based on data from the Public Defense, the CCT (2012) estimated that the system, which held a total of 29,060 inmates by late 2012, was short by 10,420 spots. The continued increase in the detainee population was associated to a combination of different phenomena: rising crime rates as well as harsher penalties for possession of narcotics, among others. What remained true according to civil society organizations was that persistent overcrowding contributed to widespread incidents of violence and human rights violations (Comité contra la Tortura 2012).

4.2.1.2 Explaining *Verbitsky*'s Impact

Verbitsky is the second of two cases – alongside C-383, which I will discuss later – where there was a dense legal constituency but no oversight mechanisms. This section first describes each of these two elements in turn. I then explain the process through which the presence of legally empowered civil society organizations influenced the ruling's impact.

The legal constituency is composed of two organizations that played key roles in the aftermath of the ruling: CELS and CCT. CELS was founded in the late 1970s and is one of the human rights NGOs with greater tradition and experience in Argentina. As the twenty-first century advanced, they expanded their work – from focusing on issues around human rights violations during the Argentine dictatorship to advocacy and strategic litigation on political and economic rights, including the living conditions of inmates. CELS was the organization that filed the original claim on behalf of the inmates in the Buenos Aires Province. The second NGO that played a crucial role throughout this whole process, but especially in the aftermath of the ruling, was the *Comité contra la Tortura*. The CCT was created in 2003 within a larger organization, the *Comisión Provincial por la Memoria*, which had been working since 1999 promoting human rights. The CCT focuses its work on promoting and monitoring human rights in the prison system in the Buenos Aires Province. Both are established and well-funded NGOs.

These organizations had a preexisting work relationship due to their experiences working with human rights issues in Argentina, and more specifically, advocating on behalf of inmates in the Buenos Aires provincial system. The aftermath of this ruling provided an opportunity in which their agendas once gain converged.

Immediately following the ruling there were responses from the PSC and government. Within days, the PSC issued a resolution requesting information on detention conditions from provincial judges and ordering that the practice of pretrial detention be put to an end. Almost simultaneously, the working group tasked with studying policy reforms to the legislation, *Mesa de Diálogo*, had its first meeting. Upon closer inspection, however, not all the activity or all the legal reforms translated into what the Court had requested or into improvements for the living conditions of the prisoners. Let us consider this in more detail.

Overall, the Mesa lacked clout. A first indicator is the absence of consistency in the meeting schedule. In 2005, the year the Mesa was inaugurated, meetings were sporadic. After that, and until 2009, they were even less frequent, sometimes with seven-month intervals in-between. The initial participants were representatives from the PSC, the Procuraduría, the Provincial Ministry of Justice, the Bar Association, the Association of Judges, and the Senate and Lower Chamber of the Province, as well as CELS. These organizations were not always present. Additionally, the Mesa did not have the required information needed for its activities. For example, the meeting records show that CELS noted repeatedly that the executive refused to make available the detailed information on the detention conditions of all the provincial inmates as had been requested by the Court. One of the lawyers who participated in these meetings concluded: "[the government was] faced with our demands for information, and with such striking differences in the evaluation of the situation [among the participants] ... (the Mesa) was very difficult to sustain." The Mesa's weakness was a common theme in my interviews, a point that was also highlighted by Puga (2012) in her study.

Despite the languishing of the working group, early 2006 brought with it one of the highlights of the aftermath of the ruling: the reform to the criminal code (Law 13,449). By November 2006, there was a 9 percent reduction in the number of people detained in police stations. Puga (2012) suggests that changes in the formal norms are not explained by the Court's intervention but rather by the support of political elites, particularly the presence of the Governor Felipe Solá, who was willing to cooperate. While it may be true that compared to his predecessor – Ruckauf – Solá appears less hawkish, this alone does not mean that he was a fully and willingly cooperating political ally. Given his position, the options available to Solá were limited at this particular juncture. Security was one of the biggest problems throughout his term, particularly in 2004; growing public discontent with perceived levels of insecurity were accompanied with massive mobilizations calling for harsher government responses. Solá's response was more amicable than someone like Ruckauf's would have been, but that does not explain compliance with the Supreme Court's decision. The reticence of the provincial Ministry of Justice to the Mesa and the chronic instability in the leadership of that unit clearly indicate that all of the provincial government's resources were not placed in support of this initiative. The situation was very delicate for Solá: It was not politically profitable, nor viable, for him to be a fully cooperating agent.

Beyond changes to the formal norms and the consequent outcomes, my theory suggests that a dense legal constituency, on its own, can have a particularly crucial effect in generating new related legal decisions, more information, and mobilization to raise awareness and put pressure on the targets. What role did CELS and CCT play in the judicial cascade of related rulings and in fostering the ideational effects that were described earlier?

From early on, CELS mobilized to bring attention to the ruling through their publications and advocacy work; they also tried to generate attention and awareness about detention conditions in the Buenos Aires Province beyond the national borders to create pressure on the government. To this end, CELS filed a claim with the Inter-American Commission on Human Rights (ICHR) underscoring problems with the implementation of the ruling. In June 2010, the Commission's Rapporteur on the Rights of Persons Deprived of Liberty visited Argentina to follow up with this process. To members of CELS, the involvement of the ICHR was a positive development, because it brought international attention to the problem, put pressure on the government, and gave them access to this tribunal.

CELS members also worked with legal operators to generate ideational change within the judiciary. Years earlier, they had undertaken a similar process: Through advocacy and educational campaigns they spread international human rights norms among judges as part of their efforts to bring former military members to justice for crimes against humanity during the dictatorship (Gonzalez-Ocantos 2016). Following a similar script, they decided to promote the *Verbitsky* ruling and educate some judges:

> What did we do? We set out to promote the spirit of the ruling. We promoted the ruling among the defenders. We gave talks and did presentations among provincial judges. We developed a system to monitor how judges implemented *Verbitsky*. We asked for reports. (. . .) We wanted the legislative reform, but we also wanted to talk to judges, have them stop jailing people. (. . .)[14]
>
> We undertook support and defense efforts with judges and defenders that wanted to file collective habeas corpus claims. We have a lot of connections and a thick network with the judicial system. One of our members led workshops, gave talks. (. . .) For the judges this was a true learning process. It generated many discussions. Not everyone considers that there is something good here; on the contrary, they believe the courts risked their legitimacy over nothing.[15]

Both NGOs also engaged in their own monitoring of the ruling's implementation, which resulted in numerous publications and public engagements.[16] Once the

[14] Interview with former CELS lawyer. Buenos Aires. November 15, 2012.

[15] Interview with CELS lawyer. Buenos Aires. November 11, 2012.

[16] See, for example, CELS (2009, 2012), Comité contra la Tortura (2012). See also: "Hay que empezar a discutir las reformas institucionales pendientes," Página 12. December 15, 2005; "Crítico informe sobre la situación de los presos bonaerenses," Clarín. November 11, 2006; "Cada tres días, un preso muere en una cárcel bonaerense," La Nación, August 6, 2009 (among others).

Office of the Undersecretary for Human Rights was up and running, CELS and CCT also dedicated efforts to drafting suggestions for the protocol guiding judges' visits to detention centers.[17]

CELS also tried, unsuccessfully, to get the Supreme Court and/or the PSC to take up monitoring the case. Indeed, if we were to guide ourselves by the letter of the ruling, it would appear that *Verbitsky* is a case with some monitoring mechanisms. In its decision, the Supreme Court charged the provincial executive with creating a working group that should include the targets of the ruling as well as civil society organizations – this appears similar to the follow-up commissions discussed for Riachuelo and T-760 in Chapter 3. Also, the Court asked the PSC to act if detention conditions were to deteriorate in the future. Though there were no detailed provisions for monitoring in the ruling, the remedies just described could come close to institutions that fall somewhere to the right-hand side of the monitoring continuum presented in Chapter 2.

Studying *Verbitsky* is particularly important precisely because of this murkiness. It is a prime example of a case that is lauded for its innovative legal approach, which can look like it included court-promoted monitoring. Upon careful inspection, however, it becomes clear that the provisions included do not amount to the type of monitoring that could constitute a collaborative oversight arena and that there is no active engagement on the part of the Court. For example: The ruling did request progress reports, something not that uncommon in structural rulings. However, as one of the Supreme Court clerks at the time explained with reference to *Verbitsky*: "Things were so that the reports arrived (at our office) and nothing was done with them."[18] Therefore, the fact that the Court requested reports on progress meant little in the way of monitoring because there was no meaningful engagement with them (for a discussion of why this is important, see Chapter 2). Furthermore, the Mesa de Trabajo, which could be taken as a follow-up commission, was set up as a place to provide commentaries on policy recommendations. It was not – despite the efforts by CELS – an organization actively charged with monitoring and one that provided a communication channel with the court.

There was no active monitoring by the court in *Verbitsky*, but the ruling can be seen as an early precursor, a first attempt at a different way to approach structural problems by this tribunal. This ruling was one of the first that the Court handed down after the reconfiguration that it underwent with President Kirchner (see Ruibal 2009). Supreme Court judges were trying to strike a delicate balance between asserting their strength by differentiating themselves from their predecessors (judges who were seen as subservient to the executive) and not upsetting things too much. CELS was particularly insistent in its efforts to get both the federal and

[17] Interview with member of Comité contra la Tortura. La Plata. March 25, 2013.
[18] Interview with former Supreme Court clerk. Buenos Aires. February 28, 2013.

provincial supreme courts to intervene. What they perceived as lack of responsiveness was a big source of frustration to one of the lawyers who was very familiar with the case:

> The Court did not foresee how to handle this space. (. . .) Our strength in the Mesa was that we had been put there by the Court. But the Court never defended our place in it.[19]

Efforts to gain any traction in this direction with both the supreme and provincial courts failed. The absence of an institutional space backed by the court – which active members of the legal constituency felt so acutely – highlights the importance of an institutional venue where civil society organizations and the targets of the rulings might interact. Had the institutional channels for court-promoted monitoring been created, the monitoring information produced by CELS and CCT could have been formally presented before the court as part of ongoing efforts to exercise oversight and hold government agents accountable for their actions. What little response CELS got, came from the PSC and it resulted in a public hearing in La Plata in late 2007. In it, the provincial tribunal moved in the opposite direction than the legal constituency would have wanted and declared the case closed as far as the detention of minors and the sick, as well as in terms of the need to update the provincial legislation on pretrial detention and early release. It is in this context that the PSC created the office of the Undersecretary of Human Rights, although it would not be staffed until a year later. While the creation of the Undersecretary was good news, the closing of the case was not. With the PSC's decision, members of the legal constituency saw that institutional opening close off.

All in all, in the case of *Verbitsky*, the court's intervention was able to generate some changes to formal norms, even though these were not as encompassing as they could have been if the international standards (or the legal constituency's ideal aspirations) had been fully embraced. These changes generated important shifts in terms of regulation, though not all of them were permanent. Ultimately, the changes led to the discontinuation of the use of police stations as permanent detention sites. The quality of detention conditions remained a problem in the province, however.

As we saw, the work done by the legal constituency took the ruling into other realms: *Verbitsky* was used to apply similar standards in other provincial detention systems, it generated changes in the legal operators within the province and gave civil society organizations leverage to access other international policy spaces. Given the almost asphyxiating political relevance of security concerns in the Buenos Aires Province which made departures from hawkish approaches unlikely, had the court not intervened, the changes I described would have been hard to come by. Although limited, the impact of the ruling was not negligible.

[19] Interview with CELS lawyer. Buenos Aires. November 11, 2012.

Next, I present a case decided by the Colombian Constitutional Court in 1999. It shares with *Verbitsky* the lack of court-promoted oversight mechanisms and the presence of a dense legal constituency.

4.2.2 *Right to Housing: C-383 (Colombia)*

In the late 1990s Colombia faced an economic crisis that had dire consequences for the housing market: Thousands of families defaulted on their mortgage and lost their homes. The mortgage crisis generated financial disruptions and social unrest. During this time nominal interest rates increased, and unemployment grew to 20 percent. By the end of the decade, the economy reached negative growth rates. The changes in the reference rates had a particularly strong effect on those who had acquired housing loans through the government-regulated mortgage system, known as UPAC (acronym for *Unidad de Poder Adquisitivo Constante*, its name in Spanish). As Clavijo (2007) explains, "the way that monetary adjustment was calculated between the years 1993 and 1999 represented an increase of between 10 and 25% in the outstanding debt of mortgage loaners by December 1999."

As a result, thousands of individuals saw their debt and their monthly installments skyrocket while their income was adjusted only at the rate of inflation or disappeared entirely. At the same time, the market value of their properties dropped sharply. By late 1998, 18 percent of all housing loans had been overdue for more than four months (for an overview, see Forero 2014).

In 1999, in response to a citizen's legal challenge to the regulatory framework that governed the mortgage system, the Constitutional Court handed down a ruling that declared the unconstitutionality of the formula used to calculate the cost of monthly mortgage payments. More specifically, the court struck down a portion of the housing bill that tied the calculation of UPAC mortgage loans to market interest rates. In its C-383 ruling, the court specified that the new formula should be tied to increases in the consumer price index, not to market rates, so it might more closely track with homeowners' incomes. The ruling required that all future loans be calculated under this new formula and that pending installments in loans be recalculated following the same criteria. With this decision the court sought to protect the right to housing as guaranteed in the constitution and ultimately, to democratize access to housing credit. This was one of the three key rulings that the constitutional court handed down that year on the topic of UPAC. The second, C-700 – directly related to, and partly a consequence of C-383 – declared unconstitutional the UPAC system itself.

4.2.2.1 C-383's Impact

I classify C-383 as Medium in terms of Immediate Effects and Low/Med in terms of Outcomes (Table 4.2). As for immediate effects, high levels of changes to formal

TABLE 4.2 *Summary of impact dimensions for C-383*

Dimension	Indicator	Assessment
Immediate effects		
Formal norms	- Housing Bill (*Ley 546 de 1999*) - Decree 2703 (30 Dec 1999) approved new methodology for calculating mortgage loans (UVR). - *Resolución* 2896 by the Finance Ministry established the new values of the UVR that should be used to recalculate installments between Jan 1, 1993 and Dec 31, 1999. - A series of high-profile constitutional challenges and tutelas on the issue (chiefly, C-700 1999).	High
Resources	- 1.5 percent of GDP in 1999 (Clavijo 2007). - No information gathering	Medium
Organizational changes	- Spurred legal mobilization to seek further enforcement of right to housing.	Medium
Ideas	- Shifted conceptions for activists, but non-existent beyond.	Low
Immediate effects overall		Medium
Outcome (rights effectiveness)	Relief for mortgage holders.	Low/medium

norms are observed along with medium changes in terms of resources and organizational changes. C-383 generated little by way of ideational effects among government officials or elite actors. Interestingly, its outcome perfectly illustrates the difficult trade-offs of unintended consequences. As I will show, although the relief measures that were made available to thousands of UPAC debtors positively impacted their livelihoods, the reforms to the mortgage lending framework limited, in the long run, the availability of credit for less well-off segments of the population.

4.2.2.1.1 IMMEDIATE EFFECTS The ruling had significant effects in terms of formal norms. In compliance with the CCC's rulings, the Ministry of Economics and the Central Bank tied the UPAC rate to the inflation rate, not market rates. Further, the new housing law passed by Congress in 1999 (Law 546), which introduced a new mortgage loan system known as UVR, made this change permanent. Law 546 also made provisions so that adjustments on outstanding debts and installments would be calculated with the Court's requirements in mind (Calderón Lopez 2002, 84–86). In observance of the court's indications, the Central Bank reduced interest rates for future installments on debts originally negotiated under the UPAC system, a measure that gave relief to thousands of families.

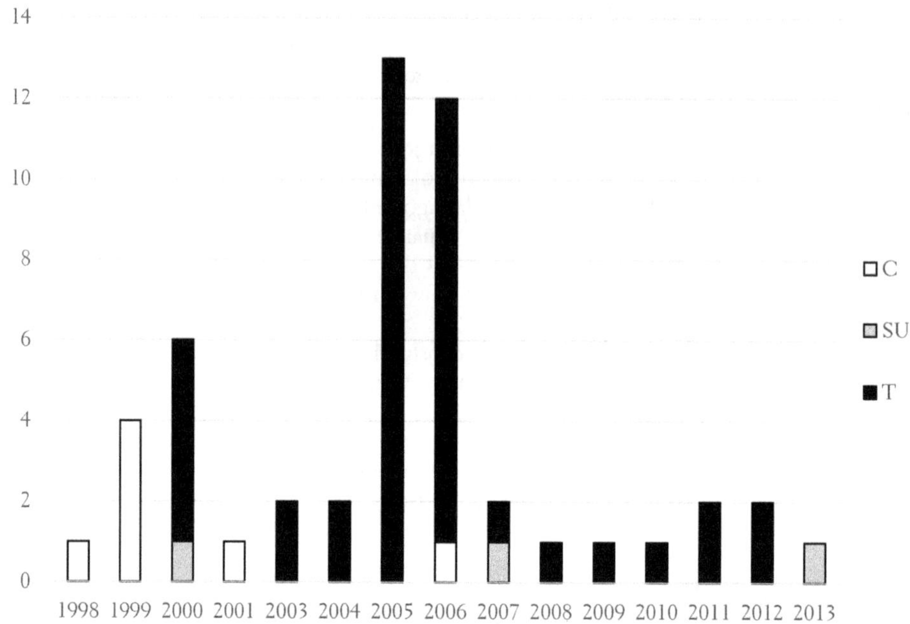

FIGURE 4.2 Rulings on UPAC by the constitutional court. T, tutelas; SU, unification rulings; C, constitutional review. Total number of rulings: 51.
Source: author's elaboration based on data in the CCC's website.

Another aspect of the ruling's effects in terms of formal norms is the related cascade of jurisprudence that built upon it. To illustrate, I will focus this brief discussion on the Constitutional Court's rulings on the issue. Figure 4.2 shows that the majority of constitutional challenges to the housing mortgage framework were handed down in 1998 and 1999; particularly those in the latter year were all in the direction of safeguarding the debtors' right to housing. C-383 is part of that group of rulings which was inaugurated earlier in 1999 with decision C-122. C-122 found unconstitutional an executive decree providing financial relief to users and financial institutions in the midst of the economic crisis. Two key rulings followed C-383: First, C-700 of the same year, in which the court struck down the entire framework that configured the UPAC system. C-700 ordered Congress to issue a bill creating a new mortgage system. Crucially, the new system built on C-383 by forbidding the exclusion of any elements other than inflation in the financial calculus of mortgage credits. Second, C-747 declared the capitalization of interests for mortgage loans unconstitutional. The criteria set out in C-383 were not only re-affirmed, but actually built into the nation wide regulatory framework through these decisions. In turn, organizations in the legal constituency used these rulings to continue mobilizing and pushing, for example, the renegotiation of outstanding debts in the lower courts.

The dimensions of the judicial cascade can be observed by looking at the number of rulings the CCC decided on these topics. Unfortunately, there is no data kept on the total number of cases that reach the Constitutional Court, in other words, we do not have information on the demand side of housing rights. However, a look at the supply side is helpful. Figure 4.2 graphs all the rulings that the court decided on the issue of housing mortgages/UPAC between 1998 and 2013. The darker areas designate tutela rulings, the white areas constitutional challenges, and the gray ones unification rulings (decisions where the court groups separate several legal challenges and hands down a decision that clarifies its position on a specific area). The relatively high number of constitutional cases (C) in the late 1990s, the presence of several tutela rulings, and the existence of three unification decisions on this issue alone (a rare occurrence) shows the relevance of the topic in the court's docket and serves to illustrate the importance of that legal strategy for legal aid and legal advocacy organizations. After the victories in 1998 and 1999, only two rulings on constitutional challenges were handed down, and the bulk of the court's activity on the issue came in the form of tutelas. The tutelas that the court decided on between 2000 and 2006 were part of a wave of legal claims that made their way to the court due to legal mobilization efforts that the UPAC debtor organizations pursued in their attempts to further extend the benefits of C-383. I will discuss these efforts in more detail further ahead.

In response to the ruling, the government mobilized a significant amount of financial resources: The cost of renegotiating outstanding mortgage loans in order to provide relief to mortgage holders in the terms ordered by the court amounted to 1.5 percent of GDP in 1999 (Clavijo 2007). However, as Clavijo notes, it is not possible to determine what portion of these resources were mobilized exclusively as a result of the court's order, as some related measures had been put in place starting November 1998, before the court first decided on the topic. In any case, this rough figure gives us a very clear sense of the high cost of complying with the court's criteria when providing relief to mortgage debtors.

The ruling also had a profound impact on the organizations that already existed and were mobilizing around UPAC issues. These organizations were relatively young and did not originally have a specific rights-based focus. In this sense, my own interviews with lawyers and activists and previous scholarly work coincide in highlighting the significance of the ruling's organizational effects. According to Jiménez Gil (2010), when the Constitutional Court recognized the issue of massive foreclosures, the people who had these loans shifted from an attitude that was initially passive and contemplative to an offensive attitude. Legal mobilization was the primary strategy of these organizations – the legal victories, which they were behind or mobilized in support of, gave them political visibility and motivation, increasing their numbers.

These observations are in line with what I heard from lawyers who founded some of the most important legal advocacy NGOs for "victims of the UPAC," as they called themselves. When I inquired about how the legal victory impacted their work, I heard stories that shared a common theme: The initial legal victories, including C-383, fueled their efforts and shifted their views. For example, "A lot of *tutelas* were generated. I went to different cities to work with lawyers. Let's be honest: [to us lawyers] this was a professional and a job opportunity. But we cared about defending those rights and giving these people access to justice. (...) The scheme of advocacy lawyers [for UPAC] spread throughout the country. I personally toured the country [giving talks and leading workshops]. We created a national network [of lawyers] that still exists."[20] As the previous quote illustrates, and other research has shown, the victory in court also altered the meaning of engagement for these lawyers, infusing their efforts with the language of constitutional and social rights (Jiménez Gil 2010; Uprimny and García Villegas 2004). There was a shift in how the members of the legal constituency perceived the issue, a phenomenon whose importance has been studied and documented by McCann (1994) in other settings.

Unlike the previous case (*Causa Verbitsky* in Argentina) where the legal constituency engaged in efforts to educate and spread the ruling and rights-based ideas among governmental legal operators, these efforts were not undertaken by legal advocacy organizations on mortgage issues in Colombia. Lower court judges in Colombia, who handled the bulk of the individual legal claims against the banks, remained insulated from rights-based perspectives with regard to housing. Vasquez Alfaro (2014) sums up this view most eloquently: "[lower court] judges don't think that the law is a tool to solve these economic and social problems. It is up to the government, the Bank of the Republic and the legislators to provide solutions. [To lower court judges] The judicial system must stay neutral...".

4.2.2.1.2 OUTCOME The outcome of this ruling clearly illustrates some of the trade-offs that may result from the unintended consequences of policy decisions. As has already been mentioned, the court's decision to require that mortgage loans not be tied to market interest rates meant concrete relief for thousands of debtors by reducing the burden of extra debt and it also made lending conditions more transparent going forward. Clavijo's research (2007) also highlights the positive effects of requiring the renegotiation of existing mortgage loans to reflect the original (non-market) interest rate. In doing so, the real value of the loan was restored and so was the debtor's capacity to repay it.

Note, however, that whether individual debts were appropriately renegotiated by the banks or not remained a highly contentious issue for several years (Barreto Valderrama 2012). My interviews with lawyers who represented and organized UPAC debtors in the late 1990s and 2000s coincide in stating that banks did not fully follow the court's specifications, and that they and their clients continued to

[20] Interview with founding member of the Association of Financial System Users, *Asociación de Usuarios del Sistema Financiero*. Bogotá. July 26, 2012.

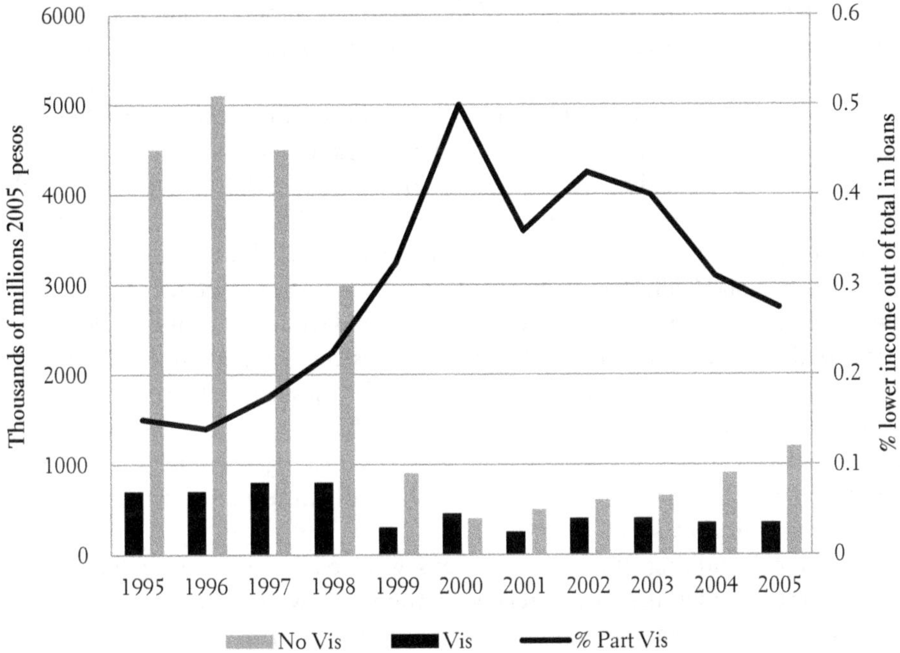

FIGURE 4.3 Mortgage loans 1995–2005. VIS: Vivienda de Interés Social (lower-income housing).
Source: Cuellar (2006)

seek redress in the tribunals for this lack of compliance.[21] At the same time, reforms to the mortgage regulations meant tightening the requirements, which made conditions more transparent, but also reduced the demand. According to Clavijo (2007), "Even between 2003–2004 when the economy was recovering, mortgage credits continued to be depressed and that portfolio now represents only 5% of the GDP, after having reached a peak 12% in the mid 1990s." Ultimately the changes also made it harder for certain sectors of the population, particularly lower-income households, to access mortgage credits (Barreto Valderrama 2012; Clavijo 2007). Figure 4.3 shows the drop, after 1999, in the overall number of mortgage loans taken. Note also that the percentage of loans taken by lower-income households (VIS in Spanish) is lower compared to previous years.

4.2.2.2 Explaining C-383's Impact

In this case as in the previous one (Argentina's *Causa Verbitsky*) no effective oversight mechanisms were deployed, but there was a dense legal constituency that

[21] Interview with founding member of Asociación de Usuarios del Sistema Financiero. Bogotá. July 26, 2012; Interview with founding member of ANUPAC. Bogotá. April 23, 2012.

contributed to the impact of the ruling by continuing to mobilize after it was handed down, seeking to extend the benefits more widely. To better understand how the ruling impacted upon the right to housing of UPAC users in the late 1990s and what organized civil society brought to the process, it is important to characterize the legal advocacy organizations that made up this dense legal constituency.

Some of the most important organizations were: ANUPAC, Asociación de Usuarios del Sistema Financiero, and ANUSIF.[22] These NGOs were set up between 1996 and 1999 in different areas of Colombia (but especially in larger cities like Bogotá, Cali, Cúcuta, and Barranquilla) bringing together citizens who had acquired mortgages under the UPAC system and witnessed their debt skyrocket. Organizations like *Asociación de Usuarios del Sistema Financiero* and ANUPAC emphasized legal mobilization strategies to fight foreclosures and renegotiate debts. In late 1998 and 1999, they also began to mobilize to raise awareness of the problems faced by UPAC debtors and turned to placing key tutelas and constitutional challenges before the Constitutional Court (Jimenez Gil 2010; Uprimny and García Villegas 2004).

From the beginning, these organizations were connected among themselves. Note, however, that they were relatively young (they had been around for a maximum of three years by 1999), hence their networks had had a similarly short life. The activities of these organizations were funded through the contributions of their members, who paid dues in exchange for legal advice and services.

In talking with lawyers who led some of these organizations, it is clear that they purposefully combined different strategies in their efforts to create political and social awareness around the issue. These organizations pursued legal mobilization before the lower courts, strategic litigation before the CCC combined with political mobilization, though the latter was done to a lesser extent.[23] The initial victory in court in 1999 changed the dynamics of their mobilization. In the words of a lawyer who worked for one of the banks with the biggest share of mortgage loans in the Colombian market: "[After the ruling] people felt that they had rights and they could organize. (...) There were legal claims before [the ruling], but in very individualistic terms ... without legal and technical knowledge."[24]

[22] The case file at the Constitutional Court includes amicus briefs and over 320 support letters from representatives or members of ANUSIF and ANUPAC. From my interview with a founding member of the Asociación de Usuarios del Sistema Financiero (Bogotá, July 26, 2012) it is clear they were also involved with this case and that most of the other organizations (REDEUPAC, Liga de consumidores y usuarios del Sistema Financiero, Fundación Damnificados del Sistema Financiero, Comité de Defensa del Consumidor Financiero) were also involved with legal mobilization efforts to extend the benefits of C-383 or file similar claims.

[23] Interview with founding member of Asociación de Usuarios del Sistema Financiero. Bogotá. July 26, 2012. Interview with founding member of ANUPAC. Bogotá. April 23, 2012.

[24] Interview with former mortgage litigation lawyer for CONAVI Bank. Bogotá. May 4, 2012.

C-383 was a key ruling for two main reasons: It ordered the government to link the indexing rates to inflation and it ordered that debts be renegotiated. The first point was a matter of changing formal norms – in this respect, compliance fell upon the government and entailed changing policy. However, since the broader goal for civil society organizations was to question the entire system, the NGOs pressed ahead by filing other constitutional challenges that eventually resulted in the other three key constitutionality rulings previously mentioned. I will first briefly highlight the quick positive response from the government in terms of updating the legal framework, and then discuss how the legal constituency mobilized after the ruling, as this was an area to which they devoted significant energy.

The government complied with the indexing of the rate swiftly. Just days after the ruling was announced, the Bank of the Republic and the Minister of Economy declared that the formula would be updated following the court's criteria within a matter of weeks.[25] Simultaneously, the controversy over the court's actions reached its climax. During the economic crisis there was consensus that political action was needed, but by no means were the court's choices the reflections of change that was already agreed upon by the ruling political elites, as Rosenberg's theory would suggest. The path the court chose was definitively not that which the government or the financial sector would have preferred. In this heated context, public attacks on the court were frequent. High-profile economists and public officials accused the justices of co-governing and meddling in matters outside their area of expertise. For example, in reference to C-383, a leading economist referred to the current state of affairs as a "constitutional dictatorship," calling the justices "donkeys" (*burrisconsultos*) and incontinent, since they were unable to control their ideology and passions.[26]

Shortly thereafter, the court handed down C-700, another ruling in which it declared the entire UPAC framework unconstitutional. In it, the court asked Congress to legislate on a new housing bill. At the time this ruling was handed down, the government had already been discussing a draft of the new housing law. The court's decision, which incorporated and built on the criteria specified in C-383, forced the Minister of Economics to reformulate the bill.[27] In compliance with the court's mandates, the new housing law that was approved in 1999 specified that mortgages could not have their interest rate tied to market rates but instead, required that they follow the rate of inflation.

After the ruling was handed down, legal aid organizations continued mobilizing. They expanded their efforts to other areas of the country[28] and they filed related legal claims, several of which led to important decisions from the CCC as I showed earlier. Importantly, they also mobilized around C-383 specifically. Members of the legal

25 "La corrección de Junio se queda en 13.7%," El Tiempo. May 31, 1999.

26 Hommes, Rudolf. "Dictadura Constitucional," El Tiempo. July 7, 1999.

27 "Aterrizaje de emergencia del plan de vivienda al congreso," El Tiempo. September 17, 1999.

28 "Deudores de UPAC quieren más," El Tiempo. June 16, 1999.

constituency understood C-383 as key: In the words of one of the lawyers that founded and directed one of the UPCS user organizations, "C-383 was of paramount importance. . .because it is the one that indicates that debts should be renegotiated." Civil society organizations focused on mobilizing to make this effective. ANUSIP (*Asociación Nacional de Usuarios del Sistema UPAC* – National Association of UPAC Users), one of the biggest organizations, coordinated in July the simultaneous filing of 1,400 legal claims (in Bogotá alone) seeking the renegotiation benefits laid out in the ruling.[29] Through the months to come, different organizations would coordinate their efforts and threaten with similar massive filings to clog the judicial system.[30] In a more radical and controversial move, ANUSIF launched a civil disobedience campaign in which it encouraged its members not to pay their installments until the government and the financial institutions renegotiated their debt. Debt renegotiation was a deeply contentious issue that would remain largely unresolved.

The legal constituency tried to get the court's attention on the matter of how the credits were being renegotiated, but in the absence of any institutional mechanisms through which to bring up their concerns, they came up against a wall. One of the lawyers recalls, "We tried everything. We went, as a commission, before the court to complain. We managed to get a meeting and were told: 'look, we cannot do anything beyond making a decision and putting our criteria in the ruling.'"[31] Financial institutions came up against the same wall when they tried to voice their own concerns about the implications of the ruling. In other words, the discussion was closed. The legal battles would continue for years, but the lack of institutional spaces in which to hold the targets of the ruling accountable and discuss the implications of the public policy that followed from the court's decisions ruled out the possibility of the court assessing the situation and updating its position based on how the implementation unfolded.

The UPAC crisis was of such proportions that the government would have likely intervened (in some manner) even if the court had not stepped in in early 1999. Even then, if the government had stepped in earlier, the reforms would not have tied loans to inflation nor would the window for renegotiating loans have been opened. More broadly, in absence of the court's rulings, an important part of the legal and political mobilization carried out by the organizations in the legal constituency would have been cut short.

4.2.3 *Comparing* Verbitsky *and C-383*

Causa Verbitsky and C-383 show that denser legal constituencies can work to extend the benefits of a given ruling to other actors through legal mobilization and that they

[29] "Corporaciones vs deudores: comenzó la lucha jurídica," El Tiempo. July 7, 1999.

[30] "Los deudores amenazan con demandas," El Tiempo. November 3,1999.

[31] Interview with founding member of Asociación de Usuarios del Sistema Financiero. Bogotá. July 26, 2012.

can mobilize to diffuse effects to other spheres, maintaining issue visibility. These all enhance impact. In the case of *Verbitsky*, CELS' advocacy work took this ruling as a starting point for other legal claims that would expand similar benefits to other populations. Their work, as well as that of the CCT, was crucial in keeping social and political attention on detention conditions in the Buenos Aires Province. The dense network of organizations of UPAC users also mobilized forcefully around mortgage debt. Beyond the mechanisms at work, the two rulings I just presented share interesting features. On the one hand, we observe ideational changes in both, but they are limited to the spheres of activity of the civil society organizations. In the case of *Verbitsky*, because of the work of CELS with legal operators in the provincial system, the rights protective framework was diffused in that sphere, albeit in a limited manner. Organizations in the legal constituency of the UPAC case did not have a similar focus (nor reach into the legal system), but the ruling did entail an important change in their mobilization strategies and the use of the rights-based discourse in their work.

On the other hand, both rulings illustrate well the implications of the absence of oversight mechanisms. In both cases there is a dense legal constituency that continued to mobilize after the ruling and had information about and input on the implementation of the decision. However, as there were no institutional spaces for interaction, there was no possibility for the court to consider this additional information external actors produced (the legal constituency or others) once the decision had been handed down. In short, these decisions are one-shot games: There is no possibility for the court to learn from the implementation of the ruling over time.

4.3 CASES WITH MONITORING MECHANISMS

The second half of this chapter zooms in on two cases with low density legal constituencies and court-promoted monitoring mechanisms: a 2006 ruling handed down by the Supreme Court of Argentina safeguarding the rights of pensioners and a 2010 ruling by the Colombian Constitutional Court safeguarding the right to prior consultation of four Indigenous groups. This second paired comparison is meant to help identify the distinct contribution to impact of monitoring mechanisms in the absence of a dense legal constituency.

As I suggested in Chapter 2, monitoring mechanisms have two kinds of effects: They impose costs on the target(s) of the ruling, and they generate resources so that the court can offset informational and power asymmetries. Court-promoted monitoring imposes costs on the target(s) of the ruling by requiring reports and information on implementation, as well as by setting deadlines, and doing so publicly. Public, institutionalized venues for discussion extract information from the target(s) and draw the attention of key related actors to the issue and, also, of actors beyond those involved originally in the case: the public, other key players, and the media.

Second, monitoring also helps the court alleviate informational asymmetries and gain more knowledge of the issue. Oversight generates information, which provides the court with expertise – and the authority that comes with it – on specific technical topics. However, in the absence of a dense legal constituency, civil society organizations do not become alternative source of information for the court, simply because the legal constituency is nonexistent, or less dense.

Going back to the monitoring continuum presented in Chapter 2, it is worth noting that the type of monitoring that is exercised in these cases is of dramatically lesser scope than the one present in the cases analyzed in Chapter 3 (environmental and health rights). The Argentine and Colombian high courts relied on reports, public hearings, and requests for information in the cases we are about to discuss, *Badaro* and T-547.

4.3.1 *Right to Pension:* Causa Badaro *(Argentina)*

The Argentine pension system underwent a series of reforms in the mid-1990s and in the early 2000s. Among other changes, one of the reforms removed the sections that provided for the automatic adjustment of monthly payments to retirees according to a fixed universal rate.[32] In practical terms this meant that important segments of Argentine pensioners received the same fixed monthly pension until their death, with no adjustment to reflect fluctuations in the macroeconomic environment. Congress was designated as the only institution authorized to issue one-time raises, but since no blanket raise was ordered through the 1990s, hundreds of thousands of retirees saw the real value of their pensions diminish as the economy crashed in the early 2000s. The decline in real value for pensions was such that by mid-2002 a single male retiree earning the minimum benefit was below the poverty line (Rofman 2002). Between 2003 and September 2005, seven increases in pension payments were ordered through presidential decree but none of these applied to those whose pensions were greater than 1,000 pesos (Herrero 2011).[33] In that context, thousands of Argentines turned to the judicial system to demand that the value of their pensions be adjusted.[34]

In August 2006, the Supreme Court ruled in favor of Adolfo Badaro who had filed a lawsuit against ANSES (Agencia Nacional de Seguridad Social, National Agency for Social Security) requesting that his pension be adjusted. His lawsuit raised the issue of whether pensions over 1,000 should be automatically adjusted, starting when and how. Since 1985, when he retired, Badaro had been receiving the same monthly amount: 1,141 pesos. In its ruling, the court decided that Badaro was

[32] For historical overviews, see Herrero (2011) and Bertranou et al. (2011).

[33] As of 2010, 78 percent of beneficiaries received the minimum pension (895,15 pesos); 17 percent of total pension recipients (881,771 individuals) received pensions of over 1,000 pesos (average value, 1,064 pesos). (García Rapp 2010).

[34] For example, the *Sanchez* ruling ordered the adjustment of payments between 1991 and 1995.

entitled to automatic adjustment, safeguarding his constitutional right to an adjustable pension. But, the Supreme Court went further: Since the crisis had affected many others like Badaro, it concluded that "more general and harmonizing" measures were necessary to implement an indexation scheme. Consequently, it urged the executive and Congress to legislate in that direction "within a reasonable amount of time."

4.3.1.1 Badaro's Impact

Table 4.3 provides an overview of the immediate effects and outcomes of this ruling.

4.3.1.1.1 IMMEDIATE EFFECTS As Herrero (2011) has shown, with this ruling the Supreme Court made a decisive difference in the reforms to the regulatory framework of pension policy and in the construction of a legal framework for the protection of the rights of pensioners. In the case of *Causa Badaro* in particular, shortly after the ruling was made public, Congress included a 13 percent increase to all pensions in the 2007 budget bill – the raise would cost the government $4,100 million pesos.[35] Several adjustments had been made previously but always limited to certain segment of the pensioners, and none had been built into the national budget between 1995 and 2005. As a result of the court's pronouncement, the system shifted to blanket raises that were incorporated into the yearly budget.[36] This shift marked an important departure. In 2008 the government announced that the adjustment would be 15 percent for all pensioners.[37] In October the *Ley de Movilidad* (Adjustment Bill) was passed. This bill provided for the Pay-as-You-Go scheme to be automatically adjusted twice a year following a combined index including wages and earmarked tax growth. However, the bill did not provide for retrospective adjustments: It only applied to future pension payments.

Rofman, Fajnzylber, and Herrera (2008, 278) pointed out shortly after the adjustment bill was passed that the lack of provisions regarding past indexation of benefits or reference wages left significant space for future legal action. This turned out to be true: The number of citizens suing ANSES so that the value of their pensions would be adjusted according to the guidelines set out by the court in *Badaro* skyrocketed. That being said, even before the Adjustment Bill was passed, thousands of pensioners were already turning to the judicial system to request that

35 "Desde enero aumentan un 13% todas las jubilaciones," La Nación. September 9, 2006.

36 Shortly after the ruling was announced and President Néstor Kirchner declared that a raise would be forthcoming, his closest collaborators explained the policy shift as a response to the ruling. ("El Presidente sorprendió hasta a sus propios funcionarios," Clarín. September 9, 2006). When announcing the raise, Economics Minister Felisa Miceli admitted that the decision was made to comply with the *Badaro* ruling (as quoted in "Desde enero…," La Nación: Ibid.).

37 "Subirán 15% todas las jubilaciones," La Nación. February 18, 2008.

TABLE 4.3 *Summary of impact dimensions for* Badaro

Dimension	Indicator	Assessment
Formal norms	- Oct 2008: Ley de Movilidad - Oct 2010: Law 26.649 is approved (the law authorizes a pension that is equivalent to 82 percent of the minimum *vital and mobile wage*). This law was vetoed by President C. Kirchner. - March 2008: Defensoría de la Nación, in collaboration with CABA Defensor for senior citizens, files a claim with the Social Security Court of Appeals.	Medium
Resources	- Law 26.198, 2007 Budget, which mandated a 13 percent raise. Congress delegated the definition of the specifics of how the mobility of pensions would be calculated going forward to the Executive. - Feb 2008 15 percent raise - Jul 2010: 17 percent raise	Medium
Organizational changes	—	None
Ideas/discourse	- Visibility	Low
Immediate effects overall		Medium
Outcome (rights effectiveness)		Medium

ANSES apply the criteria defined in *Badaro* to their case. In other words, they asked that the value of their pension be set to 88.3 percent of the wage variation index [*índice de variación salarial*] between 2002 and 2006.

To be sure, legal action in the realm of Social Security was not new in Argentina; since the 1990s, citizens were turning to the system to request adjustment to their pensions after hyperinflation devalued them. Yet the number of legal claims after *Causa Badaro* signaled something different. In an interview, a member of the Buenos Aires City Ombudsman team with extensive experience in the matter explained: "[L]itigation for pensions happened before, but not with the magnitude that it does today [2013]. This tribunal [The Social Security Appeals Court, whose sole jurisdiction is social security matters] was created in 1989. That year, it handled 18,000 cases. Today, there are around 600,000 cumulative."[38] Different sources put the number of new cases that entered the system seeking the *Badaro* benefits between 480 per day[39] and 1,000 monthly (Garcia Rapp 2010). As of 2011, 465,000 lawsuits related to this matter were still in the system, according to

[38] Interview with Buenos Aires City Ombudsman Official. Buenos Aires. March 20, 2013.

[39] "Los jubilados inician 480 juicios por día para ajustar sus haberes," Clarín. October 16, 2010.

government sources.[40] The phenomenon is noteworthy not only because of its scope, but also because of the response it elicits from the government: Every decision that is unfavorable to the government is challenged in all possible instances. Several interviewees described this litigious response as a tactic to "wear out" the litigants, or even worse: drag out legal procedures long enough for the litigants to die.

I observe no organizational effects in the aftermath of the *Badaro* ruling. This is partly explained by the lack of any organizations mobilizing around the issue in the first place. My interviews with experts[41] and previous research show that although there were some organizations mobilizing on behalf of the rights of pensioners in Argentina in the 1990s, none were active at the time *Badaro* was handed down, nor until the mid-2010s. The Supreme Court's ongoing attention to this issue in the context of follow up provided a public forum that helped keep the topic visible. Indeed, as a result of the court monitoring implementation, for example, the public's attention shifted in the years to follow toward the government's decision to use ANSES funds for other programs, instead of diverting them to pay off its debt to pensioners.[42]

4.3.1.1.2 OUTCOME The first blanket raise that was ordered as a result of *Badaro* in early 2007 reached 4,244,741 people (Herrero 2011); these individuals had not seen a raise in their pension payments in over a decade. From this perspective, the increase in their pension payments undoubtedly had a positive effect in their quality of life. However, the government's refusal to provide guidelines according to which pensions awarded before 1995 might be updated, added to its lack of compliance with pending lawsuits, shows that a stable legal framework to regulate pension updates was not forthcoming as a result of *Badaro*. That was the court's original request of the government, and it was not granted.

4.3.1.2 Explaining *Badaro*'s Impact

Badaro and the next case are examples of rulings where oversight mechanisms are present and legal constituencies are absent. In *Badaro*, the Argentine Court relied on a combination of requiring information and reports from the government accompanied with holding hearings to monitor. There is no evidence of a dense legal constituency that was closely linked to supporting the litigation of the case – no amicus briefs were filed, for example – nor were there any organizations working to follow-up with implementation in a coordinated manner after the decision was

40 "No se paga la deuda más grave," Clarín. August 28, 2011.

41 Interview with director of legal advocacy NGO, Buenos Aires, February 14, 2013; Interview with specialist in pension law. Buenos Aires. March 15, 2013.

42 "Cuestionan a la ANSES por el uso de la plata de los jubilados," Clarin. March 14, 2012.

made known.[43] There is no record of any intervention from an NGO before the court, no mention of their actions in the newspapers and my interviews further confirmed their absence from this process. We observe, however, many individuals seeking to use *Badaro* as a precedent to favor their own case. Note, however, that this is not necessarily a judicial cascade in the sense that these cases are not the result of a coordinated effort, and they surface in the context of heightened litigiousness around social security in general. In the words of one of the experts I spoke with, "What you do see is a kind of cottage industry for producing legal claims related to pensions, which is different (from organized mobilization by an NGO)."[44]

The next section will reconstruct the process following the handing down of the decision. I show how the ruling prompted the reforms we saw to the legal framework, how monitoring allowed the court to stay updated on the case over time, maintain pressure, and how external information influenced outcomes. As I will show, this combination where oversight by the court is present but there is no dense legal constituency has some implications for the impact of the ruling: The court's monitoring is more limited in its ability to have external actors – other than the targets of the ruling – provide more information. At the same time, there is no mobilization by civil society organizations that could help create information, put additional pressure on the targets, and extend other types of effects to other populations. Relatedly, there are no organizational changes.

Badaro, in its attempt to prompt comprehensive legislative action from the executive and Congress in favor of all pensioners in Argentina, caused a stir when it was announced. By urging Congress to legislate on the topic, within a reasonable amount of time, the Court sought to respect the balance of powers while at the same time prompting a dialogue. In the words of Chief Justice Lorenzetti: "Our choices were to set a precise deadline or use the expression 'reasonable' which is the one closest to fostering dialogue among powers."[45] The court's approach generated controversy and took many in Congress by surprise. One of the leaders of the Kirchnerista senators was quoted as describing their reaction to *Badaro* in the following terms: "It fell on us like a bucket of cold water, as if it was the middle of winter and we were outdoors."[46]

The government's response although quick, was far from actually proposing a bill that laid out a mechanism through which pensions would be automatically updated. As stated earlier, a blanket raise was included in that year's budget, but no bill was forthcoming. From early on, the government's reticence to legislating on the matter

[43] This ruling was the result of an individual claim filed on behalf of Badaro by a lawyer, Gabriela Stasevich, who specializes in this type of claims. This lawyer was not part of a human rights or legal advocacy NGO – her profile was that of a litigating lawyer and remained such at the time of fieldwork.

[44] Interview with director of legal advocacy NGO, Buenos Aires, February 14, 2013.

[45] "Es urgente, hay un derecho violado," Pagina 12, August 10, 2006. p. 12.

[46] "En el Parlamento, desorientación y sorpresa," El Clarin. 8.9.2006.

was clear, as reports surfaced that legislators in President Kirchner's party were ordered to not sign on any of the multiple bills introduced on the topic in the months following the ruling.[47] The government's position on this, voiced through ANSES in response to queries from the court, was that the yearly executive-mandated raises guaranteed a mechanism to update pensions and therefore constituted compliance with *Badaro*.[48] Critics, on the other hand, argued that the lack of an automatic mechanism made the raises, which were subject to the executive's whim, something entirely different from what the court ordered.

Seeing that a bill which provided for an automatic update mechanism was not making its way through Congress one year after the ruling, the court stepped in again. In a follow up to its initial pronouncement, in late 2007 the Court declared unconstitutional, in the case of Badaro, the portion of Law 24,463 that left the decision of the updating mechanism in the hands of Congress and ruled that his pension should be adjusted according to the consumer price index. Additionally, the tribunal appealed to Congress again, asking it to legislate. The court's insistence came as a reminder to Congress and the executive that although the adjustments had been made through the budget law, they had not yet legislated on an automatic adjustment mechanism bill.

After this follow-up move by the court, the Seniors' Ombudsman intervened in the process in a way that would facilitate the court's continued oversight of the issue.[49] In response to many citizens who approached the Ombudsman's office seeking legal advice for filing claims to get the benefits laid out in *Badaro*, the Seniors' Ombusdman, Eugenio Semino, took legal action.[50] In early 2008, Semino's office filed a legal claim that sought to make the benefits of *Badaro* extensive to some 300,000 pensioners in similar conditions. The actions initiated by Semino were crucial, since they put pressure on the government and opened up the legal space for the court (and other lower tribunals) to continue requesting information and actions. In early 2009, it was in the context of follow-up with the court's request for information as part of this process that a federal judge ordered a search be conducted in the ANSES offices. The aim was for the search to furnish the raw data that supported the calculations of the new index.[51] In a way, the actions of the Ombudsman "fill in the gap" for the legal constituency. They perfectly illustrate some of what organized and legally empowered civil society groups could

[47] More than twenty bill initiatives were introduced in the Lower Chamber and thirteen in the Senate. See "Nadie cumple las sentencias," La Nación. July 27, 2007. "Sin leyes para subir jubilaciones," La Nación. November 28, 2007.

[48] "El Gobierno se ampara en la emergencia," La Nación. April 2, 2007.

[49] The Seniors' Ombudsman (*Defensoría de la Tercera Edad de la CABA*) is an office within the City of Buenos Aires' Ombudsman's office.

[50] Interview with Seniors' Ombudsman. Buenos Aires. March 12, 2013.

[51] "Allanan la Anses por no brindar información sobre el cálculo del alza en las jubilaciones," La Nación. March 9, 2009. "Buscan la 'formula de la movilidad'," Página 12. March 10, 2009.

have brought to the process: information gathering, support, public action, and a feedback loop into the court.

In October 2008 parties in the government coalition passed the Adjustment Bill through Congress. This piece of legislation formally complied with the Court's requirements in *Badaro*. It put into place a mechanism for automatically updating all pensions through semi-annual raises according to a set formula. It was criticized by the opposition as faulty, and its implementation generated much controversy, garnering significant media attention. In any case, the bill's approval marked the attainment of a mechanism for automatic updates that had been lacking since the mid-1990s. After it passed, the public's attention shifted to an aspect that remained contested: the retroactive adjustment of the value of pensions.

In mid-2010, parties in the opposition worked on different draft bills that sought to link the value of the pension with that of the minimum wage by setting the former at 82 percent of the latter.[52] When some of these bills were first filed in July of that year, the government announced that they would veto all initiatives of that nature.[53] When a bill was approved in Congress in October, President Fernández de Kirchner vetoed it announcing that "this law would have led us to bankruptcy and I cannot allow that."[54] The politically charged discussion made clear that the government refused to comply or discuss readjusting the value of the pensions. Why the reticence?

Badaro did touch upon the retrospective adjustment of the value of pensions. My interviews show that the political economy issue behind the lack of compliance with this aspect was the government's desire to have free use of the financial resources at the disposal of the ANSES. I interviewed both government-friendly and opposition experts on this topic and all agreed that the executive did not want to relinquish control of the ANSES coffers. In the words of a Kirchner-affiliated lawyer who was a nationally renowned expert on the social welfare regime, "It is not in the interest of the executive to tie its hands (with regards to the use of ANSES moneys). The central issue is the use of these financial resources, the executive is not willing to give those up."[55] Others, who self-identified as sympathizing with parties in opposition to then ruling Kirchnerismo, were more specific in stating that since the nationalization of the pension system in 2008, the executive was using ANSES funds to finance government programs and internal debt.[56] Kirchneristas needed that money and were unwilling to have it be directed elsewhere.

52 Different projects proposed modifications or alternatives. Eighty-two percent of the minimum wage was a historical claim, and thus the most common formula in the different ones presented.

53 "El Gobierno anticipó que vetará el 82% móvil para las jubilaciones," Clarín. July 5, 2010.

54 "Bodou calificó al proyecto aprobado de "estafa" a los jubilados," Página 12. October 14, 2010. "Era una ley de quiebra y no lo puedo permitir," Página 12. October 15, 2010.

55 Interview with litigating lawyer, specialist in pension law. Buenos Aires. March 22, 2013.

56 Interview with specialist in pension law. Buenos Aires. March 15, 2013.

Accusations in this direction intensified in late 2009 when the lead opposition newspaper stated that the government's conditional cash transfer program was being financed with funds from ANSES.[57] Through 2010 journalists and members of the opposition as well as the independent General Auditor voiced concerns regarding the government's decision to finance debt as well as the CCT program and an ambitious new initiative to provide laptops for school children with funds from the pension system.[58] The implication was that the resources that resulted from the nationalization of the pension system as well as the ANSES surplus were not being used to pay the pensioners, but to finance government expenses.

The court was unable to overcome the hurdle of the government's refusal to pay pensions retroactively. In 2011, and then again in 2012, the Court requested information from the ANSES – on litigation related to pensions, on financial resources devoted to paying pensions, and on resources spent on complying with judicial rulings that favor pensioners – and called for a hearing.[59] It succeeded in keeping the issue alive, but the government continued to refuse to update the value of the pensions. While mechanisms to automatically update pensions were put into place, the judicial system continued to bear the weight of numerous outstanding lawsuits. Thousands of citizens who had received their pensions after 1995 but before 2010 and wanted to see the value of their monthly payments raised to 82 percent of the minimum wage filed legal challenges, which often languished in the pipeline for years.

The lack of a dense legal constituency mobilizing before institutional venues on behalf of the pensioners left the court acting solo. The Seniors' Ombudsman alleviated that absence in part, as this office was able to coordinate a collective effort to extend the benefits more widely. Yet, some dynamics were missing. In the alternative scenario where a dense legal constituency was present, the court could have relied on the information provided by it for its oversight efforts and put pressure on the government to produce affirmative, expansive compliance. Given that the issue of pensions became such a contested political topic, a dense legal constituency could have also put pressure on Kirchnerista legislators so they too might have had incentives to support a bill.

I now turn to the second case, this time from Colombia, where monitoring by the court is present but there is no dense legal constituency: T-547, handed down in 2010.

57 "ANSES da para todo: tapa deudas y ahora banca el plan hijos," Clarín. Oct 31, 2009.

58 "Cuestionan a la ANSeS por el uso de la plata de los jubilados," Clarín. March 13, 2012.

59 "Cuestionan a la ANSES por no pagar," 8.11.2011 La Nación. "Lorenzetti pidió terminar con el "padecimiento" de los jubilados," Clarín. 6.15.2012. "El enojo con Bossio fue lo que disparó el pedido de la Corte," La Nación. 6.16.2012. "Lorenzetti: 'No podemos intervenir en la política en materia de seguridad social' 7.3.2012. "Lorenzetti y los jubilados," 7.4.2012, p. 12. 8.11.2012: "La Anses respondió al pedido de la Corte," Página 12. 10.23.2012 "La Corte citó a Diego Bossio por el reajuste de las jubilaciones."

4.3.2 *Right to Prior Consultation: T-547 (Colombia)*

Prior consultation is the fundamental right that Indigenous people and other ethnic groups have to decide over projects, activities, or any work to be done within their territory as well as over any legislative or administrative measures relevant to them (Rodríguez 2008). Together with self-determination, participation, and prior consent, this set of rights – established in the WTO 169 Convention – seeks to guarantee the ethnic and cultural survival of Indigenous peoples and ethnic groups (Sanchez Botero 2012). In 2010 the Colombian Constitutional Court ruled favorably on a tutela filed jointly by the four *cabildos* (political authorities) of the Kogui, Arhuaco, Wiwa, and Kankuamo Indigenous peoples of the Sierra Nevada de Santa Marta in northern Colombia. The four *cabildos*, grouped under the umbrella organization Territorial Council of Indigenous Cabildos (CTC), sought protection of their communities' right to prior consultation with regard to the construction of a large-scale seaport on the Caribbean called Puerto Brisa (see Figure 4.4).

Puerto Brisa was conceived as a multipurpose port for handling containers, oil, coal, and other minerals. This deep-water port was envisioned by its designers as a key trading post for building materials and minerals for Colombia's then burgeoning mining industry.

In the original tutela, the CTC argued that the port's location in the municipality of Dibulla, in La Guajira, overlapped with that of an Indigenous sacred site. According to the Court's own jurisprudence on the matter, when a proposed development project is planned on an area where there is Indigenous presence, the process whereby the environmental license is granted must include prior consultation with the relevant communities.[60] In this case in particular, the plaintiff argued, the environmental license that the government had issued in 2006 authorizing the project should have been subject to prior consultation with the Kogui, Arhuaco, Wiwa, and Kankuamo Indigenous peoples because the hill within the perimeters of the port area was sacred to them. According to the Indigenous communities, the project had not been subject to prior consultation with them, and, furthermore it was causing grave environmental harm to the area.

The company steadfastly maintained that their project was legal. They underscored the fact that in 2006, when they first requested an environmental license, the Ministry of Justice certified that there was no Indigenous presence in the area. Outside the direct parties to the case, local politicians expressed their support of the project as an alternative that would create much needed jobs and revenue.[61]

[60] Prior consultations for local projects are to be organized by a specialized unit within the Ministry of Interior. These processes are usually costly and only financed by the government when it has a direct stake in the project. Otherwise, it is usually up to the company requesting the environmental license to cover the bill. See Orduz Salinas (2014) for an overview of the procedure for consultation as it worked at this point.

[61] For example, in 2008, the Governor of La Guajira, Jorge López Bernier stated: "The most critical problem for us is the lack of job opportunities, which is why we must bet on this kind of

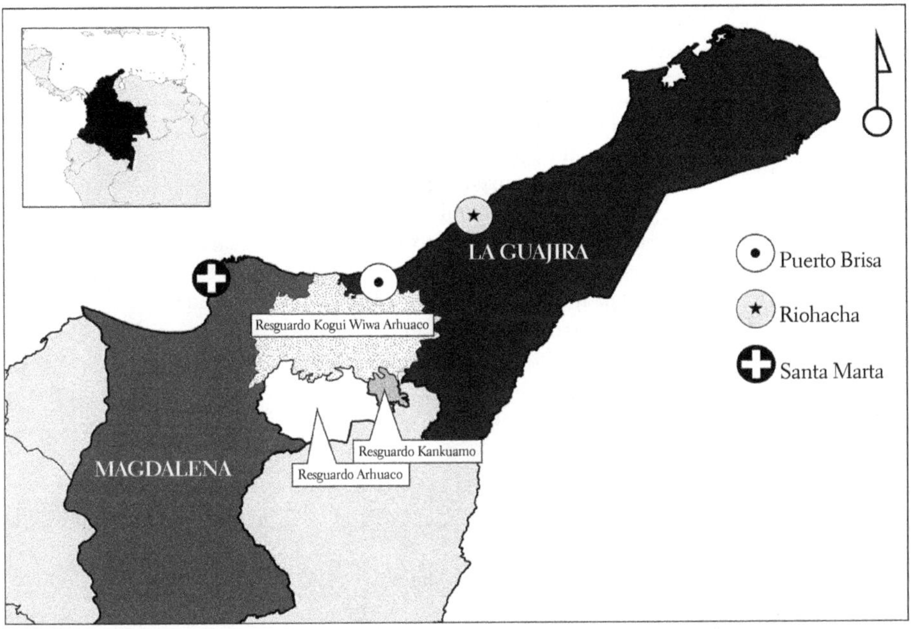

FIGURE 4.4 Puerto Brisa, Colombia

In March 2011 the Constitutional Court overturned the decision of a lower court and protected the right to prior consultation of the four Indigenous groups. In its ruling, the court required that construction of the port stop. Additionally, it gave a ninety-day window for authorities to undertake consultation with the Indigenous groups to determine the project's impacts and work with the company and the Indigenous groups to determine measures that would mitigate them.

4.3.2.1 T-547's Impact

Table 4.4 summarizes the key effects of the rulings in terms of immediate effects and outcomes. I classify the ruling as medium in terms of immediate effects and low in terms of outcomes.

4.3.2.1.1 IMMEDIATE EFFECTS As for formal norms, the ruling's impact was low. The ruling mandated a formal temporary stop to construction in the area, which was observed. In early April 2011, shortly after the parties were notified, work on the port

projects to lift *guajiros* from poverty. The industrial development of our department (La Guajira) is in this project," "Levantan suspensión a puerto multipropósito de Dibulla (La Guajira)," El Tiempo. May 12, 2008.

TABLE 4.4 *Summary of impact dimensions for T-547*

Dimension	Indicator	Assessment
Formal norms	- Updating of the environmental license was blocked, but eventually approved. - The ruling recognized legal rights to prior consultation on ancestral territory that is not within the limits of Indigenous territory.	Low
Resources	- The ruling required that a consultation process be undertaken (although the different parties involved found it unsatisfactory, for different reasons). - Work on the port stopped while the consultation process took place.	Medium
Organizational changes	–	None
Ideas/Discourse	–	None
Immediate effects overall		Medium/low
Outcome (rights effectiveness)	Consultation process took place.	Medium/low

officially halted.[62] The ruling sought to keep the company from making any further modifications/additions to the project, since the environmental license was brought into question. For a period of time, the license was suspended and work on the port was halted. However, work on the immediately neighboring sister project for a free zone continued, under the logic that this was a different endeavor. This controversial move by the company limited the ruling's impact, since anything related to the duty-free zone was, legally, not a part of T-547.[63]

Beyond putting a temporary halt to work on the port site, the ruling and the guidelines set there did not have further effects on the legal framework surrounding prior consultation. The constitutional court's rulings on prior consultation are of the utmost importance since the court's jurisprudence has shaped the legal framework for prior consultation in the country, in the absence of formal governmental

[62] Although the Ombudsman verified that activities had ceased, in the months to follow, journalistic accounts and written communications from the CTC to official authorities archived in the case file at the Environmental Ministry claim that work in the port did not come to a complete halt.

[63] The duty-free zone was granted an environmental license in the interval between when the ruling was handed down and when the court took up monitoring. According to one of my interviewees, "The duty free zone is the crucial thing in Dibulla. The order to halt operations was a huge blow to Brisa (the company) due to multimillion pesos commitments they had already made with CEMEX (Mexican cement giant) to trade cement through the port." Interview with environmental activist and scholar. Bogotá. May 15, 2012.

guidelines.[64] As an expert on prior consultation that has researched and worked with Indigenous communities since the early 1990s put it: "[T]here is a lack of normative clarity, a lack of clarity as far as the procedure for prior consultation (in Colombia). It is an extremely difficult topic."[65]

This expert and the lawyer for the Indigenous people of the Sierra Nevada coincided in highlighting that one of the noteworthy features of the ruling was that it recognized the right to prior consultation with regard to ancestral territories that are not located within Indigenous territories.[66] At the same time, they both called attention to what they saw as the limitations of the ruling: the short time frame it allowed for conducting the consultation (not in accordance with international standards, which are much longer) and the confusion it generated between prior consultation and consultation.

In terms of resources, the ruling facilitated the mobilization of human and financial resources that made possible a consultation process on the port. As will be described in more detail below, the consultation process took place in a series of meetings between late October and mid-December 2011 in La Guajira. Indigenous people and their *cabildos*, the company, representatives from the Environmental Ministry, the Ministry of Justice, the Ombudsman's Office, and the Procuraduría were in attendance. Although the sessions took place, in the end the Indigenous peoples of the Sierra Nevada refused to sign the minutes for the final meeting. This difficult ending reflected an extremely controversial and rocky process throughout. In this sense, the extent to which the right to prior consultation was effectively protected is not easy to ascertain, as I will discuss ahead. In my research I found no evidence of the ruling (and the mobilization in its aftermath) having altered the organizations working with them, nor did I find evidence of ideational effects.

4.3.2.1.2 OUTCOME The court's intervention in the case of the tutela against Puerto Brisa resulted in a consultation process (immediate effect) that facilitated a space in which information about the project was presented to the Indigenous peoples of the Sierra Nevada and where the different stakeholders – government, Indigenous groups, company – met for a discussion. In late 2014 the court deemed the consultation process finalized. In that communication, the court granted partial

64 In its rulings on the issue since the early 1990s, the Court's position has consistently been in favor of the protection of the rights of Indigenous minorities (Orduz Salinas 2014). In addition to the Court's pro-rights position, Colombia recognizes the international treaties and conventions that declare prior consultation a right (chiefly, IO 169) since 1991. The government attempted to regulate prior consultation (or aspects of it) through the following directives: Decreto 1320 in 1998 and again in 2013 with two important pushes: Directiva Presidencial 10 and an executive decree (Decreto 2613 de 2013).

65 Interview with expert on prior consultation. Bogotá. August 2, 2012.

66 Interview with ILSA lawyer. Bogotá. April 12, 2012. Interview with expert on prior consultation. Bogotá. August 2, 2012.

approval to the measures suggested by the Environmental Ministry (ANLA).[67] One year later,[68] it followed up on the modifications it had requested with new demands for information and directions for Puerto Brisa to hire personnel to supervise and monitor the projects related to the Indigenous people and the sacred sites. Does the end of the consultation process mean that the Indigenous people's right to prior consultation was made effective? In other words, what was the ruling's outcome?

There is no easy answer to this crucial question because there are no agreed-upon criteria by which to assess the situation. The consultation was controversial from the start, given the nature of prior consultation, of this particular situation, and of the court's order. Prior consultation, as the name itself indicates, should take place before the projects have begun, so that communities can have a say before projects take off. The specifics of how the procedure should be conducted are not set in stone, in Colombia or in many other countries that recognize this right.[69] In any case, an important dimension of prior consultation is to seek mechanisms that generate intercultural dialogue and information about the projects in formats and timing that are in accordance with the Indigenous people's customs, always before the project is carried out. Some argue that flexibility is needed to accommodate the needs and cultural differences among Indigenous communities, local realities, and different projects.[70] In contrast, uncertainty in the legal framework is a major concern for private companies seeking to undertake costly development projects (Orduz Salinas 2014).

Aside from instability in the local normative framework, adding to the complexity are the ongoing international and national discussions about the content of this right: Are the results of prior consultations binding? When is consent required for a project to move forward?[71] In many ways, local and national governments, judiciaries, minorities, and stake holders in numerous countries are still grappling with the complex multicultural, social, economic, institutional, and political issues that

[67] The court closed the case in Auto 189 de 2013, dated September 2013. Note, however, that the *auto* was made public, and the parties were notified only ten months later, in mid-2014.

[68] Corte Constituconal, Colombia. Auto 410A de 2015. September 14, 2015. M.P. Gabriel Eduardo Mendoza Martelo.

[69] According to Sandoval Rojas (2021), this ambiguity in national frameworks regulating prior consultation can be beneficial to marginalized Indigenous populations, allowing them to redirect the institution's goals, if they are able to turn to other institutional venues to contest the process and if they can credibly signal they have the power to mobilize in that same direction.

[70] Interview with former director of Grupo Consulta Previa Ministerio de Justicia. Bogotá. July 18, 2012.

[71] Orduz Salinas (2014) identifies two key moments in the court's jurisprudence regarding prior consultation: First, in the early 1990s and afterward, when the tribunal first recognized prior consultation as a fundamental right, but did not require their consent. Second, a later stage starting in 2009 (following a key decision from the Inter-American Court on Human Rights) when the constitutional court set a new standard. Since then, consent is required when the measure or project to be consulted is of such a magnitude or has such an impact that it could endanger the group's survival.

implementing prior consultation entails. Sandoval Rojas (2021) identifies in that ambiguity a space that Indigenous peoples have been able to use, under certain circumstances, to expand the scope of this right.

The oftentimes contested nature of prior consultation at the national and international level is reflected in the Gordian Knot that was Puerto Brisa. The Indigenous peoples of the Sierra Nevada went to court precisely because the construction of Puerto Brisa began without them having been consulted; by the time the case reached the Constitutional Court, work on the port was well underway. The court ordered that a consultation process be undertaken – not to evaluate whether or not the project's environmental license stood, but in relation to the impacts of the project and possible ways to avoid them or mitigate them. For some, this decision requesting a consultation after the fact was a setback vis-à-vis some of the court's earlier positions. For others, it opened a different avenue for a mechanism to incorporate these groups, by providing for a consultation mechanism that had already been used, at least once, when projects had already started.[72]

In the last stage of the consultation process that the court ordered and got off the ground, the Indigenous people decided to withdraw. This was in response to the refusal by the Ministry of Interior to certify the existence of sacred sites during a walk-through of the area. From the perspective of the Indigenous groups, their right was not effectively guaranteed by the process and only a permanent stop to the construction of the port was a satisfactory resolution. In contrast, for the company and the Ministry of Environment, measures could be taken to mitigate negative consequences to the extent possible, allowing Indigenous groups of the Sierra Nevada to continue to have access to the sacred sites.

Once the Indigenous people withdrew from the consultation process, three very different written versions of what ensued emerged: First, the formal report that the court had requested from the Environmental Ministry. In it, the Ministry recommended that the project be given the environmental authorization, but also suggested that some mitigating measures be taken, as I will explain later. Second, a report from the company and a third report from the Indigenous people. According to the Ombudsman and the Indigenous' lawyer, the formal report filed by the Environmental Ministry did not accurately convey the entirety of what transpired in the final meetings of the consultation process. In any case, from the controversial report it is clear that at that point, the company and the Indigenous people were no closer to an agreed-upon solution than they were before:

> ...for the indigenous people the preservation of their cultural integrity can only be guaranteed through measures like revoking the environmental license and the definitive suspension of all activities; for the company (Puerto Brisa) there are measures that can be taken to correct, mitigate or make up for the physical, biotic

[72] A similar case (in the sense that the project was already underway) was decided by the court in T-693-2011.

> and socio-cultural consequences that that project may have. Since the proposals could not be reconciled, the meeting ended without there being an agreement among the parties.[73]

The Ministry's recommendations were to uphold the environmental license, maintain the site closed for an additional four months, and ask Puerto Brisa to redesign the social component within its environmental plan (*Plan de Gestión Social*) to incorporate the information and discussions during the consultation process. Crucially, the Ministry concluded that the Indigenous groups did not face the danger of extinction and that their response to and participation in this process was proof of their political cohesion, their resources, and their capacities. If the existence and livelihood of an Indigenous group were threatened by the project in question, then (according to the court's jurisprudence) their consent is required for the project to occur (Orduz Salinas 2014). What this clarification implied was that the agreement of the Indigenous people of the Sierra Nevada was not necessary for Puerto Brisa to move forward. This position was something that the Ministry's decision to uphold the environmental license implicitly condoned.

In its follow-up *auto*, the court noted the seemingly irresolvable differences between the parties. It concluded that the Indigenous people's refusal to consider any alternative besides stopping the project and revoking the license was not in accordance with their mandates as judges of the constitutional court to find a way to weight the rights of the Indigenous groups and those of the company and have them somehow coexist.[74]

Close attention to the sequence of events by which the consultation process took place is crucial to a discussion about rights effectiveness. Whether or not some objective standpoint exists from which the ruling and the actions that ensued effectively advanced the rights of the Wiwa, Kankuamo, Kogui, and Arhuaco is not the question here. The central question for this book is whether the results of the ruling are effective from the perspective of the claimants. As a result, what interests me is understanding whether or not (and why) the process that occurred could be deemed effective by the right bearers. From that perspective, the evaluation of the consultation process is not positive.

The lawyer for the Indigenous people, the Indigenous people's Ombudsman, and an expert on prior consultation who followed the process closely attributed some of the difficulties of the consultation to the approach taken by the government officials in charge of coordinating prior consultations. The Ombudsman, for example, emphasized the lack of a rights-based perspective:

> There is a pro-private company intentionality in the governmental entities (Ministry of Justice and Environment). They understand their role as that of being

[73] Ministerio de Vivienda y Medio Ambiente, Colombia. "Resolución 218 del 21 de Diciembre de 2011."

[74] Corte Constitucional, Colombia. Auto 033 2012. M.P. Mendoza Martelo, Gabriel Eduardo. February 17, 2012.

> intermediaries that will make the indigenous people's position shift into being more favorable towards the company. It's not a pro-rights position.[75]

This dissatisfaction with the prior consultation process was echoed by other actors. The environmental lawyer put it in terms of a lack of training and preparedness for the task of facilitating an intercultural dialogue: "The Environmental Ministry does not have a clue about interculturality or dialogue. Public officials need special training. It is not the same thing to sit down and talk to the company than to sit down and talk to the indigenous people."[76] My conversation with the lawyer for the Indigenous people who, like the other interviewees mentioned here, also had experience with other prior consultations ended on a very pessimistic note: "...the tutela is not useful to guarantee rights. Yes, we can get people to sit at the table, but the Ministries (meaning, government officials) do not change."[77]

The institutional instability that plagued the governmental agencies in charge of coordinating the process complicated the situation further. The problem was particularly acute with regard to the unit within the Ministry of Interior that was in charge of coordinating consultations. This unit was created in 2010: In just four years it had changed names twice and changed director four times. Despite institutional instability and lack of clarity in its functions, this unit had to process a growing number of requests to coordinate prior consultations in light of the mining boom in Colombia at the time. In a training workshop I attended in Bogotá for public officials and representatives from companies working on projects related to prior consultation, one of the presenters (with over five years of experience facilitating these processes) stated: "[C]ompanies are extremely confused by the lack of coordination in the government agencies: for example, the lack of clarity with regards to in which areas of the country there is/is not indigenous presence. (...) In general, there is a lack of unity of criteria among the different [government] agencies."[78]

The consultation process was unsatisfactory to the Indigenous people and to their representatives. There was frustration at this instance in particular, but also with the larger structural problems with prior consultation. With that in mind, what should also be noted is that in the absence of the court's intervention, the Indigenous people would not have seen any consultation process at all. Ultimately, there would not have been procedures put in place for them to be able to access the sacred site, which the court required in its decision and follow-up *autos*. In a similar line, Sandoval Rojas (2021), who defines the result as bittersweet, highlights another aspect: The Indigenous people were unable to stop the port from being built, but a

75 Interview with the Defensor Delegado para los Indígenas y las minorías étnicas. Bogotá. July 4, 2012.

76 Interview with expert on prior consultation. Bogotá. August 2, 2012.

77 Interview with ILSA lawyer. Bogotá. April 12, 2012.

78 "Consulta Previa" Workshop, part of the program *Diplomado en Consulta Previa*, organized by the Universidad Nacional de Colombia. Bogotá, June 6, 2012.

benefit was gained in that the ruling was crucial to redefining and expanding the notion of what counts as territory for future prior consultation processes.

4.3.2.2 Explaining T-547's Impact

Like the previous case, *Badaro*, this is a ruling where the Court maintained attention on implementation through monitoring mechanisms. That the consultation process occurred at all – with all its faults – is linked directly to the court's monitoring in the aftermath of its decision. Initially, the court designated a lower court, the *Tribunal Supremo de Bogotá*, as the institution in charge of monitoring the results of the consultation process with the Indigenous groups. Notwithstanding, over the course of the following years, the CCC would actively exercise monitoring relying on direct requests for progress reports and a public hearing.

In contrast to the thicker network of organizations that come together in cases like *Causa Mendoza* and *Verbitsky* in Argentina as well as the health (T-760) and housing (C-383) rulings in Colombia, this particular ruling does not have a dense legal constituency. A lawyer from the legal advocacy NGO ILSA (*Instituto Latinoamericano para una Sociedad y un Derecho Alternativo*) was linked with the case from the beginning and worked with the Indigenous people throughout the process.[79] There are other human rights NGOs in Colombia who have handled prior consultation cases. However, I did not observe any coordinated and sustained mobilization efforts after the ruling in conjunction with other organizations, or the formation of a network around the issue of the port on Puerto Brisa.

The absence of a dense legal constituency limited mobilization around the ruling. ILSA and the Indigenous peoples participated in the public hearing and had some access to the court, but I did not observe the cross-cutting legal advocacy and political activity evident in *Verbitsky* or the Colombian housing rulings, for example.

On the other hand, the court's sustained engagement after the ruling made possible updating aspects of the implementation in response to requests from stakeholders. For example, the court changed the deadline for the consultation to take place. The battle between the stakeholders over its timing is worth exploring in some detail. In this back-and-forth some of the deeper tensions surface clearly, particularly around access to information and agreement over the purpose of the consultation process itself.

Initially, the court asked for the consultation process to take place within thirty days of its pronouncement. Soon after the court handed down its decision, both the Ministry of Environment and the Indigenous people filed separate requests for an extension to the time frame in which the consultation process should take place. In

[79] The Indigenous peoples of the Sierra Nevada are among the most cohesive Indigenous minorities in Colombia.

its request, the Ministry explained that these processes usually take anywhere from six months to a year.[80] In my interview with the ILSA lawyer she explained:

> One of the things that became clear, immediately, was the need to request an extension of the target date by which the consultation process should be held. This generated a lot of discussion and controversy among the actors. The indigenous people wanted an extension. (…) It was not going to be possible to reach an agreement with regards to timing.[81]

This was confirmed by other actors who participated in the discussions. According to the official within the Ombudsman office who at the time was in charge of Indigenous affairs and followed this process closely, "Within this limited time frame the conditions were not appropriate for their [the indigenous people's] timing to be respected."[82]

In mid-July, the parties agreed to meet in La Guajira for a preparatory meeting geared at defining the agenda and methods of the consultation process. Over the course of the next two months the lack of a common ground between the government agencies, the company, and the Indigenous people was evident. In meetings and in written communications, Puerto Brisa officials emphasized that they went ahead with the project because the Ministry of Justice had certified in 2006 that there was no Indigenous presence in the area. In their view, the deadline originally set by the court had already expired, and what had been mandated was a consultation (merely informative) and not a full-fledged prior consultation process. In parallel, the CTC contacted the court several times seeking clarification that the deadline had not passed and informing it of Puerto Brisa's unwillingness to cover the cost of specialists who would review the impact reports and provide independent assessments. As this suggests, access to information was a particularly thorny issue. The Ministry of Interior had to remind Puerto Brisa that they could not deny the requests of the Indigenous people to have access to the studies on the social, cultural, and technical impact of the port.[83]

Generating coordination among all the actors involved in carrying out the consultation process ordered by T-547 was an uphill battle. A short-lived "Interinstitutional Committee" met several times to coordinate efforts among the Ministries of Justice and Environment and the Ombudsman's office. When asked about this initiative, the Ombudsman, who participated in all meetings, stated: "This Committee came up with a joint plan (for the consultation) which did not come into being (…) It was able to advance only in clarifying what role each

[80] Corte Constitucional, Colombia. Auto 083-11. May 17, 2011. M.P. Gabriel Eduardo Mendoza Martelo.

[81] Interview with ILSA lawyer. Bogotá. April 12, 2012.

[82] Interview with the Associate Ombudsman for Indigenous and Ethnic Minorities, *Defensor Delegado para los Indígenas y las minorías étnicas*. Bogotá. July 4, 2012.

[83] Expediente caso Puerto Brisa (Fallo T-547) folder no. 17. Available at the Ministerio de Vivienda y Medio Ambiente. Bogotá.

institution should play in the consultation. It was very difficult to get the Ministries of Interior and of Environment on the same page."[84] In August, as the deadline loomed near, the Ministry of Environment had to notify the court that there had been insurmountable difficulties getting the consultation process off the ground.

Shortly after, the court heeded the requests and extended the deadline for thirty additional days. It mandated that the Environmental Ministry should reach a decision by this new deadline and make it known to the court, who would in turn decide if it stood or not. Ultimately, between late October and early December 2011 the consultation process took place through a series of meetings in La Guajira.

At this point, in the last stage of the consultation process, the Indigenous groups decided to step aside and not sign the final memorandum certifying that the consultation process occurred. Following this conflicted end to the consultation process, in early 2012 the court held a public hearing in Dibulla, La Guajira, so the justices could hear reports from the parties and personally inspect the port site. When I asked experts, lawyers, and government officials who were close to this process to describe and assess the public hearing, there were two common themes: The hearing was described as a positive experience that allowed the parties to provide the court with more information and for them to see the site and the cultural dimension. At the same time, there was agreement that the hearing did not provide enough space for interaction and discussion.[85] The lawyer for the Indigenous people put it in the following terms:

> What I think is positive is that the court requests an evaluation from all interested parties, because the report presented by the Ministry of Environment was not enough. (…) The court realized its initial order had been too narrow. The court asked all involved to conduct a balance of the consultation process. We didn't hear anything new, but the court did."[86]

Ultimately, the process failed to generate coordination among the different actors involved. As discussed earlier, the Arhuaco, Wixa, Kankuamo, and Kogui peoples refused to engage in the process further. They retained access to the holy sites, but the port was ultimately built, against their wishes.

4.3.3 *Comparing Badaro and T-547*

Comparing Badaro and T-547 suggests that monitoring can enhance the impact of the court's intervention. In both cases the court stays engaged with the issue after the

[84] Interview with the Associate Ombudsman for Indigenous and Ethnic Minorities, *Defensor Delegado para los Indígenas y las minorías étnicas*. Bogotá. July 4, 2012.

[85] Interview with the Associate Ombudsman for Indigenous and Ethnic Minorities, *Defensor Delegado para los Indígenas y las minorías étnicas*. Bogotá. Jul 4, 2012; Interview with ILSA lawyer. Bogotá. April 12, 2012. Interview with expert on prior consultation. Bogotá. August 2, 2012.

[86] Interview with ILSA lawyer. Bogotá. April 12, 2012.

decision was handed down, revisiting implementation through information requests and/or through public hearings. Monitoring can increase the costs for the targets of the ruling: In the case of Puerto Brisa, the high-stakes port was already under construction; without the court's sustained attention, the consultation process with the Indigenous people would not have taken place. In the case of Argentina's pensions, the court's sustained attention and political pressure made possible the eventual approval of a semi-annual automatic update mechanism which, given the government's reticence, was highly unlikely at the outset. Despite the shortcomings of changes to the formal norms and to the outcomes themselves, we observe noteworthy changes after both interventions.

I also proposed at the outset that monitoring could enhance impact by overcoming some of the court's information asymmetries. In both cases, we observed that in public hearings both courts were able to evaluate information on implementation and heard from actors other than those charged with compliance, including the rights claimants. In the absence of monitoring mechanisms, which invite input and create space for other actors at different points in time, a court's "field of vision" tends to be narrower.

Still, the absence of denser legal constituencies limited the impact of both Badaro and T-547. If we think about these in contrast to the cases discussed in Chapter 3, where monitoring mechanisms are active and dense legal constituencies can engage them, we begin to see that monitoring can be significantly enhanced by a dense network of civil society organizations. There is monitoring in these cases, and it made important contributions, but there is no mobilization around the rulings that can do coordinated follow up, nor can civil society organizations help further diffuse information and effects into other spheres.

These cases also suggest that state-based oversight agencies can play decisive roles in the aftermath of these decisions. The Seniors' Ombudsman in *Causa Badaro* was able to engage in the type of mobilizing – including entreaties with the court – that generated information, opportunities for follow up, and political pressure.

4.4 CONCLUSIONS: THE FOUR CASES IN COMPARATIVE PERSPECTIVE

The case studies in this chapter highlighted the distinct contributions that legal constituencies and monitoring mechanisms can make to impact, lending support to the theory I outlined earlier. I showed how dense legal constituencies helped in the cases of *Verbitsky* and C-383 by carrying out legal and political mobilization that further diffused the ruling's effects to other spheres and areas beyond the actors directly implicated in the original claim. I also showed how monitoring contributed to increasing the costs for the targets in Badaro and T-547 as well as helped each court acquire and use information it would not have had access to in the absence of institutional tools for follow-up.

Earlier I highlighted some insights we could glean from the paired comparisons. In the final section of this chapter, I would like to underscore what we can learn from thinking about the two pairs of cases side by side. Taken together, the four cases suggest interesting patterns. First, the pair of rulings with dense legal constituencies – prisoners' rights in Argentina (*Causa Verbitsky*) and housing rights in Colombia (C-383) – stand in contrast with the two rulings that had monitoring mechanisms – pension rights in Argentina (Badaro) and prior consultation in Colombia (T-547) – because the presence of legal constituencies in the first pair made possible noteworthy ideational and organizational effects. In contrast, the absence of legal constituencies limited the spheres where we observe impact following Badaro and T-547. Through monitoring, the court works in legal and institutional spaces. Civil society organizations, in contrast, work in social spaces. When civil society organizations are present, they can magnify the ruling's ripple effects into those areas. The work of legal constituencies can potentially extend effects into social spaces, help put political pressure on government agents, legislators, and other organized groups in civil society thus keeping the issue alive.

Second, the court's intervention and monitoring in Badaro and T-547 meant higher levels of impact in terms of formal norms and resources than would have been observed in the absence of the court's intervention and its sustained oversight. In the Argentine case, the ruling altered the regulatory framework for pensions, particularly because it triggered the passing in Congress of a bill providing for biannual updates to the monthly payments. Until then, updates depended on the executive's initiative and Congress' will coinciding: They were not annualized nor scheduled. In the Colombian case, the court's sustained intervention got off the ground and oversaw a consultation process for the Kogui, Wiwa, Arhuaco, and Kankuamo Indigenous groups with regard to Puerto Brisa. In both cases monitoring helped do this by increasing the amount of information the court was receiving about events on the ground and it helped put greater public pressure on the targets. The comparison suggests, however, that the effect of monitoring is partly conditional on the presence of a denser legal constituency. Though monitoring can make a difference on its own, without a dense legal constituency its reach is more limited. Where monitoring tools were in place, civil society was able to funnel (even) more information from other external sources to monitoring venues and mobilize in other spaces, creating the type of synergies we saw in Chapter 3.

5

Low Impact Cases

5.1 INTRODUCTION

In this chapter I focus on two rulings where we observe neither oversight mechanisms nor dense legal constituencies. As I discussed in Chapter 2, my theory suggests that impact in such cases would be lower when compared to cases where both of these elements, or one of the two, are present. The first case is *Chaco v. Defensor del Pueblo*, hereafter *Chaco*, a ruling by the Supreme Court of Argentina seeking to safeguard the rights of the Qom Indigenous group in the Chaco Province. The second case is a ruling handed down by the Colombian Constitutional Court seeking to protect the right to a healthy environment for the inhabitants around the Bogotá Canal, in Cúcuta.

In the pages that follow I provide, for each ruling, an overview of the case, an assessment of its impact, and an analysis of the aftermath of the decision. I show that these two cases had lower levels of impact overall, although they did prompt some effects. In both cases, the effects were restricted mostly to the devolution of specific resources to the area and the creation of precedent for similar efforts in the future. The nature of the effects is explained partly by the absence of dense legal constituencies and monitoring mechanisms. A dense group of legally empowered civil society organizations could have contributed to the follow-up process, to the production of information, and to keeping political pressure on the targets. Monitoring mechanisms could have created spaces for the court to receive external input on implementation and potentially created institutional scenarios for all actors related to the ruling to interact.

Both rulings in this chapter are exemplars of judicial interventions that try to address a complex public policy issue with one-time specific interventions providing detailed one-shot orders. They stand in contrast to approaches like those taken by the courts in the cases studied in Chapter 3 (*Mendoza* and T-760 on health) and Chapter 4 (*Badaro* and T-547 on prior consultation) where more flexible orders provided for ongoing participation of different stakeholders in supervising the aftermath and implementation.

Although in comparison to the other cases analyzed in this book the impact of the two cases under consideration in this chapter is lower, among the two, *Chaco*'s impact was higher. Looked at side by side, immediate effects in the Argentine case were medium, whereas those in the Colombia case were low. As I will show in more detail below, greater immediate effects in the *Chaco* case are associated with the work of an independent governmental agency, the Defensor del Pueblo – the national human rights institution based in Buenos Aires. The human rights subunit within the Defensor worked with Centro Mandela, a Chaco-based organization to bring the case before the Supreme Court, and afterward continued working on it. The advocacy work that the Defensor did was central to the relatively higher impact in the *Chaco* case. Once again, just like with the work of the Seniors' Ombudsman in the *Badaro* case (Chapter 4), we see that independent government agencies can play a key role mobilizing around the ruling after it has been handed down.

What little ideational effects the *Chaco* ruling did have were also restricted to the Defensor itself, whose views of Indigenous rights shifted through their work with the Qom. The absence of ideational effects beyond those directly implicated in the ruling in both cases, and their total absence in the Colombian case (T-231), is indicative of their importance. In sharp contrast to previous research that has placed the biggest emphasis on the implementation of rulings (that is, in changes in terms of formal norms and resources), both *Chaco* and T-231 suggest that ideational effects are not mere inconsequential by-products, but are actually central to the process of generating rights effectiveness and broader political and social change.

5.2 RIGHTS TO FOOD AND HEALTH: *CAUSA CHACO* (ARGENTINA)

In mid-2007 the dire humanitarian conditions of the Qom in the forested area known as "El Impenetrable" (The Impenetrable) made national news in Argentina with headlines such as: "Ethnic Genocide in El Impenetrable"; "Eight are dead in El Impenetrable"; "In a month, hunger killed five in El Impenetrable" and "Humanitarian disaster."[1] Difficult and long-standing socioeconomic conditions fueled the outbreak of preventable diseases (like chagas and tuberculosis), malnourishment, lack of water and basic sanitary services. The Qom are the second largest Indigenous group in Argentina (roughly 60,000). They inhabit regions of the Chaco and Formosa provinces (see Figure 5.1) and have also migrated to the outskirts of Rosario and Buenos Aires. Their situation in El Impenetrable was aggravated by

[1] Página 12, "Genocidio étnico" en El Impenetrable, 5/21/2007. La Nación, "En un mes el hambre mató en El Chaco a cinco personas," 8/3/2007. Página 12, "Desastre humanitario," 8/8/2007.

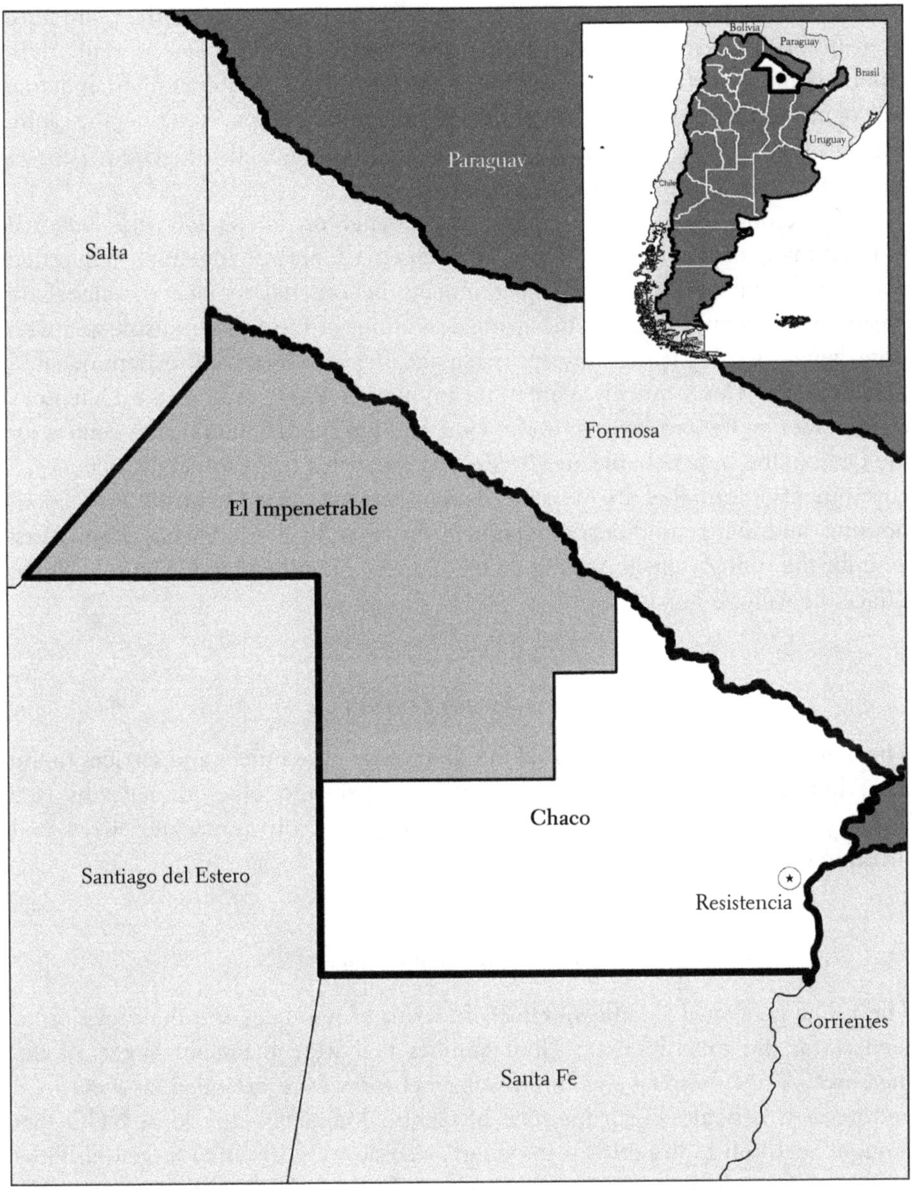

FIGURE 5.1 Map of Chaco and El Impenetrable, Argentina

difficult conditions in Chaco more generally. The province consistently ranks as the lowest in human development indicators on a national level: In 2008[2] and 2013, roughly half of the province's one million inhabitants were poor (CIPPES 2013).

2 "Chaco, donde la pobreza es más pobre," p. 12, May 22, 2008.

Like other Indigenous people in Argentina and in Latin America, the Qom have been historically excluded and marginalized. This history of socioeconomic difficulties, political exclusion, and extreme marginalization contributes to an endemic lack of institutional visibility of Argentinean Indigenous groups, including the Qom. Though the 1994 constitutional reform explicitly recognized Indigenous peoples and certain rights, marginalization persists.

In September 2007, the Defensor del Pueblo de la Nación (the national Ombudsman) filed a lawsuit before the Supreme Court of Argentina requesting that the federal and provincial governments be ordered to take the necessary measures that would improve the living conditions of the Indigenous people who were being "silently, progressively, systematically, and inevitably exterminated."[3] The Supreme Court quickly granted an injunction in response to the Defensor's claim, ordering the provision of water, food, and transportation to health centers for the Qom in the Impenetrable area. It also requested that the provincial and national governments inform it of the measures being taken with regard to health, education, housing, and living condition programs in the area. In the following pages I first describe the ruling's effects, relying on the framework outlined in Chapter 2. Then, I trace the ruling's impact.

5.2.1 Chaco's *Impact*

The court's pronouncement spurred the devolution of resources and services to the area, but its ripples did not reach much further into other dimensions (see Table 5.1). I classify the impact of this ruling as low on immediate effects and medium on outcomes.

5.2.1.1 Immediate Effects

The ruling generated significant effects in terms of resources and the provision of services for the roughly 2,000 Qom families that were the main targets of the measures. A new hospital was built, water networks were extended, as were food and pension benefits. For a member of Centro Mandela – the local NGO that brought attention to the crisis – the court's decision was essential to getting these resources: "...it had tremendous importance. Particularly in three aspects: water, food, and access to sanitary services. (...) [The aid that was funneled to the area] entails, on average, for each family three boxes of food, pension and drinking water. It is insufficient [vis a vis optimal conditions], but it generated a substantial change."[4]

[3] "Mondino denunció el exterminio de Tobas en el Chaco," Perfil. August 29, 2007.
[4] Interview with member of Centro Mandela. March 20, 2014.

TABLE 5.1 *Summary of impact dimensions for* Chaco

Dimension	Indicator	Assessment
Immediate effects		
Formal norms	- Small judicial cascade of related rulings.	Low
Resources	- Water pipelines were extended to the judicialized area (which comprises the following municipalities: Espinillo, Bermejito, Miraflores, Juan José Castelli, and part of Pampas del Indio; 2,000 families total) - A new hospital was built in Castelli. - New resources were channeled to the region via two existing programs: *Asistencia Alimentaria* and *Pensiones no contributivas*	Medium
Organizational changes	–	None
Ideas/discourse	- Changes within the Defensor del Pueblo.	Low
Total immediate effects		Low
Outcome (rights effectiveness)	- Access to health services. - Enjoyment of food and pension benefits.	Medium

The court's pronouncement was also directly linked to the flow of resources into the area, including breathing new life into long-standing plans to extend access to drinking water. A member of the Defensor del Pueblo team described it in the following words: "Plans to build the aqueduct had circulated for the last 50 years. But [because of the court's intervention] they were accelerated."[5] Such efforts made an important difference in the context of the living conditions of the Qom, given their historical marginalization.

The ruling also generated a very modest legal cascade, reflected in the low assessment for formal norms in Table 5.1. More specifically, the *Chaco* ruling served as precedent to seek the judicial enforcement of the rights of other Indigenous groups in other parts of Argentina, particularly Santuario Tres Pozos in Jujuy and the Qom Navogoh in Formosa. Because the immediate effects were circumscribed largely to generating resources, I classify *Chaco* as low on immediate effects. However, as discussed earlier, the devolution of resources and other material effects was in turn linked to certain improvements in living conditions for the Qom in the affected area, which explains that the outcome is medium, as I will discuss later.

Finally, this ruling (along with others) contributed to an ongoing ideational transformation within the Defensor del Pueblo, whereby this institution began working with and on behalf of Indigenous peoples from a rights-based perspective.

[5] Interview with member of the Human Rights Area of the Defensor del Pueblo de la Nación. Buenos Aires, March 18, 2013.

5.2.1.2 Outcome

In terms of outcomes, the assessments of those who are deeply familiar with the situation in El Impenetrable speaks of improvements, but partial. On a general level, conditions were so bleak when the court intervened, that the influx of assistance marked a significant difference. The hospital that was completed in Castelli in 2010 saw more than 55,000 patients in 2012.[6] However, a report by the Defensor del Pueblo that year (2012) noted staffing difficulties and other challenges to the hospital's functioning at its full capacity, including problems with its integration with rural health centers. The same report also surveyed families in the municipalities who were beneficiaries, all of whom reported receiving food assistance, pensions, and water (at varying rates).

The measures provided important and needed relief, but structural inequalities remained. A member of the Centro Mandela stated: "[The court's decision] alleviated the poverty that stems from a lack of income. [But] the more structural poverty only slightly (. . .structural poverty) remains largely intact."[7] Overall, the ruling had real and important consequences for the Qom inhabitants at that particular juncture, in light of the severity of the crisis and the previous condition of total abandonment. However, its reach in terms of a long-term solution was limited. As a result, I classify it as medium in terms of outcome.

5.2.2 *Explaining* Chaco's *Impact*

In contrast to the cases discussed in Chapter 3 (*Causa Mendoza* and T-760), the *Chaco* ruling did not provide for court-promoted monitoring mechanisms and the legal constituency that had a stake on the rights and overall well-being of the Qom was much less dense in comparison to the web of associations directly invested in the cleanup of the Matanza-Riachuelo River basin, for example. Though the Supreme Court held hearings to listen to the provincial and national governments on the programs they put in place, there was no monitoring of progress over time, no periodic reporting to the court. Indeed, as Benedetti and Sáenz (2016) note, the only audience held in 2007 specifically did not require or invite the active participation and input from the Ombudsman (which had lodged the original complaint) nor from any other related actor. Furthermore, we do not observe the creation of institutional spaces where the court, the targets of the ruling, and a dense legal constituency did follow up on the ruling.

6 "El Hospital del Bicentenario de Castelli atendió a más de 55 mil pacientes en 2012," Diario Norte. January 18, 2013. Argentine provincial hospitals are classified in levels according to their complexity and the type of care they can provide. The Castelli one was level VI, where the highest possible classification was VIII.

7 Interview with director of Centro Mandela. March 20, 2014.

As for the legal constituency, in this case there was only one locally based organization, the Centro Mandela, closely associated with the ruling. The Centro worked for months prior to filing the legal claim to get media attention on the crisis and collaborated with the Ombudsman in preparing the brief. Its advocacy was important in bringing attention to the situation in Chaco – and afterward, so were its attempts to continue to draw attention to the area. The Centro is a small volunteer-based human rights NGO created in the late 1990s. At its core was its director, Rolando Nuñez. By the time this claim was filed with the Supreme Court, the Centro did not have experience with Indigenous groups or Indigenous rights, nor had it done any previous work with the Qom. They became aware of the situation in the Impenetrable while researching on fraud and deforestation issues in national lands. In that context, they brainstormed informally on ways to raise awareness.[8] The Centro worked out of Resistencia (in Chaco) and did not have a presence in or ties to Buenos Aires. In a country like Argentina, where resources and access revolve around the capital city, regional organizations face certain barriers when doing advocacy before political institutions. In short, their reach and resources were limited, and for this reason I classify it as a low density legal constituency.

The Defensor del Pueblo, with whom the Centro collaborated, played an important role in the aftermath of the ruling, as the team decided to do basic follow-up on the implementation of the court's decision. They monitored the situation from a distance through reviews of national and local news outlets, by traveling to the region, and producing reports of these visits. The role of this agency in keeping the issue alive, while not equivalent to the presence of a dense legal constituency, generated a conversation with the regional authorities and maintained some level of national attention on the issue. By doing these things, this independent government oversight agency partly filled a gap, in a manner akin to what the Seniors' Ombudsman did in the *Badaro* case (Chapter 4).

Interestingly, several of my interviewees coincided that the biggest obstacle to the full realization of the Qom's rights was them being viewed as subjects of rights. The head of the human rights team within the Defensor, who was involved with this institution's work in the area since 2006, put it as follows: "There is a discriminatory bias (. . .) What continues to be a problem? [The lack of] a framework to think of the indigenous person as a subject of rights. We need to sensitize the police, the judge, the person who works at the hospital. What's happening today? That the person on call at the hospital makes the indigenous person wait and sees to the *criollos* first."[9] Public policy that incorporates a rights-based perspective can contribute to rights effectiveness, but officials and providers need to be aware of it too. This key

[8] The general characterization of the Centro Mandela and its resources is based on author's interview with the director of Centro Mandela. March 20, 2013.

[9] Interview with member of the Human Rights Area of the Defensor del Pueblo de la Nación. Buenos Aires, March 18, 2013.

ideational shift (which occurred in the case of the Colombian health ruling described in Chapter 3, for example) did not happen here. The lack of awareness with regard to rights-based discourse among government officials and bureaucrats has very real consequences, like the ones mentioned by the head of the Defensor's human rights team above. In that sense, this experience suggests that the ideational effects that rulings can trigger are not mere inconsequential by-products of judicial intervention in the enforcement of rights.

The importance of a rights-based perspective can be illustrated further by looking within the Defensor del Pueblo itself and its own prior experience with becoming conversant in and advocating for Indigenous rights. It is telling to note that the Defensor del Pueblo de la Nación had no specialized subunit focusing on *pueblos originarios* in 2007, when this case started. The head of the team at the Defensor explained that an important part of the reason why the original legal claim on *Chaco* was filed focusing on human rights, in general – and with no reference to Indigenous rights – was that their lawyers were not familiar with the latter: "At that time [2007] that framework [indigenous rights], that sensibility, was very foreign to our lawyers here in Buenos Aires."[10] An expert on Indigenous law and rights recalled that those who were following the discussions around the Defensor's choice of legal strategy were particularly concerned that the Indigenous rights perspective might be foreign to a very important subset of lawyers: the justices sitting on the Supreme Court.[11]

In my conversation with the head of the human rights office, the discussion around the *Chaco* case prompted him to note that working with this case and similar ones on the rights of Indigenous communities had resulted in important learning experiences for his team: "Now we have to do fieldwork, we have to think about the cultural dimension and we have to privilege consent and agreement with the indigenous people."[12] The type of change that was triggered within the Defensor began to bring into perspective *pueblos originarios* as special subjects of rights. The transformation also shifted the officers' perspectives. This kind of change, if it happens among key decision-makers and other bureaucratic agents, can make important differences in terms of policy, implementation and everyday interactions.

I now turn to the second case in this chapter, a ruling on environmental rights handed down by Colombia's Constitutional Court in the early 1990s. Like *Chaco*, in this ruling there was neither monitoring by the court nor a dense legal constituency. Both offer an informative contrast to the other rulings studied in this book.

10 Interview with member of the Human Rights Area of the Defensor del Pueblo de la Nación. Buenos Aires, March 18, 2013.

11 Interview with expert on Indigenous law and rights. March 14, 2014.

12 Interview with member of the Human Rights Area of the Defensor del Pueblo de la Nación. Buenos Aires, March 18, 2013.

5.3 ENVIRONMENTAL RIGHTS: T-231 (COLOMBIA)

In 1993, the Colombian Constitutional Court reviewed a tutela that had been filed against the office of the mayor of the city of Cúcuta and its municipal public services company, EIS (*Empresa de Acueducto y Alcantarillado de Cúcuta*, Cúcuta Water and Sewage Services). An inhabitant of Cúcuta called the judiciary's attention to the grave environmental deterioration of the Bogotá Canal, which runs across the length of the city. Luis Alberto Rodríguez filed the tutela seeking to protect his right to a healthy environment, endangered by the extensive contamination in the canal.

Cúcuta is Colombia's sixth largest city. With roughly 650,000 inhabitants, it is located on the border with Venezuela (see Figure 5.2 for a map of its location), and its economy depends heavily on the ebbs and flows of commerce with Colombia's neighboring country. The Bogotá Canal was built in the late 1960s as the main rainwater collector for the city's aqueduct system (Velandia Caicedo 2002). As it makes its way through Cúcuta's heart, the canal touches fourteen different neighborhoods.

The contamination and environmental degradation of the canal and its surrounding area were serious in the early 1990s and remain problematic. Between the 1970s and 1990s, Cúcuta grew rapidly and in a mostly informal and unplanned manner, which resulted in numerous infrastructure defects, among them the construction of sanitary and rainwater aqueducts without any technical planning (Torres Tovar 2009). As a result, thousands of illegal sewage connections dumped their waste directly into the Bogotá Canal, contaminating it.[13] The situation was aggravated by the persistent use of the canal and its banks as garbage and solid waste disposal sites (Muñoz, García, and Lara 2007). Solid residues often block the canal passages; the contaminated water and waste generate foul smell, and disease.

In response to Luis Alberto Rodriguez's tutela, the Constitutional Court ordered the EIS to initiate a program for the cleanup and upkeep of the canal within thirty days. At the same time, it ordered the mayor's office to undertake educational campaigns with inhabitants along the canal's banks to involve them in the maintenance of the canal's surroundings.

5.3.1 *Impact of T-231*

Table 5.2 summarizes the impact of this ruling, which I describe as low overall.

5.3.1.1 Immediate Effects

According to the case file that rests in the Regional Appeals Court in Cúcuta and to David Bonells, the director of EIS at the time,[14] cleanup activities were executed in

[13] The infrastructure project that separated rainwater from sewage was not finished until 2014.

[14] Interview with former director of the EIS. Cúcuta. August 29, 2012.

FIGURE 5.2 Cúcuta, Colombia

TABLE 5.2 *Summary of impact dimensions for T-231*

Dimension	Indicator	Assessment
Formal norms	No modifications to legal or regulatory framework. Used as precedent in other efforts to guarantee judicial protection of water at the national level.	Low
Resources	Basic cleanup and maintenance operations were executed. Little evidence of educational campaigns directly associated with the ruling (and less of their duration over time). No informational resources were created.	Low
Organizational changes	–	None
Ideas/discourse	–	None
Total immediate effects		Low
Outcome (rights effectiveness)	Did not improve contamination or overall environmental conditions around the canal.	Low

the Bogotá Canal. Photographic and paperwork evidence proves that $50 million pesos were spent executing the court's orders.[15] However, there is less evidence that the educational campaigns were a sustained effort over time. The few campaigns that are mentioned in newspapers or in the records of the regional environmental agency in Cúcuta, CORPONOR, are sporadic and do not seem to be related directly to the ruling, not even in terms of their timing. Furthermore, discussions with staff at CORPONOR did not link these campaigns with the judicial decision, but rather suggest that they were the results of other programs.[16]

In terms of formal norms, this tutela generated a modest legal cascade. It was one of the first filed and won in Colombia protecting environmental rights, particularly the right to water. As such, it is recognized and has been used as a precedent in other efforts to enforce the judicial protection of water (Rodríguez, Gómez, and Lozano 2011).There was no evidence that T-231 triggered organizational changes or ideational effects.

5.3.1.2 Outcome

In terms of rights effectiveness, the balance in the medium and long term after T-231 was not positive. While the actions undertaken in 1994 meant temporary and welcome relief, the canal deteriorated again after these initial cleanup efforts.

[15] Case File 01-93 at the Tribunal Superior de Cúcuta.

[16] Interview with two Program Managers at CORPONOR (Corporación Autónoma Regional de la Frontera Nororiental). Cúcuta. August 27, 2012; Interview with director of CORPONOR. Cúcuta. August 28, 2012.

In 2012,[17] and at the time of writing, the canal continued to pose an environmental hazard. An important part of the problem with the canal, as with many of the cases under study here, is the lack of information. From the case file (which includes photographic evidence of the canal's condition) and from my review of local and national newspapers (which continue to report on the canal's poor condition at different points in time after 1993) we can conclude that there was no significant improvement to the environmental conditions. A review of the articles published on the canal in two local newspapers between 1994 and 2016 (when this investigation closes) shows that it was described by local news sources as a sewer and the gravest environmental problem in Cúcuta.[18] There was no specific agency or organization in charge of cleaning and monitoring conditions along the canal, and there was no single institution or organization with jurisdiction over its length. Different entities were, allegedly, in charge of different sections of the canal at different times – who was responsible for it was a disputed matter.[19] To summarize, given the preceding discussion, we can score this ruling as low on impact in both dimensions.

5.3.2 *Explaining T-231's Impact*

As in the previous case, *Chaco*, there were no court-promoted oversight mechanisms nor is there evidence of a dense legal constituency for T-231. The ruling includes pro forma dispositions requesting a report (as do most tutela rulings) but there is no disposition for public hearings or any follow-up activities.[20] In this case, there was no legal constituency associated to the ruling. The tutela was filed by an individual inhabitant of Cúcuta without legal representation and there is no evidence of him having been linked to any rights advocacy organization. Unfortunately, I could not locate him for an interview – it seems he had passed away. More generally, I found no evidence of any civil society organization doing legal or rights advocacy around environmental or related issues in Cúcuta at the time of litigation or in the decade thereafter. This has changed more recently, with a vibrant environmental movement coalescing around conservation of the Santurbán Páramo. However, for the time span following the ruling, the lack of a legal constituency in this case was absolute.

17 Interview with Program Manager at Aguas Kpital (water provider for the area). August 30, 2012. Cúcuta. See also Muñoz, García, and Lara (2007).

18 "Contra los malos olores" El Tiempo. January 18, 1996; "Limpian Canal Bogotá," EL Tiempo. January 18, 2001; "El Lunar de Cúcuta," El Tiempo. January 7, 2003; Canal Bogotá toda una cloaca," La Opinión. August 22, 2011.

19 Interview with director of CORPONOR. Cúcuta. August 28, 2012.

20 The file at the regional appeals court in Cúcuta included some of the reports since 1993. The physical file did not show evidence of wear or heavy use at the time I consulted it. Since all records from the 1990s are only accessible physically, this suggests that it had not been consulted much since it was created.

In its ruling, the court had given the EIS thirty days to undertake the cleanup and maintenance operations of the canal. Program managers at CORPONOR confirmed that the EIS spent resources and services on this endeavor,[21] signaling some compliance with the Court's decision. As explained earlier, compliance with what was ordered was partial, as the education campaigns were not carried out. In short, the ruling requested and generated a very specific response from the main target – namely EIS, the service provider – in terms of a one-time effort.

However, the reasons behind the canal's environmental deterioration ran deep; so much so, that a one-time cleanup effort could hardly be expected to address them for good. My interviews with former and current staffers of the water service providers in Cúcuta, officials at the regional environmental agency, and existing research coincide that the environmental hazard needs to be understood as the result of multiple factors: first, lack of resources for cleanup and maintenance; second, a lack of civic culture around proper waste disposal; and third, larger structural problems related to Cúcuta's urban planning, or more precisely, its lack thereof.

Cleanup efforts, which were the focus of the court's ruling, need to be sustained over time for them to have a meaningful impact. The director of the EIS at the time of the ruling explained that he complied with it knowing fully well that this was not a long-term solution: "I cleaned up the canal knowing that this was not going to do any good [in the long run]. (…) This is a huge problem that becomes particularly acute [every year] during the rainy season [when the filters in the canal become clogged with solid residues]."[22] Maintaining the canal involves not only efforts to keep it clean, which need to be frequent, but also resources to address larger issues like finishing up construction of its last leg and continued efforts to upgrade the sewage network in Cúcuta. Importantly, it also necessitates the involvement of the people who live close to it.

Problems with maintenance of the canal were also rooted in citizens' behaviors, particularly with how the people who live near and around the canal relate to it. In the words of the director of CORPONOR, "[the canal] is a problem of resources and also a problem of civic culture because people continue dumping solid residues, dead animals etc. directly into the canal."[23] The ruling tried to address this part of the equation by requesting that educational campaigns be carried out. Unfortunately, as already mentioned, this was not a sustained effort.

Like in the previous case, *Chaco*, this ruling is a one-shot decision that left untouched some of the more structural aspects behind the rights violation – in particular, the sources of the canal's contamination. Monitoring mechanisms – had

[21] Interview with two Program Managers at CORPONOR (Corporación Autónoma Regional de la Frontera Nororiental). Cúcuta. August 27, 2012.

[22] Interview with former director of the EIS. Cúcuta. August 29, 2012.

[23] Interview with director of CORPONOR. Cúcuta. August 28, 2012.

they been deployed for this kind of ruling – could have offered oversight over time and given the court a chance to become aware of the larger problems and perhaps adjust its intervention.

Equally crucial could have been the presence of a dense legal constituency. A common theme throughout my interviews was the negative impact of the lack of citizen mobilization around the canal and environmental issues in Cúcuta. A program manager at CORPONOR stated: "What is the problem with the Bogotá Canal? Yes, efforts are not maintained [over time]. There is a lack of resources and support for activities. There is [also] a lack of citizen mobilization. Only today are there areas [in the city] where the citizens are beginning to organize."[24] This lack of mobilization is probably linked to the nature of Cúcuta's urban growth. As mentioned earlier, the city's urban history was characterized by lack of planning and by informality. As one "Cucuteño" put it in a conversation on the topic during my time there, city dwellers in precarious positions vis a vis the city government (for example, those who do not have property titles, or those whose houses are not connected – or are illegally connected – to the sewage system) seem unlikely to formally or informally demand better services or connectivity. Informality and precarious living conditions in this urban setting appear closely linked to persistent contamination of the Bogotá Canal.

What lessons can we draw from the *Chaco* and Bogotá Canal ruling taken together? In the next and last section of this chapter, I put the insights gleaned from these two cases in dialogue with the other case studies in this book.

5.4 CONCLUSIONS: LEARNING FROM *CHACO* AND T-231

In comparison to all of the other cases studied in this book, the impact of these two rulings is overall lower and circumscribed firmly to the realms of formal norms and resources. It bears underscoring, however, that although low in the aggregate, the rulings did have some impact. The humanitarian crisis had been building up in Chaco for some time without any attention from the provincial government – that inaction might have easily continued. The Court's intervention thus helped focus national and provincial efforts, in coordination, and with speed. Efforts by an independent government oversight agency (the Defensor) to monitor and engage the targets of the ruling helped build accountability by maintaining political pressure and national attention. Such efforts highlight, once again, the important role that independent government agencies can play in these processes, bridging gaps and doing some of the mobilizing that a legal constituency could do.

Both *Chaco* and T-231 illustrate well the nature and limits of judicial interventions on complex SER cases in which the court hands down a final decision

[24] Interview with Program Manager at CORPONOR (Corporación Autónoma Regional de la Frontera Nororiental). Cúcuta. August 27, 2012.

detailing what needs to be done and then "disengages." Both rulings tried to alleviate complex circumstances that were caused by a constellation of factors, and they did so through decisions that provided very concrete and finite instructions to the targets – in both instances, government agencies.

Interventions like the ones in these two rulings – which provide one-time, specific, and usually centralized orders – have often been criticized for being too close to a command-and-control model of intervention in social policy. Critics consider that when courts intervene in this way, they are often too narrow in their approach to the problem and too shallow, since they cannot fully reach the different actors involved (Sabel and Simon 2004). Such interventions have also been criticized for their lack of effectiveness and because they raise issues of legitimacy (Rodríguez Garavito and Rodríguez Franco 2010). For others, the problem is of a different nature: When courts decide on SER cases in this manner (specifying what needs to be done) they are treading into areas that are the purview of majoritarian elected actors. The two cases in this chapter confirm some of these problems and suggest that courts might benefit from different approaches to deciding on socio-economic issues. In the case of the canal in Cúcuta, for example, the court ordered a one-time cleanup, but this measure could have hardly made a dent in what was clearly a much larger issue. The Qom's plight in Chaco, the result of structural discrimination and decades of institutional abandonment, was also only partially and temporarily alleviated by the resources that flowed to the area as a result of the court's ruling. Chapter 3 analyzes rulings that try to tackle large complex issues by incorporating a more structural approach and monitoring mechanisms that explicitly involve different actors and generate discussion and involvement over time. These approaches are not silver bullets either, but they do generate different dynamics and can result in higher levels of impact.

At the same time, it is clear that the answer not only lies on how courts decide and what they do, but also – importantly – on the presence of civil society actors, particularly legal constituencies. Legal constituencies are not only crucial in getting cases before the court (Epp 1998), they are absolutely central to the aftermath and implementation of the rulings. The wake of these two cases suggests that the absence of legally empowered civil society organizations may severely limit the impact that judicial interventions can have.

Finally, it is worth underscoring the low levels of ideational effects in the *Chaco* case and their absence in the Bogotá Canal ruling. In this area, the contrast with *Causa Mendoza* and T-760 is illuminating. As we saw in Chapter 2, in those cases subsequent judicial cascades diffused rights frameworks, government agents became exposed to and could become conversant on rights-based policy ideas in the context of extended monitoring or oversight-related activities. This can shift discussions and change policy, but almost as importantly, it can produce changes in individual attitudes and norms that color myriad interactions between the newly recognized subjects of rights and government bureaucrats, other citizens, etc. In short, the responsiveness of key decision-makers and bureaucrats is crucial in the process of making rights effective. In the absence of monitoring spaces and in the absence of dense legal constituencies that can mobilize and do follow-up after the ruling has been handed down, it is harder to configure spaces and discussions that can facilitate such changes.

6

Collaborative Monitoring in India

The Colombian Constitutional Court and the Supreme Court of Argentina are not the only tribunals deciding on socioeconomic rights, and the cases under study in this book are not the only structural rulings in the Global South. Is my argument applicable beyond the cases discussed in previous chapters? In other words, is there evidence that the presence of monitoring mechanisms and legally empowered organizations in civil society help us understand whether and to what extent other structural rulings can have significant impact? My aim in this chapter is to explore these questions in a bounded manner, by conducting shadow case studies of rulings with collaborative oversight arenas decided by the Supreme Court of India, a Global South tribunal with an active jurisprudence on socioeconomic rights. Identifying and gathering data for multiple cases that fulfilled all the different configurations of absence and presence of monitoring mechanisms and legal constituencies was an enterprise beyond my capabilities for this book. Hence, this chapter uses insights from the theoretical framework developed and illustrated in the Latin American context and applies them to the analysis of two rulings handed down by the Supreme Court of India with similar causal configurations as T-760 and *Causa Mendoza*: the Right to Food (RTF) case and the Delhi Vehicular Pollution case.[1]

Studying the Indian high tribunal presents two compelling advantages: First, since it was the first to make use of monitoring mechanisms worldwide, the aftermath of its cases can be observed over a lengthy period. Second, it has been widely studied by scholars, which provides a wealth of secondary literature and rich findings to learn from and dialogue with. I rely and build on existing research on these cases and on the Supreme Court of India, supplemented by my own fieldwork, to provide key points of comparison to the Latin American cases. These two shadow case studies offer an opportunity to witness the potential and the perils of collaborative oversight arenas over an extended stretch of time.

[1] *M.C. Mehta v. Union of India*, WP 13029/1985.

Like the Argentine and the Colombian courts, the Supreme Court of India has a noteworthy track record advancing socioeconomic rights, particularly during the 1980s when it was especially receptive to workers' and environmental concerns. This activism came after the court had played a more quiescent role by legitimizing Indira Gandhi's declaration of Emergency Powers in 1975. Post-Emergency, the court "reached out" to the ordinary person seeking to deepen the democratic project in India (Nigam 2014), and it did so through a new judicial instrument called public interest litigation (PIL). PIL is a very flexible legal tool through which any citizen can approach the court in informal writing, to call its attention if the constitutional rights of marginalized persons are being violated. Court-promoted monitoring of implementation emerged in the context of the procedural flexibility that was built into PIL during the 1980s and 1990s. During this "golden era," the Supreme Court made extensive use of PIL to hand down rulings safeguarding socioeconomic rights and, specially, the rights of the most destitute in India.

The legal claim that started the Delhi Vehicular Pollution case was filed in 1985, during this very period of the court's history. This PIL, filed by an environmental lawyer, called attention to the growing air and water pollution in Delhi. The claim asked the Supreme Court to order the Indian government to implement existing environmental regulations to curb pollution in the capital city. The Right to Food Case came before the court years later, in 2001. It was filed by a human rights NGO who sought redress from the Indian government for inhabitants of Rajasthan and neighboring states who were at the time facing extended droughts and famine. This PIL emphasized the right to food and asked for food security and aid for these populations. After almost two decades monitoring it, in February 2017 the court declared this case closed.

The chapter shows that the creation of collaborative monitoring spaces in India can enhance accountability and has the potential to shift the balance of power between a reluctant government and the litigants, allowing civil society actors, as well as others, access and an unprecedented platform. These dynamics were bolstered by a very strong social movement, working in conjunction with civil society organizations, in the Right to Food case. In contrast, the collaborative oversight arena that was configured in the Delhi Vehicular Pollution case was less open to civil society to begin with and had a less dense civil society as its counterpart, which limited the possibility for mobilization, diffusion, and growth on that end.

Tracing the particularities of the Indian cases raises questions about lengthy time frames: How long should courts stay at the center of extremely complex social problems? It also highlights the dangers of procedural leniency. Both cases, but specially the vehicular pollution ruling, confirm what research in the area of structural litigation on slums has shown (Bhuwania 2017): that procedural leniency can lead implementation in directions unrelated to the original legal claim. Too much autonomy coupled with long monitoring processes and a lack of accountability may endanger the positive synergies created by collaborative oversight.

6.1 RIGHT TO FOOD CASE

The first case I analyze is known as the Right to Food case. In the early 2000s the state of Rajasthan went through years of consecutive drought and as a result, famines. In 2001, the People's Union for Civil Liberty (PUCL) of Rajasthan filed a legal claim before the Supreme Court arguing the government should take responsibility for providing redress and guaranteeing food for inhabitants of Rajasthan and other five states. In response to this legal claim, lodged by the PUCL with the Human Rights Law Network (a human rights legal advocacy organization), the Supreme Court handed down an interim order in November 2001 recognizing the constitutional right to food and directly addressing food insecurity in India by ordering national and subnational governments to effectively implement preexisting government food schemes.

The legal claim was initially aimed at and addressed to the Indian government, the Food Corporation of India, and six states, but the Supreme Court expanded the reach of its orders to all Indian states and made of the existing governmental schemes as constitutional entitlements. These are the governmental food schemes that the SC concerned itself with: (1) Targeted Public Distribution System (TPDS), a system which distributes rations of food grains and other basic commodities at subsidized prices through special local shops; (2) the Adtyodaya Anna Yojana (AAY), a program that provides food assistance to destitute households through special ration cards; (3) the National Family Benefit Scheme (NFBS), a program that provides cash assistance to a BPL (below the poverty line) household on the death of the household's breadwinner; (4) National Maternity Benefits Scheme (NMBS), which secures maternity benefits and cash assistance to BPL pregnant women; (5) Integrated Child Development Services (ICDS), a program that provides supplementary nutrition, education, and health care for children under six years of age; (6) The Midday Meal (MDM) Scheme, a program that entitles every child in primary and upper primary levels of government and government-assisted schools to a hot cooked meal; and (7) The Indira Gandhi National Old Age Pension Scheme (IGNOAPS).

The case was active between November 2001, when the first of many decisions was handed down, and February 2017, when the court closed it. The specific orders were multiple, with a significant portion providing concrete guidance with regard to the implementation of existing food schemes. What kind of impact did the RTF case have? Just as previously, I will disaggregate impact into two broad categories: immediate effects and rights effectiveness, starting this overview with the former. As should be clear by now, the geographic and administrative scope of the case (dealing with multiple programs, on the national as well as the subnational level, in a huge country like India) as well as its sixteen-year time frame, make it massive. Mainly due to space constraints, but also in light of data availability, I will focus the bulk of my attention here on two of the programs: the MDM scheme and the TPDS.

6.1.1 *Impact*

The policy impact of the court's intervention was huge; the November 2001 order and subsequent ones dramatically altered the legal framework governing the right to food and specific features of the food scheme programs (see Appendix B for a list of the main orders on TPDS and midday meals). The majority of studies on this topic (Guha-Khasnobis and Vivēkānanda 2007; Hertel 2015; Rutledge 2012), even the more critical ones (Banik 2010), agree that in the area of altering the formal legal framework and defining the constitutional right to food, the court's intervention was the game changer. The right to food did not exist before this decision; yet, in the aftermath of the first interim order it was constitutionally enshrined and its contours defined. The many SC orders and their related policy decisions ranged from everything between defining how much grain was to be provided, to calls for action in the face of noncompliance by some states. An additional high watermark in terms of changes to formal norms was the passage of the National Food Security Act (NFSA) in 2013, as Dixon and Chowdhury (2019) also point out. This bill, directly linked to the actors and the process that sprung up in the aftermath of the court's intervention, as we will see, is one that orders poorest households be given 5 kg of food grain per person per month at a subsidized price.

Although compliance was slow and varied depending on the state and the food program, the court's intervention spurred the devolution of national and state-level financial resources to breathe life into the existing programs. For example, budgetary allocations for the ICDS program increased to 372 percent, from 0.6 million inhabitants at the time of the initial order to 1.4 million inhabitants in the following years. According to Mander (2012), the rise in allocations for the midday meal program was even more pronounced: in 2002/2003 the total allocation was Rs. 10,000 million and it had increased eightfold by 2009. The effects in the area of organizational changes were perhaps some of the most striking. The group of activists and lawyers that were originally involved with filing the legal claim did not do so hoping for a positive outcome – the court's decision took them, as much as anyone else by surprise (Guha-Khasnobis and Vivēkānanda 2007). One of the biggest effects of the decision was the creation of a nationwide network of organizations, the Right to Food Campaign, in response to the court's positive decision (more on this campaign below). This network of more than twenty legal advocacy, grassroots, and civil society organizations united groups working in local and national spaces around mobilization seeking to make the court's orders effective, and expanding their reach.

Another area in which the court's intervention had a decisive impact was at the ideational level. According to Rutledge (2012), by legitimating the issue of hunger – focusing public and governmental attention on malnutrition – the court created information, knowledge, and the social expectations increased around the issue of right to food. As she shows, the court dramatically increased national and regional media coverage on these issues and created popular support for the midday meal program (p. 541). The court's decisions were also crucial to the creation of a rights-based discourse, just as we have seen in other cases in this book. Jean Drèze (2006), an economist who was involved in the oversight process and in activism surrounding the right to food, emphasizes that the diffusion of the rights-based perspective is critical in welfare issues like food. According to him, in the absence of a rights-based discourse, welfare measures are seen by bureaucrats and the public as signs of the benevolence of the state, not as legal entitlements.

Did all these immediate effects result in an improvement in rights effectiveness? Or should we see this ambitious case as a failure? As with most discussions around achieving the fulfillment of socioeconomic rights, results are rarely optimal. My conversations with activists and lawyers involved in the monitoring, as well as existing academic assessments agree that the court's intervention facilitated the greatest change through the midday meal program. Midday meal programs are widely used around the world and are believed to aid educational enrollment by easing a financial burden and/or providing an incentive for disadvantaged families to send their children to school. By 2005, four years after the initial court order, a program that had been around since 1975 and was not even in operation in several states reached almost universal coverage throughout India. Jayaraman and Simroth (2011) found that implementation across states after 2001 led to large and statistically significant increases in primary school enrollment; by their estimates there was a 13 percent increase in enrollment, equivalent to about fourteen additional students in each primary school. More recently, Dixon and Chowdhury (2019) show that the scheme not only expanded, as the court effectively pushed for its rollout in parts of India where it was not active, but that it generated gains in educational advancement, child nutrition, and social equity where it was deployed.

As for the TPDS program (which distributes grains directly to poor families), Dreze and Khera (2013) find that at the national level, the TPDS reduced the rural poverty index by 18%–22%. Reetika Khera, who has studied this issue widely, argues that the TPDS guarantees food security and has a key stabilization role, especially for vulnerable and isolated populations, because "it ensures regular supplies of food grains even in the remotest parts of the country" (2011, p. 49). TPDS has not solved all problems, though. Not surprisingly, improvements in the rural poverty index are better for states were the TPDS functions better: like Tamil Nadu (from 61 to 83 percent) and Chhattisgarh (from 39 to 57 percent); in both states, the TPDS had been functioning for a considerable time. Some of the issues that remained a matter of public contention were problems with the system for updating the beneficiary lists, the exclusion of needy households from the program and, relatedly, a discussion of who qualifies.

As mentioned earlier, the Right to Food case was not just the TPDS or the ICDS; yet, there is much less information on progress and setbacks in other fronts. The lack of information and visibility suggests what interviewees, direct observations, and previous research also highlight: that the degree to which the court's intervention was able to move the needle is smaller precisely in those areas. It is not a coincidence that TPDS and ICDS are the two issues that civil society organizations under the RTF Campaign umbrella chose to prioritize, through active monitoring and mobilization, after the first interim order (Guha-Khasnobis and Vivēkānanda 2007). As I will show below, the RTF Campaign purposefully and forcefully engaged with the institutional tools and spaces that court-promoted monitoring opened up to create the synergy that facilitated many of these changes. The unevenness in implementation within this case's different areas perfectly illustrates a larger point I have made about collaborative oversight arenas in this book: A dense, engaged, and organized legal constituency can effectively channel the attention and resources of a collaborative oversight arena toward meaningful movement.

6.1.2 *The Collaborative Oversight Arena in the RTF Case*

The creation of a collaborative oversight arena is essential to understanding the impacts this ruling had. To better comprehend who participated in monitoring, and how, I will first briefly describe the institutional setup the SC usually deploys when monitoring (across cases), characterize some of its unique features in the RTF case, and then discuss the main features of the legal constituency mobilizing around the case.

Like its counterpart in Colombia and Argentina with the T-760 and *Causa Mendoza* cases, the Supreme Court of India deployed its full toolkit of monitoring mechanisms: It requested reports, held periodic hearings, and set up institutional spaces where it invited civil society actors to participate in collaborative monitoring of implementation. In the Latin American cases, we saw that the tribunals devoted some internal resources within the court to handling the monitoring of big structural cases – units within the court coordinated with a monitoring commission in which different civil society organizations took part.

In contrast, the Indian SC deploys a different setup when it monitors, and different cases can have different monitoring bodies. In this case, the Court appointed two special commissioners to work with it. These individuals, who were not staffers in the court, had their own team and were charged by the court with doing follow-up on it's orders. The judges in the bench have absolute discretion in appointing the commissioner(s) and they in turn have a great deal of autonomy; they report directly to the court and often serve as the bridge between it and civil society organizations invited to monitor implementation, as well as other stakeholders in the rulings. In sum, in India, as in Colombia and Argentina, the court makes possible institutional spaces for accountability and for the different stakeholders in the ruling to interact periodically. These spaces exist in all the cases, but within what I call collaborative oversight arenas, in India there can be an additional actor, the commissioner(s), and the monitoring commissions can take on varied forms across cases, as we will see in the Delhi Vehicular Pollution case discussed further ahead.

As mentioned, the RTF case has two commissioners: N. C. Saxena and H. Mander, who have a great deal of functional autonomy (Birchfield and Corsi 2009). Both had backgrounds in legal advocacy around rights and activism before their appointments. Together they headed the monitoring commission, which formally included twelve civil society organizations invited to join in monitoring by the court in 2002. Mander (2012) described their work as follows: to produce implementation reports on the interim orders; review and analyze the performance of central and state governments in implementing food schemes; investigate and report on local complaints and reports on food programs; and make suggestions to different levels of government on next steps. In an interview, Biraj Patnaik, special advisor to Mander, described the role of their office in similar terms, offering some important additional details: "We produce yearly reports to the court (…) attend meetings [related to the orders]; and sit in on different committees with the government. We work very closely with the RTF Campaign, and we do a lot of media work."[2]

In his description, Patnaik is clearer than Mander on the importance of coordination and close linkages with social organizations. The closeness between the commissioners and the RTF Campaign is more evident if one considers that Patnaik, like the commissioners and most of the state advisers (individuals selected to honorary positions to report on developments at the state level), had a background in and deep connections with civil society organizations and social movements. Patnaik had been a part of the PUCL and worked for years with food schemes before joining the Office of the Commissioner. Just from the structure of the commission and that of the commissioner's office it is clear that one cannot understand the impact of the RTF ruling without understanding the interaction and the close connections between the court and civil society actors. The commissioners' relevance and their deep connections with civil society are confirmed in Bryerley's (2019) case study of the RTF, which describes their role as three-pronged: crucial to the monitoring strategy, important as an advisory body to the court, and also as mediators with the central and state governments.

With the monitoring structure clear, I now turn to describing the legal constituency in the RTF case. As mentioned earlier, initially, twelve civil society organizations were included in the monitoring commission as state-level advisers.[3] As Hertel

[2] Interview with Biraj Patnaik, special advisor to the Commissioner on RTF. Delhi. July 29, 2016.

[3] Hertel (2015) summarizes the list of organizations initially invited to the monitoring commission: "Among them are coalitions involved in advocacy on food, water and livelihood security (including the Right to Food Campaign itself, along with Samaj Pragati Sahayog of Madhya Pradesh); local affiliates of international development organizations (e.g., ActionAid); research and academic organizations (such as the Hazards Centre of Delhi, the Institute of

(2015) notes, there is some overlap between the groups appointed by the court to do monitoring and groups that are members of the Right to Food Campaign. However, they are not equivalent, though their relationship was close from the beginning. As Srinivasan and Narayanan (2007) explain, it is difficult to pinpoint the origins of the RTF exactly, but they go back to activist organizations in Rajasthan (including the PUCL Rajasthan chapter, which filed the PIL claim before the SC) meeting and mobilizing around mid-2000 when the drought in the state worsened. After the first interim order was handed down, the group that had coordinated the legal claim intensified their mobilization efforts, agreeing to use the order and the political juncture to advance food security issues in India. Dipa Sinha, the co-convener of the RTF Campaign, described her organization and the decision to structure it as such in the following terms:

> The initial orders of the court enthused a lot of people: "now there's something we can use", we thought. [In a convention in Bhopal, we had] different thematic sessions discussing how to take this forward. We said: we don't need another NGO, but we should have an umbrella organization that we can all go under. Women's organizations, agriculture organizations, dalit groups; [let's] have an informal grouping to bring everyone together. (...) So: I can't tell you a list of fixed members [for the RTF Campaign], but I could get you 2,000 people [to show up to an event] next week![4]

What happened after the court's initial order is a good example of what I call organizational effects of a ruling: In the context of continued monitoring, the organizations participating in it strengthened their networks and capacities further. A bigger and stronger RTF Campaign was one of the most significant offshoots of the RTF case.

Dipa Sinha, whom I just quoted, embodies the close networks among activists and the connections between commissioners and the Right to Food Campaign: She had prior experience as an ICDS grassroots advocate, and before entering the RTF Campaign, she worked in the Office of the Commissioner doing monitoring and research at the state level. The legal constituency in this case was incredibly rich and dense: multiple organizations working on different fronts (particularly in early 2000s) with the court and some government institutions. As Bryerley (2019) notes, one of the advantages of the RTF Campaign was that it had a strong presence in Delhi, but it also reached into multiple states. This dense network of diverse, but experienced and interconnected, organizations quickly sprung to life and to action in response to the court's favorable ruling.

Development Studies of Jaipur, and Ranchi University); legal aid organizations (Committee for Legal Aid to the Poor, based in Orissa; Sahyog a legal cell, based in Allahabad); and farmers groups (e.g., Paschim Banga Khet Mazdoor of West Bengal)."

4 Interview with Dipa Sinha, RTF Campaign co-convener. Delhi. August 9, 2016.

In November 2001 the court ordered states to start providing cooked midday meals in primary schools.[5] Of the states that did not have them (three already did), only Rajasthan complied by the deadline. Many alleged financial constraints or logistical difficulties handling food and asked the court to revert the order. In India, as well as in Colombia and in Argentina, the court's pressure through follow-up orders with specific directives, compounded with mounting pressure and follow up from civil society organizations, were crucial to getting responses from the governments. Let us study how.

6.1.3 *The Role of Collaborative Oversight in the RTF's Impact*

Over the next three years, the court, the commissioners, the RTF Campaign, and government officials were engaged in a back-and-forth over the lack of compliance and the features of the MDM scheme. The mechanisms that resulted in an almost universal MDM scheme by 2005 were the same we already saw at work when other collaborative oversight arenas were analyzed in this book: reports, public hearings, mobilizing media attention, and increasing information on the issue. The commissioners, relying heavily on grassroots monitoring done by civil society organizations linked to the RTF Campaign, reported back constantly to the court on gaps with implementation and ideas. Civil society organizations contributed with monitoring but also mobilized outside the judicial space, including protesting and putting pressure on governments at the national and state level (Krishnan and Subramaniam 2014). The RTF Campaign, building on its coalition of multi-issue organizations, successfully mobilized public opinion and applied pressure on bureaucrats and elected officials through collective action, thus exposing government inaction (Birchfield and Corsi 2009).

It is worth noting that here too we see the Supreme Court of India (like the CCC and the SCA) relying on the information produced by external organizations in the context of collaborative monitoring and reports from the follow-up commission to tweak its own orders and update the policy proposals. Two excellent examples of this mechanism at work are: (1) the insistence on *cooked* midday meals on site and (2) the requirement that Dalit cooks be hired for MDM programs. To illustrate, I will elaborate here on the feedback loop that was activated between civil society organizations, commissioners, and the court with regard to cooked meals.

Recall that a lot of the initial pushback from the states on implementing midday meals hinged on the argument that setting up the infrastructure for cooking and/or maintaining the minimum sanitary conditions to avoid food poisoning was an insurmountable barrier. Organizations within the RTF Campaign insisted that it

[5] This section draws heavily from an interview with S. Vivekananda (July 2016), who participated in the process, and from the thorough account published in Guha-Khasnobis and Vivēkānanda (2007).

was possible to set up midday meal programs as long as minimum infrastructure and quality norms were met. Members of the campaign designed and successfully implemented a survey in three states that already had such programs to learn from their experiences. They presented a report to the commissioners in which they argued that provided minimum quality norms were met, safe midday meal programs were possible (Drèze and Goyal 2003). The commissioners in turn used this data to request on their own report that the court stick to the requirement that meals be cooked on site. The court followed the recommendations in its April 2004 interim order, and as non-compliant states began rolling out their programs, all of them did so with cooked meals as a central feature.

Setting up a collaborative oversight arena also allowed civil society organizations to have access to policy discussions venues to participate in and influence the policy process. A good example of this process was the conception of the National Food Security Act. The first years after the court's involvement in 2001, the RTF's follow-up efforts and most of the court's attention were focused on guaranteeing implementation and expanding some of the food schemes (Pande and Houtzager 2016). In parallel, activists capitalized on electoral years (2004 and 2013) to raise the issue of passing a National Food Security Act (Krishnan and Subramaniam 2014). The space that the Supreme Court had created for the ongoing monitoring of the RTF case provided the perfect venue for demands for a legislative bill to be voiced. Many of the specific features of the NFSA were first tested out during monitoring of the Right to Food Case. Pande and Houtzager (2016), whose study carefully reconstructed the activist networks within and around the RTF, refer to this process as a site for creativity, crossbreeding, and information, showing how "although the law does not incorporate activists' core demand – universal access to TPDS – some of the reforms included in the new law are inspired by the creative experiments of civil society."

In February 2017, the Supreme Court of India closed the case. The tribunal argued that in view of the passing of the National Food Security Act in 2013, "nothing further survives of this petition." After its closure, Anuj Bhuwania, an expert on PILs in India described this particular PIL as a resounding success (quoted in Vishwanath 2017). This assessment coincides with recent studies which highlight the positive impact of the expansion of different programs under the court's watchful eye, as well as the continued resonance of the Right to Food Campaign, as two of its most important legacies (Bryerley 2019; Dixon and Chowdhury 2019). In this case the Court's sixteen-year intervention appears and, importantly, is perceived, as not having gone in vain.

6.2 DELHI VEHICULAR POLLUTION CASE

The second ruling I discuss in this chapter is commonly known as the Delhi Vehicular Pollution case. In 1985, lawyer M. C. Mehta filed a claim before the Supreme Court arguing that the government had to intervene to reduce air and water pollution in India's capital city in light of its dire health consequences, particularly on children. As Mathur (2004) highlights, what the claimants demanded of the Supreme Court was to order authorities to implement an existing framework, particularly the Water and Air Pollution Control Acts: "The laws already existed but the Government of India or the Delhi administration were not making sufficient efforts to implement them." The claim asked the Supreme Court to order the government to act on polluting industries, relocate the most hazardous ones outside the city, regulate and monitor emissions by vehicles, and act against drivers whose vehicles did not comply with regulations. In short, this case was an effort to hold the government accountable to its own promises with respect to environmental regulation, particularly with regard to pollution in Delhi.

To understand this ruling better it is helpful to keep in mind the transformation that the Delhi metropolitan area underwent in the second half of the twentieth century: According to the Delhi City Census, between 1951 and 2011, the population expanded from 1.7 to 16 million inhabitants. The rapid urbanization and exponential population growth fundamentally altered the physical, social, and economic landscapes of the city, generating (among others) greater industrialization and increased demand for transportation. By the mid-1980s, development had taken a heavy toll on the city's air quality and Delhi was one of the five most polluted cities in the world (Rajamani 2007).

The Supreme Court has monitored this case for more than three decades, issuing a first ruling in 1998 and hundreds of orders in the process. This is a massive, unfolding case on an environmental issue that has only grown more salient and more pressing since the mid-1980s when the court first got involved. It has been widely studied by numerous scholars and hence, we have a wealth of information and perspectives to draw from. Here, I will rely on Rajamani's (2007) periodization of events to structure my own discussion. She divides the aftermath of the Delhi Vehicular Pollution PIL into two phases: First, the initial ten years, in which compliance was scarce and there was little activity around the ruling. A second phase started in 1995, in which the bulk of the discussion and actions were focused on the conversion of public vehicles to natural gas with the objective of improving air quality. The shift to natural gas was undoubtedly the most notorious aspect of the court's involvement, and I will devote most of my attention to it, but as we will see, it was not the only one.

I posit there is a third phase in the case, post-2000s, in which environmental pollution worsened in Delhi to become a severe, chronic, and national problem. In parallel, the institution that the court had created to monitor and advise it, EPCA (Environment Pollution (Prevention & Control) Authority for the National Capital Region), took on a much bigger role as a regulatory agency of sorts, leaving behind its more limited (original) role as a monitoring body. In this third (ongoing) stage, the monitoring institution and the court's involvement have moved into realms beyond those originally envisioned.

6.2.1 *Impact*

To disaggregate the ruling's impact, I begin by looking at immediate effects. In the context of monitoring the ruling, the court created the Environment Pollution (Prevention and Control) Authority for the National Capital Region under the Environment Protection Act, 1986, or EPCA, an institution of importance to environmental governance, especially pollution, in the capital city. As the following pages show, EPCA – also known as the Bhure Lal Committee after its chairman – played a very important role aiding the court in the process of oversight. Over time, it also gained its own weight as a quasi-regulatory body, though its legitimacy and the renewal of its mandate remained tied to the court.

In terms of the legal and regulatory framework, the court's intervention had a significant influence. In early 1990s, a few years after the ruling and at the court's nudging, the government first created standards for vehicular emissions, for drivers and manufacturers. Since, more regulations and policy decisions like the phasing out of certain type of vehicles, restrictions on circulation, relocation, and/or banning of some industries have been discussed in and enacted through EPCA. EPCA has also played a significant role in the creation and flow of information on the issue. In the context of monitoring, this institution has requested from government actors, and generated through the organizations that are associated with it (like the Central Pollution Board), data on air pollution and polluting agents. As we have seen happen in other cases with collaborative oversight arenas in this book, the court's involvement and its sustained monitoring of the situation over time aided in the creation and flow of information on the topic of pollution.

As far as policy, perhaps the most influential decision that came from the Supreme Court was the order to convert all public transportation vehicles in Delhi to compressed natural gas (CNG). The process was controversial, difficult and it took more than a decade until its completion in 2002. The decision shifted public and private buses as well as rickshaws to using CNG, with the argument that this was a more environmentally friendly fuel. Other orders included the relocation of industries, and the phasing out of lead-based fuels from use in Delhi.

To discuss impact at the ideational level, it is important to note that the Delhi Vehicular Pollution PIL was part of a wave of similar environmental PILs that the Supreme Court of India took around this time. Unlike the Matanza-Riachuelo case, which was a single, high-profile case that clearly marked a breaking point for Argentina in terms of visibility of environmental matters, this case was one among many. As Rajamani (2003) notes, between the late 1980s and through the 1990s, the Supreme Court articulated and expanded the right to a clean environment through several rulings and PILs. Together, all these rulings (many of which were claims raised by a single individual, M. C. Mehta) raised the profile of such issues.

Finally, how did the previously outlined effects impact rights effectiveness for the inhabitants of Delhi? In other words, did the court's intervention and the effects that stemmed from it facilitate an improvement in air pollution? This question is best answered with attention to changes over time. As Verón (2006) notes, it is difficult to conclusively evaluate the effectiveness and ecological impact of the air-quality measures taken at the court's behest as some studies present conflicting results. Data from the Central Pollution Board suggests that pollution levels in Delhi went down between 1996 and 1999 (Verón 2006).[6] Other studies agree that pollution levels were reduced temporarily (Dréze and Goyal 2003; Narrain and Bell 2005). However, a study conducted in 2004 found that levels of some pollutants remained constant and that NO_x levels had risen (Kathuria 2004). Similarly, a study conducted by Ravindra et al. (2006) also observed a rise in NO_x, a decrease in some pollutants, and steady levels of others before and after the CNG conversion. Note, also, that this is just a sample of a wider number of studies.

Different experts coincide in pointing out that some of the court's decisions reduced air pollution for a while; however, in the long run, the gains were offset by the steady increase in private motor vehicles (Dreyfus 2013; Kathuria 2004; Ravindra et al. 2006). In recent years new organic and anthropocenic emission sources have come into the picture and influenced pollutant levels. In sum, though the court's intervention entailed some relief and it left in place a more robust and effective regulatory framework, the dynamic nature of the problem means that pollution continues to be a grave problem.

6.2.2 *Collaborative Oversight in the Delhi Vehicular Pollution Case*

Collaborative monitoring is also important to understanding impact in the Delhi Vehicular Pollution case. In this section I first describe the institutional setup that the SC deployed, then characterize the legal constituency and show how monitoring in general and collaborative monitoring in particular influenced impact. The institutional setup for oversight is somewhat different in this case from the RTF ruling. These differences highlight the extreme procedural flexibility within PIL which allows different teams at different times within the Indian Court to develop their own institutions and approaches. Such flexibility stands in contrast with the more rigid monitoring structures we see in the Latin American cases, which configure more centralized and institutionally uniform monitoring efforts.

In this case, the Supreme Court of India also made use of a wide array of monitoring tools: It requested reports, held public hearings, created expert committees as well as institutional spaces where different actors, including civil society organizations, could participate in monitoring implementation. In 1991,[7] during

6 Data from the Central Pollution Control Board (CPCB) suggest that pollution levels have come down significantly in 1999 compared with 1996, when air pollution peaked: SO_2 was reduced by 27%, NOx by 12%, particulate matter by 25%, and lead by 97% (Verón 2006, 2099).

7 Through *M.C. Mehta v. Union of India*, WP 13029/1985 (1991.03.14).

what Rajamani calls the first phase of implementation, the Court set up the Saikia Committee, a group of experts that provided policy recommendations to tackle Delhi pollution. Seven years later, in 1998, came the creation of the institution that has been at the center of monitoring for close to three decades. In January of that year, the Court ordered the Ministry of Environment and Forests to follow section 3 of the 1986 Environmental Act and create a statutory committee. The EPCA was "constituted with the sole objective of assisting this Hon'ble Court for protecting and improving the quality of the environment and preventing, controlling and abating environmental pollution in the NCR." In contrast to the Saikia Committee or the *Peritos Constitucionales* committee created by the Colombian Constitutional Court in the national health system case, the EPCA in India had the standing of authority – the other two are advisory. The EPCA was, initially, the functional equivalent of monitoring commissions in the RTF, T-760, and Matanza-Riachuelo cases in this book, with the added ability to file criminal complaints. Over time, its members and profile have changed. An especially important transformation is that it morphed into an advisory and regulatory body working closely with the court, one that is involved in all manner of environmental issues in Delhi.

As with other cases with collaborative oversight arenas in this book, a key reference point is to look at which external actors, particularly civil society organizations, were invited to participate in the joint monitoring space. Those with a seat at the EPCA table originally included the chairman after which the committee is named, Bhure Lal, a well-respected and long-time civil servant who was, at the time, a member of the Central Vigilance Commission. Additionally, it included "Anil Agarwal from Centre of Science and Environment which was spearheading a campaign for cleaner Delhi; Jagdish Khattar from Maruti Udyog (car manufacturer) representing the automobile industry; DK Biswas, chairman of the Central Pollution Control Board; and Delhi's Transport Commissioner, K Dhingra" (Mathur 2004). The committee met once weekly and sometimes invited other stakeholders to present information and argue in favor of a particular position (Narrain and Bell 2005).

If we compare the kinds of actors that were part of the EPCA and had access to the collaborative oversight arena with those similarly positioned in the RTF case and in the Latin American cases, we note that though some government control agencies were included, only one NGO had a permanent seat at EPCA: the Centre for Science and Environment. CSE is one of India's most prominent environmental NGOs. Created in 1980, CSE is important to understanding this case. In 1995 they launched a campaign that sought to raise awareness and create policy change around the need for regulations to curb vehicular pollution in India. This effort gave them national notoriety and, as mentioned earlier, gained them entry into this case's collaborative oversight arena, of which they have been an active participant since. Note however, that as Verón (2006) underscores, though CSE played a dominant role in pushing through vehicular air pollution regulations, it was not the only NGO working on environmental issues in Delhi. According to him, somewhere between 200 and 300 organizations were active at the time of his research, ranging from community-based initiatives to professional rights advocacy organizations. Though numerous, these organizations were not connected among themselves (Verón 2006). In contrast to the very dense, networked, and organized legal constituency in the RTF case, for example, the legal constituency in the Delhi Vehicular Pollution case is less dense: Though there were numerous civil society organizations, there were no dense coordination networks among them, especially not in the early years of the case.

The very existence of EPCA and the fact that it included government and external actors was an improvement over prior regulatory stasis and a lack of any external input – yet, there was a lack of broader participation. The court did not initially invite a wide selection of civil society organizations or other external actors to participate in this, the main collaborative monitoring venue. Early on, members of the EPCA argued it would be beneficial for this institution to consult with other actors and the public (Bell et al. 2004). As Rajamani's analysis underscores (2007), there was a participatory deficit, evident in different aspects: "[T]he decision to consult particular organizations was made on an ad hoc and discretionary basis. Not all stake holders were identified and consulted, and no avenues for wider public consultation were explored. Some with a direct stake in the proceedings, such as private bus operators, felt frustrated by their lack of access to the EPCA..." Overall, external actors, but specially civil society organizations, have had much less institutionalized access and participation in the Delhi Vehicular Pollution case than they have had in the RTF case, for example. This had important consequences, as I will discuss later.

Another civil society actor of relevance for the collaborative oversight arena was the original claimant, lawyer M. C. Mehta. When he filed the claim, Mehta was chairman of the non-governmental organization Environment Protection Cell of Hindustani Andolan (Mathur 2004). Mehta played a key role in filing several prominent PILs in the 1980s and 1990s, including another case that the court took up, protecting the banks of the Yamuna River. He was asked by the court to participate in the Saikia Committee (expert group) and he submitted more than thirty reports to the SC over the years. Specially during the early years of the case, he was crucial in helping bring attention to it, as his advocacy work on environmental issues gave him a very public profile.

6.2.3 *The Role of Collaborative Oversight in the Impact of the Delhi Vehicular Pollution Case*

As I mentioned above, during the initial years after the Delhi Vehicular Pollution PIL was filed, there was very little movement toward implementation of the existing regulatory framework, which was the claim's main objective. As Bell et al. (2004)

indicate, the city administration and the national government announced a number of new policies in the second half of 1980s. These were likely in response to the court's insistence, but they were not pursued with forcefulness and were, in the end, ineffective. The perfect example was the decision to raise the fines for drivers of polluting vehicles in 1989. This initiative was dead from the start as the city lacked the testing equipment to correctly identify who had to be penalized (Bell et al. 2004, p. 26). Similarly, at least two initiatives to issue new vehicular mass emission standards were delayed and ultimately watered down until they lacked teeth.

Still, throughout the 1990s, the court's active monitoring of the case put pressure on the city government and generated some changes. In the early 1990s the court moved to order the relocation of hazardous and large polluting industries, an action item that had been in the city's second master plan for some time (Bell et al. 2004). By 2003, oil and fuel-based industries, including brick kilns, had been relocated to the outskirts of the city at the Court's orders (Guttikunda and Goel 2013). The Court envisioned a phaseout of fifteen-year old commercial vehicles which was executed in the form of several orders, deadlines, and extensions until it became a reality in December 1998 (Bell et al. 2004).

In 1991 the court created the Saikia Committee, which was charged with evaluating existing strategies for vehicular pollution control problems around the world, assessing low-cost alternatives for operating vehicles with less pollution, and making specific policy recommendations to reduce pollution in Delhi. The committee was named after its chairman, former justice Saikia, and it had as its other members M. C. Mehta (the lawyer who had filed the original PIL), the chairman of the Central Pollution Control Board, and a representative of the Association of Indian Automobile Manufacturers (Narain and Bell 2005). The Saikia Committee's mandate was strictly advisory and limited in time. However, its role is an important one because this committee recommended to the Supreme Court the use of CNG as an alternative fuel, on the grounds that it was less polluting and more widely available in India. This policy proposal would go on to have tremendous impact in the city.

In the mid-1990s came a turning point for this case with an awareness campaign launched by the CSE and the creation of the EPCA, the key institutional space for monitoring. The CSE's campaign included a book, "Slow Murder," with case studies of the causes and effects of vehicular pollution in different Indian cities, including Delhi. This campaign gained nationwide notoriety and brought the public's attention to the negative health impacts of worsening air pollution. This is another excellent example of the strategic importance of civil society mobilization to producing visibility around an issue. In Dreyfus' words, the judges and civil society encouraged each other (Dreyfus 2013, 36). It was in the context of CSE's activism that the Court renewed its pressure on the government for action around implementing and/or reforming the extant legal framework. It first requested that the city government submit an action plan. In 1996 and 1997 Delhi presented the court with a plan, one that was not implemented consistently. At the end of 1997 the Ministry of Environment and Forests also presented an action plan. Toward the end of the decade it appeared as if, once again, the government was generating numerous policies but there was little effectiveness to them (Narain and Bell 2005, pp. 11–12).

In 1998, shortly after the publication of the Ministry of Environment's plan, the court ordered the creation of the EPCA. Since its inception, the EPCA was a key player in this case – the SC consistently, and almost exclusively, relied on its findings and recommendations as it monitored the case (Jackson and Rosencranz 2003). In its first report to the court, the EPCA emphasized the lack of implementation of existing policies and advised that the Supreme Court prioritize a series of measures according to a specific timetable. The court went on to adopt the recommendations and issued the corresponding orders in 1998. Chief among them were: increasing the number of public buses from 6,000 to 10,000 by early 2001, eliminating unleaded petrol from Delhi by September 1998, replacing all pre-1990 vehicles and taxis with new ones running on clean fuel by early 2000, banning buses that were more than eight years old (except if running on clean fuel) by 2001, and converting all public transportation to CNG by April 2001.

The conversion to CNG was controversial and consequential. The process illustrates the promises and perils of coming to a policy decision shepherded by the court through a collaborative monitoring space. On the one hand, as we have seen in other cases in this book, the court's intervention meant increased public accountability in the face of governmental inaction. The court created a political space for the discussion and gave it momentum; it relied on information provided by EPCA, formulated and tweaked policy with input from the external actors participating in monitoring, and was able to effectively push through changes. Notably, the limited number of stakeholders that participated in EPCA ignored the concerns of other actors. I will summarize some of the key moments of the CNG conversion decision and aftermath to illustrate some of these dynamics.

The choice to convert to CNG was, as Mathur (2004, p. 26) notes, a "techno political struggle" of conflicting narratives, scientific evidence, and multiple interests. EPCA was singularly important as the scenario in which these interests played out and the site where the decision was made. According to Bell et al. (2004), the CNG conversion idea did not originate with EPCA but it had first been experimented with by the government's Oil and Natural Gas Commission in 1988; after their initial tests, different CNG conversion pilot projects surfaced across India. As noted earlier, the Saikia Committee had previously recommended CNG conversion to the Supreme Court. In the context of EPCA, according to Shankar and to one of my interviewees,[8] the transnational auto lobby pressed strongly in favor of CSE. In his own reconstruction of the process, Mathur notes that CSE's Anil Agarwal was

[8] Interview with expert on judicialization. Delhi. July 23, 2016.

also a bold advocate for this choice. EPCA ultimately recommended a policy that was controversial not only because it was costly in terms of investment and infrastructure changes, as it required new buses and a network of gas stations. The decision was also controversial because with air pollution, as with many environmental or complex public policy problems, there is often no single solution and there is conflicting evidence with regard to the effectiveness of alternatives.

Public and private bus operators went on to express their disagreement with the decision by, first, passively resisting through inaction for the first two years and, second, via active resistance. As the April 2001 deadline for converting buses to CNG approached, the issue turned into a national political controversy as it became clear that the city government and operators were not ready to comply with the court's order.[9] Bus operators claimed that they had not been notified of the court's decision; they demanded help from the government to offset the costly investment, asked the government to request an extension, and went on strike to protest the situation. There were not enough CNG buses ready to provide transportation services by the time diesel buses were scheduled to be out, and the dispensing stations were not ready either. The court extended the deadline to 2002 in deference to availability concerns, but the standoff between it and the city government and transporters grew as did popular unrest when buses went off the road and the service worsened.

In the midst of the controversy, the Indian central government created its own expert committee and asked it to make a clean fuel policy recommendation. The Mashelkar Committee advised the government to not define a specific fuel type, but instead only propose a fuel emission standard. In response, the SC extended the deadline for conversion to March 2002, but refused to modify the order to convert to CNG. In April 2002, the court intervened more directly when, in consultation with car manufacturers, it set a schedule to convert diesel-based buses and roll out the new CNG buses. It also imposed heavy fines on diesel bus drivers, and on the central government, whom it accused of stalling the conversion process. By December 2002, the full bus fleet was converted.

I mentioned earlier several studies suggesting that conversion to CNG successfully reduced some air pollutants, a move in the correct direction. At the same time, it is important to mention the side effects this choice had on Delhi's inhabitants. The troubled implementation of the conversion impacted all commuters at the time. Beyond that, some scholars argue that the court's prioritizing CNG conversion hurt the most vulnerable in the city. Bhuwania (2018) and Baviskar (2012) contend that the court actively ignored the plight and hurt the livelihoods of poor workers and rickshaw drivers. The relocation of polluting industries was executed without paying attention to the workers of many of these factories who often found themselves unable to find livelihood and shelter afterward (Baviskar 2012). Similarly,

9 This section draws heavily on the accounts of Mathur (2004) and Bell et al.'s (2004).

Bhuwania notes that the CNG conversion decision and the steps taken to implement it were executed without giving Delhi rickshaw drivers or their representatives the chance to present their argument or chance to express how the implementation of the orders was impacting them.

Unlike the Matanza-Riachuelo case in Argentina (Chapter 3) where we saw a dense and interconnected legal constituency using monitoring spaces as openings to communicate with the Court and inform it about problems with the relocation of entire neighborhoods, here, the lack of ample representation for civil society organizations in the EPCA and a legal constituency that was less dense entailed more limited opportunities for their participation, and also more limited access to the state. This is partly because though EPCA functioned initially (and still does, in a few aspects) as a follow-up commission, its reach and profile have shifted and expanded over the thirty plus years that the Supreme Court has monitored this case. Over the 2000s, and especially after 2015, the EPCA expanded its membership to include more government representatives and academic experts on technical matters, shifting more toward a technical policy advisory body. This shift is part of what I see as the third stage of the Delhi Vehicular Pollution case. At this point, the issue of air pollution has become larger than Delhi itself, infinitely more pressing, and more complex.

Though CNG conversion worked, it was only a brief reprieve that was ultimately offset by the exponential growth of private cars and other environmental dynamics. Today, the sources of Delhi's grave air pollution are well-known – chief among them, motor vehicle emissions, certain industries, crop and wood burning, as well as dust. However, the problem continues to worsen. On the one hand, as Chandra (2018) notes, the multipronged nature of the problem makes designing policy and strategy for pollution in Delhi a moving target. On the other hand, as Dixon and Chowdhury (2019) state, the deeper problem is that in recent years, the sources of pollution have been growing faster than humans' ability to mitigate them. In more ways than one, the nature of the problem has outgrown the Court's initial ruling. It has also outgrown Delhi itself, as it is clearer than ever that it also involves neighboring states.

6.3 CONCLUSIONS

What lessons can we draw from these two Indian cases when looked at through the analytical framework I propose in this book? Both the RTF case and the Delhi Vehicular Pollution case confirm that the creation of collaborative oversight arenas opens spaces for different external actors with a stake in the ruling to converge. The court can draw on their technical expertise and the information they create on the progress of implementation, widening its perspective. Neither case presented a perfect solution to the complex problems they sought to tackle, but both made important inroads. In this last section I am interested in discussing what we can learn from these two cases in dialogue with the Argentinean and Colombian cases that also had collaborative oversight arenas.

In Chapter 2 I posited that monitoring mechanisms allowed courts to overcome informational and power asymmetries. I emphasized that we needed to look beyond the tribunals and the monitoring institutions they created to gain a deeper understanding of how impact is crafted after a victory in court. The cross-regional perspective gives us new insights into the dynamics in and around monitoring, of which I want to highlight the following: First, the differences in how the Supreme Court of India structures monitoring have implications for access and for the degree of control and discretion that the court retains. Second, the Indian cases underscore the importance of dense legal constituencies. Finally, these case studies bring to the fore the pitfalls of courts staying engaged for lengthy time horizons. I elaborate on each of these points in turn.

The differences in how courts structured monitoring can influence the possibilities for synergies between the different actors involved, as well as the level of control that the court retains over the institutions it creates to aid with monitoring. For instance, a feature that matters is who is invited to participate in oversight spaces. As I am particularly interested in tracing the role that legal constituencies play, I focus on participation from civil society organizations. Of all the rulings studied in this book, the Delhi Vehicular Pollution case is the one in which the joint monitoring commission (the EPCA, also known as the Bhure Lal Committee) was less open to civil society organizations. When compared to the others, less access by different civil society organizations resulted in reduced access points to the state for these organizations and fewer opportunities to be heard or bring their concerns before the Supreme Court of India.

In the case of RTF, the commissioners were very close to the case's legal constituency and the larger social movement working on food security issues in India. The commissioners operated in addition to the follow-up commission and provided significant support and leverage for civil society organizations whose focus was rights-based and grassroots. In the pollution case, the initial composition of EPCA (which, as mentioned above, only included one civil society organization versus several government agencies and select private industries) prioritized a different set of interests, that of industries and government agencies. Over time, the follow-up commission ended up becoming practically an institutional fixture in the pollution governance infrastructure in Delhi – one that has a decidedly technical and industrial orientation.

Structure also influenced how much control the courts had over the institutions they created for monitoring. The comparison with India is illuminating because both the Colombian and Argentinean courts retained greater control over the minutiae of the oversight process: In the Latin American cases, monitoring was coordinated by offices within the court, with court staffers, following the traditional operating framework of each tribunal. In contrast, PIL in India gives tremendous procedural leeway to the Supreme Court of India. The Indian Court used this leeway to, among other things, create semi-autonomous institutions to aid it in its task: a commissioner in the RTF case, or a committee like EPCA in the Delhi Vehicular Pollution case. In both Indian cases the "semi-autonomous" institutions are not operated by court staffers and they have significant autonomy from the court, which means they have a lot of discretion in the direction they pursue.

In this sense, the Indian experience sounds a warning. In this country, PIL's "built-in" procedural flexibility means that how monitoring looks like and the direction that the different cases take has the potential to vary immensely. It also means that the court (or court-empowered institutions) may, and have, more openly taken the driver's seat in terms of policymaking than their Latin American counterparts. In India, procedural leniency creates an extremely flexible oversight process and more semi-autonomous institutions operating in the orbit of the court, but not necessarily by and under its daily orientation and staffing. Lengthy time horizons coupled with extreme procedural flexibility create greater possibilities for the cases to diverge away from their original moorings.

Several Indian scholars have voiced strong critiques of this built-in flexibility within PIL, which they see as putting vulnerable claimants and the poor in particularly precarious positions vis-à-vis the individual preferences of the judges or those more powerful actors acting under their umbrella (Bhuwania 2017). I agree that procedural flexibility in India can create an oversight process that is extremely dependent on the individuals who have sway over it, instead of on an institutionally defined approach. In this context, there is greater room for discretion, and that discretion can cut in different directions. The RTF case had a strong human rights bent, and close connections with civil society, because those charged with running it by the Court reflected and fostered that view. That orientation was also central to the original claim. On the other hand, monitoring in the vehicular pollution case appears more in tune with other interests, especially industrial actors. Both approaches have been subject to critique. But the latter in particular led to an implementation process that placed less emphasis on a rights-based approach to environmental concerns and created less room for involvement with environmental actors.

The cross-regional comparison also foregrounds the importance of a dense legal constituency that can meaningfully engage with the court and other interested parties. In the Right to Food case, there existed civil society organizations before the ruling. That pre-installed capacity grew richer and more coordinated under the umbrella of the ruling; for example, in the spaces the court created for organizations to meet, organize, and hold government agencies accountable on their implementation (in)actions. According to Thiruvengadam, another crucial benefit of a dense network of legal advocacy organizations is that their role in holding governments and private actors publicly accountable is that they can successfully halt abuses from other players by exposing them. In striking contrast, the legal constituency in the

Delhi Vehicular Pollution case appears to have been much less dense: Though there was a key player, the environmental NGO CSE, as a whole the legal constituency was not interconnected, it lacked prior experience working together and it had less human and material resources.

We know from the Colombian and Argentinean experiences (Chapter 3) that one of the effects of participating in collaborative oversight is that the process can promote organizational changes within participating NGOs, enhancing networks and capacities within these institutions. The fact that monitoring spaces in the vehicular pollution case were comparatively more restricted to access by civil society organizations cut off possibilities for organizational growth and enhancement of mobilization capacities for civil society organizations.

The Indian case studies also allow us to reflect on and learn from the implications of sustaining collaborative oversight over long periods of time. One of the criteria that made India particularly promising as a place in which to the applicability of my argument was the fact that as the first court to deploy these mechanisms, it is also the one that has been doing it for longer. As we discussed earlier, in 2017, the Supreme Court closed the Right to Food case, after nearly two decades. The time horizon of the Delhi Vehicular Pollution case, which has been open since 1985, raises some issues that are worth examining. Three of my interviewees – environmental lawyers or activists who had followed the case or been involved with it as part of what I call the legal constituency – coincided in pointing to lengthy monitoring as both beneficial and detrimental: They agreed that monitoring fostered accountability and that it created opportunities where often none existed. As one of them described it, "Given state lethargy, just to shake them [the government] up you need a stick. (...) In that sense we welcome it."[10] The overwhelming majority of civil society actors I interviewed across cases and countries where court-promoted monitoring had been deployed agreed with them on this, mentioning that these initiatives gave them space and the opportunity to exercise accountability, which they viewed as positive. This book shows that this is not only a perception: I document multiple instances (Chapters 3 and 5) in which public exercises of accountability in the context of monitoring generated actions and responses that furthered implementation and impact.

However, at the same time that court-promoted monitoring creates spaces for accountability, over lengthy time horizons, it can do two things. On the one hand, it creates fatigue. While interviewees stressed the benefits of monitoring outlined above, they also commented on the drain in their resources that came with having to engage with the court over many years[11] and voiced frustration at changing personnel in the courts,[12] for example. On the other hand, some of my interviewees,

[10] Interview with environmental lawyer. Delhi. August 10, 2016.

[11] Interview with environmental lawyer (litigator). Delhi. August 10, 2016.

[12] Interview with environmental lawyer and researcher. Delhi. August 4, 2016.

as well as existing research, expressed concerns with the negative implications that sustained monitoring could have for separation of powers.

Interviewees commenting on the vehicular pollution case in particular highlighted that, in their view, the court's lengthy intervention led to the court "taking over the functions of the Executive"[13] and the "executive washing its hands off the issue."[14] This dynamic described by my interviewees is not exclusive to these cases: In their cross-country study, Gauri and Brinks (2008) found different instances of the executive (or even congress) taking cover in the court's interventions or standing by while the judiciary acted. They argued this could be a calculated strategic choice from government actors. In their telling, if the Court acts, the Executive risks less and exposes itself less, especially on politically sensitive topics. The key question in the context of these cases that drag on over time is if the court's involvement can become, in the long run, an excuse for the executive to consistently deflect political responsibility and even action. The Indian cases suggest that it is a possibility.

Some scholars have taken this critique further, arguing that the court's intervention weakened existing government agencies by taking over their functions (Jackson and Rosencranz 2003). As we saw, some in India express concern over this, though this chapter suggests that in both cases, a lot of the work done by court prompted action and resources into existing institutions or created new ones. In the cases I studied in depth, the two Latin American courts nudged government agencies into action and sought responses and resources from existing institutions. That was the point in the Colombian health case, for example, where the court strove to work with the Ministry of Health and its units. Even in the Matanza-Riachuelo case, where the Supreme Court of Argentina ordered the creation of a new government unit in charge of cleanup and recovery of the river, ACUMAR, the tribunal was not attached to this new institution.

[13] Interview with health and environmental lawyer and researcher. Delhi. August 8, 2016.

[14] Interview with environmental lawyer and researcher. Delhi. August 4, 2016.

7

Conclusions

In most of Latin America and in many other countries, democracy is stagnant, if not declining. It remains true today, as it was when O'Donnell (1999) pointed it out, that the effective enjoyment of civil, political, and social rights is one of the challenges to deepening democracy. Even in countries where democracy is more stable, inequalities in the effectiveness of rights (depending on region or socio-economic level) result in countless individuals who are unable to exercise full democratic citizenship. What is the role of high courts in enforcing rights, a process that is so crucial to democracy? What can the study of new legal tools for enforcing rights (specially court-promoted monitoring) teach us about the construction of judicial power in the Global South?

In recent decades, some Latin American courts became central actors in the enforcement of socioeconomic rights (SER). As documented in the preceding chapters, high courts in Colombia and Argentina played important roles in this transformation, handing down ambitious rulings aimed at expanding the sphere of citizenship. Based on the study of eight structural rulings, this book examined the conditions under which courts in developing democracies can produce political and social change. More specifically, the study focused on why some high court rulings from two of Latin America's most assertive tribunals, the Colombian Constitutional Court and Argentina's Supreme Court, have a significant impact on socioeconomic rights while others have very little. In this final chapter I review the main argument, my findings, and discuss the book's implications for debates on judicial power, as well as for normative and empirical research on judicial intervention in the realm of rights.

7.1 CAN COURTS ADVANCE RIGHTS?

Whether courts are actually capable of producing important social, economic, and political change is crucial to a long-standing debate regarding their ability to advance rights. Some argue that the judicialization of politics is at best ineffectual (Rosenberg 2008), and at worst can exacerbate preexisting inequalities by favoring individualistic, piecemeal, and irrational approaches to public policy (Ferraz 2011; Horowitz 1977). Others have a more optimistic assessment of the role of courts in these arenas, claiming that judicial intervention can contribute to mobilization (McCann 1994), alter legislative agendas, foster inter-institutional coordination, and, occasionally, advance the rights in question (Cano Blandón 2017; Gauri and Brinks 2008; Rodríguez Garavito 2010; Rosenberg, Krishnaswamy, and Bail 2019). In this book I offered a nuanced understanding of the impact that courts can have – looking beyond compliance and stressing the multidimensionality of court influence. Instead of focusing on labeling rulings as good or bad, positive or negative, I explored their role in larger, complex processes of change. The present work is in line with research on the topic that underscores the importance of redefining our notions of change (Keck 2014), highlighting that rights-protecting rulings are part and parcel of ongoing policy debates and political conflict (Botero and Brinks 2023). This requires thinking of courts – at least when they tread into the political arena – not only in terms of their function as mechanisms of dispute resolution that issue a final solution, but more as coordination devices that can facilitate change by creating spaces for the interaction of multiple actors.

To understand what explains variation in the impact of structural rulings aiming to enforce SER, I focused on the ways organized civil society mobilizes in the aftermath of these rulings and on the novel oversight mechanisms that some high courts have deployed to monitor adherence to some of their most important pronouncements. These include institutional innovations such as follow-up committees, public hearings, and information requests. I argued that judicial impact in structural cases – those that deeply affect public policy in a particular area – depends on how organized constituencies in civil society interact with these court-promoted oversight mechanisms. I develop my argument through comparative case studies of eight landmark rulings on health, environmental and social welfare issues handed down by the highest courts in Colombia and Argentina.

Cases, either before they are filed, as they run their course through the courts, or even after, generate legal constituencies (legal advocacy organizations associated with the ruling). In addition, in cases like the landmark rulings I examine, courts can sometimes exercise oversight over the post-ruling process, monitoring progress and compliance. On their own, both this kind of court-promoted oversight or active legal constituencies can use the rulings to produce some effects out in the real world. When both are present – that is, when courts make use of oversight mechanisms and a dense legal constituency engages with the court and the targets of the rulings during oversight – the impact of a ruling can be higher, reaching into different spheres. In its 2008 ruling safeguarding the environmental and health rights of the inhabitants of the Matanza-Riachuelo River basin (*Causa Mendoza*), the Supreme Court of Argentina provided for continued oversight of the ruling's

TABLE 7.1 *Cases and observed impact*

	No monitoring	Monitoring
Denser legal constituency	Medium impact [*Causa Verbitsky* and C-383]	Higher impact [*Causa Mendoza* and T-760*]
Less dense legal constituency	Lower impact [*Causa Chaco** and T-231]	Medium impact [*Causa Badaro* and T-547]

(*) The *Chaco* case had somewhat more impact than expected, and T-760 was somewhat lower. See below.

implementation and facilitated the creation of a follow-up commission including external and civil society actors to help in this process. In the years that followed, this commission played a central role in increasing the accountability of the governmental entities charged with reforming policies and implementing programs. It provided a forum for information on implementation to circulate back to the court, allowing it to tweak its policy, and it gave the members of civil society organizations access to key policy spaces. The ruling had a huge effect in changing the conversation around rights and environmental politics in the area, in no small part because of the work of the organizations involved with oversight. In explicitly examining the importance of the engagement of civil society legal advocacy organizations (legal constituencies) with courts, my argument goes beyond previous work that focuses solely on the court as the agent of change (Rodríguez Garavito and Rodríguez Franco 2010), on civil society (Epp 1998) or on the backing of political elites (Rosenberg 2008).

Monitoring mechanisms are relatively novel institutions, and this book presents the first small-n comparative study with a cross-regional perspective of them. I paired cases depending on different combinations of the two variables whose influence I wanted to understand better: presence or absence of court-promoted monitoring and low-density or high-density legal constituencies. These combinations are illustrated in Table 7.1. As explained in the Introduction, I studied two rulings for each combination or cell in Table 7.1, one case decided by the Colombian court and the other by the Argentinean court. Careful process tracing for each case study allowed me to better identify and trace the causal effects of the two independent variables and in the process unpack the black box linking judicial intervention to its "on-the-ground" consequences. The cross-case comparison and the Indian shadow case studies buttress the theory-building exercise.

At the outset of this study, I hypothesized that the impact of these two variables would lead to the outcomes depicted in Table 7.1. Over the course of the study, I found that a strong state-based actor could partially supplant the work of an organized civil society with, however, important consequences for the nature of the impact on the affected population, as we will see below. For this reason, the *Chaco* case turned out to have more impact than I initially foresaw. I also found that an all too heterogeneous and less cohesive, but still dense, legal constituency can face coordination difficulties. For this reason, the Colombian health case (T-760) had a lower impact than I expected. The insights that I gleaned from my empirical research allow me to propose some refinements to my theory in this final chapter – I explain those later, after I summarize the main findings.

The first paired comparison (Chapter 3) focused on a ruling safeguarding environmental rights (*Causa Mendoza* in Argentina) and a ruling safeguarding the right to health (T-760 in Colombia). In both cases, the joint presence of monitoring mechanisms and a dense legal constituency configured what I call a collaborative oversight arena. This is an institutional space in which the court, government agencies, targets of the ruling, and civil society organizations can interact, fostering accountability. Here civil society actors have access to the state and collaborative oversight arenas also open up the opportunity for the diffusion of policy ideas and of the rights-based framework. In the case of *Causa Mendoza*, interactions in the context of ongoing oversight of the ruling made possible the creation of tighter regulatory standards, the diffusion of information about new monitoring initiatives and about the state of the river basin. At the same time, some of this information became part of a feedback loop to the court, which was able to use it to update and revise its monitoring decisions and policy implementation.

In the case of T-760 in Colombia, where the court asked the government to reform the national public health system, the collaborative oversight arena fostered similar dynamics. The court's ongoing oversight of the implementation of the ruling created a space for external actors and government agencies to increase political pressure and act as agents of accountability, particularly in the face of corruption in the health sector. With input from civil society organizations and other external agents, change toward tighter regulatory standards became a priority and was promoted. In both cases, drawing on information from external actors about the issue and the implementation of the rulings helped the courts reduce informational asymmetries and use that input to inform its monitoring decisions.

Compared to the other rulings under study, these two have overall higher impact and they stand out for the dynamics just outlined. It should be noted, however, that the Colombian health ruling had a lower impact than the Argentinean environmental case. The legal constituency in the Colombian case was more heterogeneous (it included patient organizations, human rights groups, doctor organizations, legal advocacy organizations, and unionized workers, among others), it had less stable membership and less ability to coordinate than the legal constituency present in *Causa Mendoza*. These increased coordination costs reduced the effectiveness of their interventions in monitoring venues.

To better isolate the effects of civil society legal advocacy organizations, the second paired comparison (presented in Chapter 4) focused on rulings with dense legal constituencies but no court-promoted oversight mechanisms. There, the spotlight was on a ruling safeguarding the rights of prisoners in the Argentine province of Buenos Aires (*Causa Verbitsky*) and another safeguarding the right to housing in Colombia (C-383). Viewed in comparison with the other rulings in this book, the impact of these two and the pair in Chapter 4 is somewhat lower than those discussed in Chapter 3, but higher than those in Chapter 5; I classify them as medium. Upon closer inspection of the types of impact in comparison to the other rulings, we can see that both the levels of legal mobilization after the rulings and the type of ideational changes observed are directly linked to the work of the legal constituencies.

In both cases the presence of dense legal constituencies is associated with higher cascades of related rulings in the aftermath of the legal victory. Because there is not an ongoing, configured collaborative space for oversight, civil society organizations are forced to mobilize legally, through new litigation, and politically, in the legislative arena, to attempt to diffuse the benefits to similarly situated actors. In the case of *Verbitsky* we observe a series of similar high-profile collective legal claims (*amparos*) in other provinces and, also, the growing use of *Verbitsky* as precedent in individual *amparos* by inmates all over the country. A legal cascade such as this one, which we also observe in cases like *Grootboom* (the housing rights case in South Africa) and many others, is very often missed by researchers focusing too narrowly on the effects of a particular ruling. In the case of C-383, the Colombian housing case, the work of organizations affiliated with UPAC users was central to legal and political mobilization efforts to make the benefits of C-383 extensive to all mortgage debtors and to continue pushing for other reforms to the housing law.

Through their mobilization, both legal constituencies were also able to diffuse the rights-based framework. However, the diffusion of the rights-based framework was more limited when compared to the previous two cases since the effects were confined to the close spheres of influence of the legal advocacy organizations. For instance, in the case of *Verbitsky*, one of the organizations had close connections with officials and legal operators in the provincial legal system and worked extensively – through workshops and talks – to promote the ruling and train judges on an alternative vision of detention conditions. In the case of housing debtors' associations in Colombia, the legal victory had a significant effect in terms of how activists and members of the organization understood the issue (as one of constitutional rights) but I could not find any ideational effects beyond that immediate circle, because they did not carry out that work of diffusing the idea. In those cases where there is a collaborative oversight arena (*Causa Mendoza* and T-760), we see that the sustained interaction of different actors in oversight venues in the latter two provide for spaces where policy ideas and the rights-based framing can more easily reach decision-makers and other actors.

The third paired comparison (Chapter 4) focused on cases where the combination of factors under study is the exact opposite of Chapter 3: that is, cases with court-promoted monitoring but low-density legal constituencies. This comparison allowed me to more closely study the effects of monitoring mechanisms. The first ruling was handed down by the Supreme Court of Argentina enforcing the right to pension (*Causa Badaro*); the second was a case decided by the Colombian court safeguarding the right to prior consultation of four Indigenous groups in the Colombian Caribbean coast (T-547). In both cases the court's sustained attention meant higher levels of impact in terms of formal norms and resources than we might otherwise expect. In the Argentine case, the ruling altered the regulatory framework for pensions, particularly because it triggered the passing in Congress of a bill providing for bi-annual updates to the quantity of monthly payments (thus far these had depended on the executive's initiative and Congress' will and were not annual). In the Colombian case, the court's sustained intervention got off the ground and oversaw a consultation process for the Kogui, Wiwa, Arhuaco, and Kankuamo Indigenous groups with regard to a private project to build a large-scale industrial port in land they claimed was a sacred site.

While in both these cases we can trace concrete changes in formal norms and resources back to the court's intervention, I observed no organizational or ideational changes. This contrast to the rulings that had a dense legal constituency – where I did observe those kinds of effects – suggests that the absence of legal constituencies limits the spheres where we observe impact. While the court works in legal spaces, civil society organizations work in social spaces – when the latter are present, they can magnify the ruling's ripple effects into those areas. The work of legal constituencies can potentially extend effects to these spaces, help put political pressure on government agents, legislators, and other organized groups in civil society thus keeping the issue alive.

The final paired comparison (Chapter 5) spotlights cases without monitoring and with low density or no legal constituencies. In the first of these cases, the Supreme Court of Argentina ordered the national Argentine government and the Chaco Province to guarantee the enforcement of the right to food and health of the Qom Indigenous people inhabiting an isolated forested area of the Chaco Province known as El Impenetrable (*Causa Chaco*). In the latter, the Colombian court safeguarded the right to a healthy environment for a citizen of the city of Cúcuta and his neighbors who lived by the severely polluted Bogotá Canal, which crisscrosses the city. The Cúcuta case (T-231) has the lowest impact of all the rulings under the study both in terms of immediate effects and outcomes. Impact was circumscribed mostly to some changes of formal norms and resources. The *Chaco* case is also low in terms of immediate effects, but given the dire situation of the Qom, although the programs and changes carried out following the court's intervention could not address structural inequalities, they brought relief and entailed important improvements to their living conditions.

One feature of this case is of note: the difference a state-based actor can make when they are in the mix. Efforts by the Defensor del Pueblo (the national Ombudsman) to monitor the aftermath of the *Chaco* ruling helped build accountability by keeping political pressure, particularly on the provincial government, and maintaining national attention. The Defensor continued traveling to the area to report on the Qom's conditions and the implementation of the programs. However, despite the centrality of its work, the Defensor was physically removed from the everyday realities of the Qom in Chaco. The fact that the bulk of the advocacy and engagement with the court and other actors was carried out by an independent government actor removed from the Indigenous people further disempowered them, leading to outcomes that did not necessarily align with their preferences. Though the job of the Defensor was crucial in improving conditions for the Qom, the absence of a dense network of legal advocacy organizations that could have interacted in institutionalized oversight venues is evident.

In contrast to overly pessimistic views of the intervention of courts in advancing rights, these cases suggest that even when levels of impact are low, courts' interventions can make a difference. They bring public attention to long-standing problems, and they can prompt concrete responses from government bureaucracies. Following the Colombian court's ruling with regard to the canal in Cúcuta, the cleanup took place, and the Argentine court's intervention guaranteed resources for food aid, pension programs, and a new hospital, among others. At the same time, both cases illustrate the limits of judicial interventions in complex SER cases stemming from the way in which the court approaches its decision, as I now turn to discuss.

When we think of court decisions, most often than not we imagine them handing down a final ruling that details what needs to be done. After the decision, courts usually disengage. I refer to these decisions as one-time interventions. Such centralized orders, laying out specific procedures that need to be followed have often been criticized for being too close to a command-and-control model of intervention in social policy. The focus on this kind of decisions is on producing comprehensive and fixed procedural rules – that is, a detailed blueprint of who needs to do what, akin to the bureaucracy's regulatory function. In contrast to that model, more experimental approaches to judicial intervention combine flexible norms toward achieving general standards with ongoing participation from different stakeholders (Sabel and Simon 2004). Judicial intervention of this form does not seek to produce a detailed blueprint and often does not come in the form of a one-time final decision. Actually, some argue that experimentalism has the potential to breed dialogue between the court and other political actors (Dixon 2007). In this dialogue, the court refrains from command-and-control, but engages in calling attention to blind spots and defines goals as well as obligations, through sustained engagement with other stakeholders.

Both *Chaco* and T-231 confirm some of these problems and suggest that courts might benefit from different approaches to deciding on socioeconomic issues. In the case of the canal in Cúcuta, for example, the court ordered a one-time cleanup, within a specific time frame. This measure could hardly have made a dent in what was clearly a structural issue. In contrast, Chapter 3 analyzes rulings that try to tackle complex issues by incorporating a more structural approach and monitoring mechanisms (for example) that explicitly involve different actors and generate discussion and involvement over time. These approaches are not silver bullets either, but they do generate cooperative dynamics, interaction, and higher levels of impact.

The findings of this study highlight how court rulings are most effective (i.e., have greater impact) when courts act in concert with other actors. In those cases where the courts were able to create spaces for interaction between themselves, civil society organizations, government organizations, and other external actors – like in *Causa Mendoza* and T-760 – the impact of their rulings extended into more areas and was greater. In both these cases, the configuration of collaborative oversight arenas made possible dynamics that put political pressure on targets for greater accountability and generated information feedback loops that informed the court's monitoring decisions. The kind of monitoring that appeared to be most effective (in the context of collaborative oversight arenas but also for those cases without a dense legal constituency) was the kind that functioned more akin to a fire alarm mechanism (McCubbins and Schwartz 1984). Following McCubbins and Schwartz, by fire alarm I mean, a monitoring effort that, instead of being fully centralized and carried out directly and entirely by the Court, relies on external agents who, working within a set of rules, examine implementation, seek information, expose delays, and prod those charged with implementing.

Configuring a collaborative oversight arena can also foster repeated interactions between stakeholders in the ruling – in this context, different policy ideas and ideational effects can spread. In the case of *Causa Mendoza*, for example, the follow-up commission insisted on tighter regulatory standards for monitoring environmental conditions in the river basin. In the context of oversight, the court ordered the agency in charge, ACUMAR, to heed these standards, and the monitoring process itself also created opportunities for members of the follow-up commission to directly discuss this with the ACUMAR. Although from the point of view of the organizations that participate in the follow-up commission standards should have been stricter, their insistence led the government to adopt more results-based monitoring practices and make information more readily available for public accountability.

Getting decision-makers and government officials to consider (and eventually even implement) new policy ideas or to incorporate rights-based considerations in their bureaucratic decision-making and in their cognitive frameworks is essential to altering the way things are done in a particular policy area. The impact of T-760, the decision reforming the national health system in Colombia was significant in this sense. In its ruling, the court recognized health as a fundamental right, and insisted that an emphasis on *el goce efectivo del derecho* (a perspective emphasizing rights effectiveness) should be the guiding principle of reforms to the system. As Chapter 3 discussed, the ruling helped focus the debate on problems with the health system and on health as a right. This, in turn got the Ministry of Health and bureaucrats to frame many of the discussions and some of their decisions in those terms. Eventually, this type of change may alter the very politics of an issue, so that courts are no longer needed to put and keep the issue on the policy agenda.

7.2 CROSS-REGIONAL LESSONS

The shadow case studies of Indian rulings with collaborative oversight arenas show evidence of patterns similar to those I saw in Colombia and Argentina: These spaces created opportunities to exercise accountability, diffuse ideas, and to alleviate information and power asymmetries, all of which contributed to greater impact. Beyond confirming the usefulness of my framework to think through the politics of implementation in structural cases, the cross-regional comparison highlights other important dynamics, some of which point to the trade-offs involved in collaborative monitoring: too much procedural leniency and lengthy time horizons.

The Indian cases allow us to begin sketching what may be the frontiers of when too much experimentalism could begin detracting from the pluses in collaborative monitoring. As I show in Chapter 6, and as several Indian scholars have documented (see, for example, Bhuwania 2017), court-promoted monitoring in India is exercised within the greater flexibility afforded by public interest litigation (PIL). This means that judges have a lot of discretion in terms of where they take the cases, and, that collaborative oversight institutions in India are less under the direct control of the court when compared to Colombia or Argentina. In India, there is greater room for external actors (or go-betweens between the court and civil society) to play important roles, which can make institutions that are part of collaborative monitoring more permeable to external interests. It can also allow for court staffers, including judges, to exercise a lot of discretion. As Bhuwania (2017) notes, procedural leniency and very high levels of autonomy without accountability can result in processes that stray far away from their initial objectives.

The Indian cases, which have been monitored for decades, also underscore the potential downfalls of lengthy time horizons. The fatigue that I began to glimpse in Colombian and Argentinian cases with court-promoted monitoring was even more palpable in the Indian context, as discussed in Chapter 6. While monitoring creates spaces that are valued by civil society actors as opportunities to create accountability, extended monitoring also creates fatigue among those involved, can be costly to maintain for many civil society groups, and could result in the Executive "washing their hands" of the issue. For example, the Right to Food case closed in 2017 after nearly two decades of court-promoted monitoring, while the Delhi Vehicular Pollution case is getting close to thirty years. The longer courts maintain monitoring spaces open for structural cases, the longer they can exert pressure, but also the longer they must spend scarce resources on issues that are extremely complex. Courts can maximize the impact of their interventions by circumscribing them in time.

Despite their potential to work as accountability-enhancing mechanisms, courts that make use of court-promoted monitoring are not deploying silver bullets. When crafting collaborative oversight arenas, courts are bringing together, for a sustained over-time effort, a multitude of political and social actors. These efforts will necessarily incorporate many of the weaknesses and failings – as well as the strengths – of their contexts. The corruption allegations that surfaced around the contracts to expand the sewage and water networks in the Matanza-Riachuelo River basin included many of the well-known ingredients of local – corrupt – politics in the Buenos Aires Province.[1] At some point, the judge charged by the Supreme Court to aid with monitoring of the *Causa Mendoza* case was implicated in the scandal – a situation that critics pointed to as evidence of the hopelessness of the entire enterprise (Gargarella 2014a). An alternative reading of this situation must note that the Supreme Court quickly reacted to the accusations, removing the judge. And, perhaps most importantly, made sure that the accusations were investigated, the findings publicized, and measures adopted – steps not to be taken lightly, in a setting where impunity for this type of accusations was the norm.

The oversight process initiated by the Colombian Constitutional Court for the health ruling (T-760) was also subject to debilitating pressures by external agents and suffered under the weight of endless corruption scandals in the health sector. As seen in Chapter 3, court-promoted monitoring configured an arena in which many of these accusations could be ventilated, those responsible were exposed, and the appropriate accountability institutions (Fiscalía and Contraloría) set in motion. Yet, many rightly complain about the slow response from some of these institutions. In both Argentina and Colombia, long-drawn monitoring process of extremely complex issues expose the courts (and participants in oversight venues) to undue external pressures – processes that can easily lead to roadblocks and fatigue.

Both the challenges and the gains stemming from judicial intervention on socioeconomic rights highlight the degree to which courts are, as I have argued elsewhere with Daniel Brinks (Botero and Brinks 2023), an integral part of their surrounding sociopolitical ecosystem. Both in the sense that they cannot craft impact alone, but also in the sense that they are likely to be vulnerable to the same pressures and shortcomings of the institutional and cultural milieu that surrounds them. Courts are not perfect solutions, just like legislatures are not perfect solutions, though both are subject to different challenges and offer different advantages. In any case, the cases studied in this book illustrate the potential for impact, on different levels and taking place in different sociopolitical ecosystems, despite the constraints.

7.3 REFINEMENTS TO MY THEORY

One of the strengths of qualitative research in general, and of theory building exercises in particular, is the possibility of engaging in an iterative dialogue between theory and evidence to improve our theoretical frameworks. The findings I just summarized, and specially the lessons I learned from comparing across

[1] "El juez de la causa Riachuelo, en la mira por sospechas de corrupción" Clarín. November 2, 2012.

configurations, countries, and regions, suggest that my original theory can be refined in two important ways. First, while my own conceptualization of monitoring mechanisms in Chapter 2 highlighted the importance of thinking about the variety of tools and levels of engagement from the court, my research showed that to whom monitoring was delegated to could also influence impact. The cross-regional comparison underscores the importance of thinking about monitoring mechanisms not just in terms of how much the court does (whether it only requests reports or if it sets up a collaborative oversight arena), but also in terms of who it delegates monitoring to. In-house control, as was the rule in Colombia and Argentina, appears to have configured processes in which external actors could hold less direct sway and thus, had more limited ability to deviate the monitoring process away from the ruling.

Second, my findings also highlight the need to rethink civil society support. My theory recognizes the centrality of advocacy organizations in civil society to crafting impact, distinguishing between high and low levels of density (measured in terms of availability of funding, networks, and resources). My theory did not originally consider how other dimensions of the configuration of the legal constituency might influence impact. Two appear to be especially important: On the one hand, the potential downsides of a numerous legal constituency whose purposes were too diverse. A legal constituency that is well populated, but too fragmented in the aims and approaches of its members (as was the case in the Colombian health ruling) can have two clear negative consequences for impact: lack of coordination and reduced visibility of their work. Both in turn can hurt effectiveness and reach. On the other hand, certain government-adjacent independent organizations like the Ombudsman offices proved to be strong boosters of density among civil society. The *Chaco* and *Badaro* cases, in particular, show how such organizations are crucial to channeling resources and visibility, creating pressure points, and access to the State (which they are closer to) that improves impact.

The work of civil society organizations is a central piece of crafting impact, as this and other work shows (Langford 2021). Future research should consider a characterization of organizations' density (whether by that name or other) that is sensitive to how the organizations' purposes and missions complement themselves or create divisions and tensions. Careful mapping out of the different kinds of actors that are involved in the monitoring, particularly those that navigate the frontiers of, and build bridges between, civil society and government is crucial.

7.4 CRAFTING IMPACT THROUGH COLLABORATION

My emphasis on the convergence of two factors, court-promoted monitoring and dense legal constituencies, for there to be higher impact stands in contrast to the views that overemphasize the court's agency (Rodríguez Garavito and Rodríguez Franco 2010) as well as those that focus exclusively on the importance of follow-up litigation by a support structure in civil society (Epp 1998). In accordance with other research (Ansolabehere 2013; Brinks and Forbath 2014; Gonzalez-Ocantos 2016), the cases here suggest that courts are better understood not in isolation, but as deeply engrained in the surrounding sociopolitical dynamics (Ansolabehere 2013; Brinks and Forbath 2014; Gonzalez-Ocantos 2016). My study contributes to this literature by specifying the ways in which legal advocacy organizations and their interaction with different government and private actors can be crucial to what happens after the rulings have been handed down.

In all the cases in which they were present in this study, civil society organizations were working to hold the targets of the rulings accountable. In *Causa Mendoza* in Argentina and in the health ruling in Colombia (Chapter 3), a dense web of civil society organizations was a necessary ingredient in the configuration of a collaborative oversight arena, as was discussed earlier. Yet, even in the cases where there were no monitoring mechanisms but there was a dense legal constituency (namely, the Argentine ruling on prisoners' rights – *Causa Verbitsky* – and the housing rights case – C-383 – in Colombia) the work of civil society organizations mobilizing after the ruling was still central to generating information, building on the ruling as precedent, doing independent monitoring, and diffusing its rights-based premises. The Indian cases, particularly the Right to Food ruling (Chapter 6), reaffirm the positive effects that a robust network of civil society organizations can have.

The crucial importance of organized civil society to what happens after structural ruling holds lessons and implications beyond the study of the judiciary. Recent research on institutional weakness in Latin America underscores that flaws in enforcement can be relational, and may be overcome through cooperation with societal actors (Brinks, Levitsky and Murillo 2020). This work, however, focuses mostly on institutional landscapes that are viewed as problematic or lacking. This book speaks to how embeddedness in civil society can bolster institutional effectiveness, giving institutions strength, perspective, and bite. From this perspective, this book resonates with Rich's work (2019) on the successful implementation of Brazil's progressive AIDS policy, a feat borne out of the close collaboration between bureaucrats and the Movement to Combat HIV/AIDS. The findings also show that the creation of institutional avenues for participatory oversight can magnify societal accountability (Peruzzotti and Smulovitz 2006), giving civil society and watchdog agencies more direct access to accountability venues and opportunities for exposing problems. As Bergallo (2014) notes these participatory processes mark a sharp contrast with the usually closed-off legal procedures, even considering their imperfections. Future research on impact and implementation should explore these dynamics further, without ignoring, as Merlinsky (2016), Puga (2012), Cano Blandón (2021), Barrera and Sáenz (2020), and Ryan and Napoli (2017) remind us, the power differentials within societal groups which determine who and how can better engage with the state, as well as with private actors.

My study also raises important points when it comes to thinking about high courts as spaces that can improve participation, particularly through collaborative monitoring in structural cases. Why are these courts so accommodating to participation from other actors? And what is the role of judges in creating and facilitating those spaces? The cases studied in this book show courts structuring their working relationships with organized civil society and other external actors in a number of different ways. From a comparative perspective, the variation in institutional design is fascinating and should be explored further in other countries and at other levels beyond high tribunals. Comparing the experiences of the Latin American and the Indian high courts in Chapter 6, I concluded that the degree of control exerted by the court over the monitoring process and the procedural flexibility it is afforded can help explain why and whether the monitoring process favors certain type of actors over others. Yet, we should remember that most high courts throughout the world do not interact as closely with civil society. What makes this willingness to let external actors in more likely? This project and existing research suggests some possible answers.

First, context matters. In countries like the ones studied in this book – that is, many countries in Latin America and the Global South – courts are enmeshed in deeply unequal societies with high rates of litigiousness and were citizens have turned to judiciaries seeking to make the promises of lofty constitutional frameworks a reality (Botero, Brinks, and Gonzalez-Ocantos 2022). This creates pressure for courts to respond.

Second, institutional design and the politics of appointments matter. Some courts, like the Chilean Supreme Court as designed by Pinochet, successfully insulated themselves by virtue of design and institutional culture from the rights-based demands of their surroundings (Hilbink 2011). However, in places where institutional design allows for the conflicts and urgencies of the setting to filter in, the pressure mounts. The more open courts are to different issues and to a wider array of actors, via different institutional tools, the more they are exposed to a wider array of issues and the harder it becomes to ignore them. Faced with complex, intractable sociopolitical problems and lacking "the purse or the sword" courts may turn to civil society and other external actors as new partners that can help with implementation and in the process function as support for the court's actions.

Monitoring, working with outside actors is a choice, an enterprise that can increase impact but one that is not perfect (as we have seen), and is certainly not without risks.

In that sense, this book also shows that monitoring experiences like the ones I have described and studied here are not sustainable in the long run without purposeful agents creating the legal and political space for oversight to exist continually (Gargarella 2014a). In short, court-promoted monitoring and collaborative oversight arenas appear impossible without a third factor: judicial initiative. Deploying court-promoted monitoring and sustaining oversight efforts over long stretches of time requires judges committed, or at the very least willing, to engage in experimental approaches to remedies, and to do so with a democratic spirit. Judicial leadership is decisive to sustaining monitoring and, as Sigal, Morales and Rossi (2017) have already highlighted, such leadership is particularly important in the realm of rights enforcement.

Though I have not focused on the individual figures of specific justices, the strategies that the Colombian, Argentine, and Indian highest courts have chosen to monitor certain landmark cases show that the preferences and choices made by the judges matter a great deal. Without the judges' willingness to engage with other actors, to coordinate oversight efforts, to hold public events and to create new spaces for accountability, involving often reticent players in new dynamics, we would not observe this collaboration. More work needs to be done to understand the conditions under which institutional tools – like monitoring mechanisms – are developed by judges, as well as how and when they expand. As we seek answers to these questions, we would do well to keep in mind that judicial leadership is crucial, and that to understand it, the legal preferences and normative commitments of justices have to be explored, as well as how these change over time (Botero 2018).

7.5 RESPONDING TO THE CRITICS OF JUDICIAL INTERVENTION IN SER

Institutional innovations like court-promoted monitoring, as well as judicial intervention in the realm of rights more generally, raise some concerns and have been strongly criticized. First, let us discuss the normative critique against judicial review of rights: Unease at the idea that a minoritarian non-elected institution might decide on and define the content and realization of rights, a task usually associated with – and better left to – a representative institution like the legislature. To Waldron (2005), for example, judicial review on matters of rights tramples on principles like representation and participation and is therefore democratically illegitimate. Waldron's critique is founded on four assumptions about the functioning of any given political system that, as Roa Roa (2019) shows, do not hold in many countries around the world.

Of the four assumptions Waldron specifies for his critique of judicial review to hold (fully functioning democratic institutions, fully independent judicial institutions at all levels, generalized commitment to rights among citizens, and disagreement about rights in society) the first three are the ones that we can most easily point to not being reasonable assumptions in many democracies in today's Global South. Assuming fully and harmoniously functioning democratic institutions in the Global North is also questionable, given recent setbacks in the context of the erosion of democracy (Alizada et al. 2021). Waldron himself has recognized that the experience of countries like Colombia made him doubt his initial position criticizing the pertinence of judicial review on rights. In such countries, provided crass countermajoritarian problems are avoided, assertive courts can be crucial to fostering active democracies, not elements that undermine them.

In other words, the normative critique desperately needed an empirical perspective (Brinks and Forbath 2014; Rodríguez Garavito and Rodríguez Franco 2010). One of Waldron's main concerns was that judicial review on matters of rights would strip citizens of their right to participate – a right that he conceives of as happening exclusively in the legislature. In contrast, in recent years, many studies of the Global South have shown that litigation can be a tool for enhancing participation. My findings show that under certain circumstances, courts can act as facilitators, catalysts for change, and that they can provide spaces for participation without necessarily imposing their slanted vision. Despite the difficulties and risks, this book shows that these courts do not necessarily displace democratic politics, or elected policymakers; instead, they can create new political spaces devoted to special problems. And these spaces can call upon multiple stakeholders, including government actors. In short, as the preceding chapters showed, working with other political and social actors, courts can enhance accountability and increase responsiveness. Of course, these monitoring spaces are not perfect: They can be subject to undue pressures, they can reproduce the inequalities that shape the societies around them and those that the language of the law enforces (Barrera and Sáenz 2020). Attention to these configurations and to power differentials is, again, key. But they are a new, additional venues that can give voice to new actors and create spaces where they will be heard.

While some have criticized courts for their continued involvement on normative grounds, other scholars criticized courts for their meager or harmful results. One of the earliest critiques in this second direction was Hirschl's (2004) who saw in judicial decision-making on economic, social, and cultural rights evidence of a juristocracy bent on advancing the strategic interests of a minoritarian elite. Puga (2012), based on her work in Colombia and Argentina, critiqued the inability of the judicial system as a whole to incorporate the voices and experiences of the most vulnerable. In that sense, she found structural rulings of this nature largely ineffectual. More recently, several Indian scholars, among them Menon (2014), Bhuwania (2017, 2018) and Thiruvengadam (2014), have forcefully critiqued their Supreme Court justices for what they perceive as a move away from commitment to rights enforcement toward favoring corporate interests or more powerful actors in general. In contrast to critics like Waldron (2005), who questioned courts' involvement on normative grounds, later works like these – most more empirically based – have raised issues with some of the consequences.

These critiques are important as they demand that we remain vigilant about the volume of work we still need to do in our very unequal societies for socioeconomic rights to be accessible and effective more broadly. Puga (2012), Menon (2014), and Bhuwania (2017) remind us that law and legal institutions can be used as oppressive tools, and Hirschl (2004) in turn points out that not all the aspirational goals we have enshrined in constitutions have become reality, or are necessarily progressive. But none of those studies – nor this one, for that matter – can claim to show conclusively that no progress at all has been made in the aftermath of such interventions. This book and other research show that structural rulings enforcing rights can generate important immediate effects and outcomes, which have consequences for the advancement of the right in question. This is not an all-or-nothing debate. In working with different actors, courts can provide some fruitful openings for change.

7.6 JUDICIAL POWER

This book speaks directly to debates on the enforcement of rights, but in addition, it has implications for how we understand the construction of judicial power and with that, for contemporary discussions about assertive courts as tools for democratic erosion. In many countries in the Global South, generous bills of rights are central parts of constitutions, which high courts are charged with defending. As such, judicial involvement in the definition and enforcement of rights is part and parcel of constitutional politics – a situation which marks a distinctly different starting point from the jurisdiction and institutional design of many high courts in the Global North. Judicial disputes around socioeconomic rights continue to grow in importance as issues like preservation of and access to water, to housing, the right to health, and climate change become ever more central to political discussions. Rulings on these topics, and ambitious structural rulings in particular, have major implications for a comprehensive understanding of the role of high courts as institutions of governance.

Court-promoted oversight of structural rulings can transform the complex game between judges, the Executive, media, and the public. Creating a supervised process for compliance enlists the litigants and their support networks (where they exist) on a long-term enterprise, creates multiple opportunities for interaction, and raises the saliency of the case. As my theory discusses, this may well enhance the ruling's constituency, and will, in any case, keep the issue in the public's eye for longer, while hopefully providing the media information that both highlights the problems created by the violation and creates pressure for the Executive and bureaucracy to solve them. These dynamics can enhance impact, as we have seen throughout the book, but there might also be value in this complex balancing act to the court, particularly in terms of enhancing its power.

As Staton (2010) has shown, by enhancing transparency around rulings judges can help expand, within limits, de facto judicial power. Of course, in areas that are of great importance to the government, judges' room for maneuver is likely smaller. Even then, transparency in the context of a collaborative and somewhat flexible process offers some advantages. In the case of court-promoted monitoring, the process by which the ruling's awareness is increased involves other actors, while providing for the opportunity to adjust measures and correct course as time advances. This creates a space for collaboration where the court sets some ground rules, and at the same time (as can be seen throughout Chapters 3, 4, and 6) there is room for vagueness, since some aspects of the decision itself (like deadlines and specific objectives) are often co-constructed or co-supervised and can be tweaked.

Vagueness in judicial decisions can fulfill several purposes: Courts delegate specific choices to actors who are better informed about the details of the policy, while increasing pressure for compliance; crucially, it can also mask pockets of non-compliance or delay (Staton and Vanberg 2008). In short, the ongoing supervision of a case might allow judges to have it both ways: They can increase saliency and allow the public to identify non-compliance, or at least to make it clear that the problem continues, while at the same time avoiding a too-clear decision that creates a confrontation with other branches.

Creating a process for crafting solutions with input from external actors and room for some adjustments avoids the overt confrontation with the government that a detailed order with strict deadlines would create. Judges can, within constraints, build up judicial power through a process that can reduce friction with other branches and generate multiple opportunities for interaction with the Court. As exchanges between branches of government in the context of judicial intervention in SER cases are iterative games, overtime, the use of collaborative monitoring in structural cases can contribute to a dynamic that can diffuse conflict.

As I was wrapping up this book, some expressed skepticism of an analysis that was overall optimistic about the contributions of high courts to rights enforcement in an era in which assertive judiciaries have, on more than one occasion, facilitated the rise of populists that weakened democracy. Examples include the rise of Jair Bolsonaro in Brazil in the wake of the Lava Jato scandal, and the instrumentalization of the judiciary in Poland, Hungary, El Salvador, and Venezuela in the context of processes of democratic backsliding or outright autocratization. Judicial involvement, and at times overreach, in the enforcement of rights was, in some cases like Brazil with Bolsonaro, related to the rise of contemporary populists. But that is not an ironclad rule, nor should it be taken to suggest that the judicialization of rights has yielded purely negative results. The effects of judicialization are usually varied, and its limits (defined by both institutional and contextual factors) must be understood without ignoring its advances (for an assessment of Latin America, see Botero, Brinks, and Gonzalez-Ocantos 2022). The connection between judicial assertiveness and the threat to democracy at the hand of populist actors is a much more complex story.

Yes, judicial overreach can help populists: When courts decry politics (like in Brazil during Lava Jato), when high courts explicitly side with such leaders (like the Supreme Court in Venezuela; see Sánchez Urribarrí 2022), or when they facilitate the bending or breaking of constitutional rules (Castillo-Ortiz 2019), the leaders can use the rulings to legitimize their disregard for democratic checks on their power.

An activist court can also encourage populist attacks, as Jair Bolsonaro consistently did by claiming that the Supreme Federal Tribunal was only protecting the elite minority it represented.[2] Where courts are easily co-opted or packed by illiberal forces, chances are they will more quickly become tools that facilitate executive aggrandizement processes. Though these are possibilities, assertive high courts do not necessarily have to be detrimental to democracy by ushering in populists. These dynamics are certainly not at play in the two cases that are the main focus of the book: Argentina and Colombia.

The absence of such dynamics in these two countries thus far is not a coincidence. Precisely because of the use of monitoring mechanisms – among other tactics – these two courts maintain very different relationships with their political systems than those we have observed in democratic erosion cases. As we have seen, when these courts decide on high-profile and/or structural cases they often engage in exchanges with political actors, including opening monitoring spaces and inviting others to participate. As I have shown throughout Chapters 3–5, these courts do not demonize politics or attack the Executive: They try to foster dialogue. These courts play what Kureshi (2022) would call a *representation reinforcement role*, creating new avenues for engagement and enhancing existing ones. In doing so, they sharply reduce – though they cannot foreclose – the opportunities for the rise of populism and their own instrumentalization in the process. By monitoring, collaborating, these courts build a dynamic that is less confrontational, and that can help counteract (or at least delay) attempts to instrumentalize the judiciary.

Research on the role of courts in processes of democratic erosion stresses the importance of understanding that courts and elected powers interact over long periods of time in changing political and institutional contexts (Huq 2018). The nature of these interactions is important, as heightened inter-branch conflict and aggressive attacks are usually part of the illiberal playbook with respect to courts. My point is simply that understanding how courts build and deploy their power should also consider their track record on socioeconomic rights, as these rulings are an important part of the governance dynamic, and they do not always spell disastrous results or empty overreach. Where high-profile public policy matters are dealt with via collaborative processes that reduce (or at least diffuse) conflict, impact can be enhanced, so can judicial power and the process can buttress the maintenance of a democratic separation of powers.

The study of monitoring mechanisms and judicial impact raises fascinating issues for students, practitioners and observers of law and politics, comparative judicial politics, and rights activism worldwide. This book shows that courts can contribute to the advancement of rights, though they cannot offer silver bullets.

2 For a brief overview of the dynamics between Bolsonaro and the Supreme Federal Tribunal in Brazil, see Bustamante and Meyer (2022) and Leal and Thomaz (2022).

The Colombian and Argentine tribunals have, at times, successfully configured important new political spaces for effective pursuit of public policy goals, in conjunction and dialogue with external actors. In doing so, they have increased their power and positioned themselves as non-negligible political forces. In the end, then, when they do things right, courts can contribute to deepening democracy, and can bring the many promises contained in constitutional texts one step closer to reality.

Appendices

APPENDIX A: METHODOLOGICAL CONSIDERATIONS

Measuring and Scoring Impact

Due to the multidimensional nature of impact, its assessment requires multiple and diverse indicators. Earlier studies of impact relied on several well-known indicators: tracking legislative and policy initiatives (Feeley 1998; Keck 2009; Rosenberg 2008), looking at media coverage (Rosenberg 2008; McCann 1996; Rodríguez Garavito and Rodríguez Franco 2010), and analyzing interview material for ideational changes (McCann 1996; Feeley 1998). Mixed methods approaches are increasingly common, as scholars that are interested in exploring the wide variety of effects often rely on a combination of qualitative and quantitative indicators (see, for example, Gauri and Brinks 2008; Rodríguez Garavito and Rodríguez Franco 2010; Gonzalez Velez and Jaramillo Sierra 2020). Interviews with activists, government and private officials, litigants, affected parties, and members of the judiciary are used to reconstruct decision-making processes, litigation strategies, mobilization strategies, as well as changes in ideas. Finally, policy data on resource allocation, services delivered, procedures or actions undertaken, and development indicators are increasingly used to assess rights effectiveness.

My own measurement strategy relies on a combination of these indicators. Evidence of changes in ideas and discourse (in salience and perception of issues among informed key and elite actors associated with the rulings, for example) were analyzed by looking at coverage in key printed media outlets and through interviews. To identify and assess changes in formal norms, as well as resources, I focused on gathering primary and secondary evidence that allowed me to carefully reconstruct the policy process. This evidence included: identifying the governmental resources devoted to the specific programs ordered or modified in relation to the ruling (before and after where possible); determining the preexisting policy infrastructure in the policy area and if (and how) it was modified after the decision; identifying the mobilization of human and financial resources toward the relevant agencies and the geographical area of interest. Part of formal norms is also changes to the jurisprudence; to that end I relied on searches of the online databases of the two courts (together with specialized legal databases) and drew on interviews and secondary literature to identify key subsequent lower court decisions that referred to the ruling of interest. As for organizational changes, those were best identified through interviews with actors related to the process and secondary literature.

The open-ended interviews I conducted were particularly useful to identify effects (or their absence) on all dimensions; interviewees often pointed to new data sources and provided information that was crucial on its own, and to triangulate with other data that I had acquired from policy documents, official reports, or published research. Interviews were also useful to get at ideational effects and for more fine-grained information on the behavior of public officials, private agents, litigants, and members of social organizations.

Bringing the indicators together to provide a summary assessment of subdimensions and stages requires some scoring scheme. In this project I rely on a scoring and aggregation system based on none, low, medium, and high labels, which I use for the two subdimensions within impact: immediate effects and outcomes. I begin with the negative label: *none*. This applies to a subdimension where there was no evidence of any affect whatsoever and it would apply to a ruling for which there is absolutely no evidence of any effect in either outcome or the subcategories of immediate effects. Note, however, that the expression that a ruling had no effects or is "dead letter" is often misused, particularly with structural cases: When we look at things closely, we may find that at a minimum some change ensued at the formal level, for example.

To distinguish between degrees and types of impact, where there is some, I score each of the four subdimension within immediate effects (Ideas and Discourse, Formal Norms, Organizational Changes, and Resources) as Low, Medium, or High based on my qualitative assessment and scored the aggregate as follows:

- If I observed effects in only one subdimension, regardless of the score or the dimension, the ruling had generated some effects and would be scored as **low** impact.
- I scored the immediate effects subdimension using the following rules:
  - The most common category (3 out of 4 or 2 out of 4) applied to the subdimension
  - If one or two categories were scored as "none" the lowest category of the four applied to the subdimension

When I score and aggregate in this manner, I am collapsing a significant amount of information. This rough measurement scheme is meant to provide an approximation and a guide and does not replace, but rather complements, the rich qualitative description which is necessary to understand impact. The score helps to identify differences across categories, and invites us to look into the subdimensions to get a clear picture of how cases in that range (and in the extremes) vary across them.

Empirical Implications

Oversight mechanisms and legal constituencies, individually, contribute to impact in different ways. My argument in this book is that their joint presence can ultimately lead to even greater impact. What would we observe if this account is accurate? Here I lay out the observable implications of my theory. Process tracing methodology requires the specification of the connections between the elements under study (legal constituencies, oversight mechanisms, and judicial impact) so that their consistency with the evidence can be ascertained in the data analysis stage (Hall 2003).

For rulings where oversight mechanisms are used (but the legal constituency is low, meaning not dense):

- The use of oversight mechanisms provides courts with public venues on which to exert political and social pressure on the targets of the ruling. When oversight mechanisms are used, we should observe the court requesting information (on the issue in general and on compliance with the ruling in particular) from the targets of the ruling, and the targets of these requests responding by bringing this information before the court.
- In turn, this information should be used by the court to inform its oversight and policy decisions and to make further requests from those involved.
- The use of oversight mechanisms imposes costs on the targets of the ruling. By costs I mean financial burdens (like fines) or reputational costs (like public exposure in the media, scandals, reprimands from superiors). Thus, when oversight mechanisms are used, we should find evidence of those costs and/or we should observe decisions and behaviors that track and respond to those costs

For rulings where the legal constituency is dense (but oversight mechanisms are not deployed):

- On their own, the presence of legal constituencies is associated with judicial cascades, that is, a subsequent stream of directly related cases and decisions that try to extend the benefits of one particular ruling to other actors.
- We should observe mobilization around the ruling that can be directly linked to the legal constituency (media attention, political pressure).
- We should observe efforts by legal advocacy organizations to exercise follow-up and monitor the decision. These efforts might include, for example, petitions to government agencies or service providers, the production of progress reports by NGOs, among others.

- Where there is a dense legal constituency, we will observe the legal constituency – working on its own – generating information on compliance with the ruling and the issue.
- In line with prior research (McCann), we should observe changes in the way people involved in mobilization strategies perceive the issue.

For rulings where the legal constituency is dense AND oversight mechanisms are used (that is, where collaborative oversight arenas are configured):

- We should observe all the effects above (that is, those associated only with legal constituencies or only with oversight mechanism). In addition:
- Because collaborative oversight arenas generate spaces for interaction and the flow of information, we should see the use of monitoring information by the legal advocacy organizations and others.
- We should also see that the input from the legal constituency (and potentially other participants in the process) in the context of oversight informs the court's monitoring of the ruling.
- We should see those who participate in the oversight arena engaging in actions geared toward holding the targets of the ruling accountable either through follow-up of the court's original decisions or through crafting other related requests.
- We should observe the emergence of policy that is created and modified with participation from and in response to the input from the constituency and actors involved in oversight venues.
- We should observe the diffusion of ideas (policy and normative ideas like the rights-based framework) as the legal constituency uses institutional oversight spaces oversight to further diffuse information and ideas.
- We should also observe sustained changes in visibility of the issue in public opinion (in the media) and, importantly, in actors or groups beyond those who are direct parties to the process.

APPENDIX B: KEY SUPREME COURT OF INDIA ORDERS ON TPDS AND MIDDAY MEAL

Source: Mander 2012

Targeted Public Distribution System (TPDS) – Court Order Summary

1. Both BPL and APL are entitled to 35 kg of food grain at a subsidized price.
2. A fixed address is not a requirement to get a ration card. Homeless people are entitled to ration cards.

3. Corruption committed under the Public Distribution System is commensurate with a criminal case under the Essential Commodities Act.
4. An eligible person denied the BPL–TPDS card can apply to an Appellate Authority in a district within thirty days of the incident. The authority concerned shall reach a decision within sixty days. While the appeal is pending, the aggrieved person shall be issued a temporary BPL–TPDS card.
5. The monthly ration shall be made available in installments.
6. It is the legal duty of all FPS owners to:
   - keep their shops open regularly
   - charge only the prescribed price
   - give the BPL cards to cardholders and not keep them at the Fair Price Shop
   - not make false entries on the BPL cards
   - not store or sell the food grain on the open market
   - not hand over an FPS to other person/organization.
7. The license of a shop-owner who does not comply with the above provisions shall be cancelled.

National Programme of Nutritional Support to Primary Education or Midday Meal (MDM) Scheme – Court Order Summary

1. The State Governments/Union Territories shall implement the MDM Scheme by providing every child in every government and government-assisted primary school with a prepared midday meal with a minimum content of 300 calories and 8–12 g of protein each day of school for a minimum of 200 days (SC Order dated 28 November 2001).
2. A midday meal has to be provided to every schoolchild throughout the summer vacation in all drought-affected areas (SC Order dated 20 April 2004).
3. A midday meal has to be free of cost to all schoolchildren under any circumstances (SC Order dated 20 April 2004).
4. Preference shall be given to Dalits, Scheduled Castes, and Scheduled Tribes in the appointment of cooks/helpers (SC Order dated 20 April 2004).
5. The Central Government is directed to allot provisions for the construction of kitchen sheds and also to contribute to the cooking costs of the midday meal (SC Order dated 20 April 2004).
6. State governments are directed to apportion provisions for quality infrastructure; facilities, that is, drinking water and toilets; monitoring, for example, regular inspection; and other safeguards to ensure a nutritious

meal is provided to children at primary schools (SC Order dated 20 April 2004).

7. The Central Government is directed to allocate funds to meet the conversion costs of food grain into cooked midday meals. Provisions also have to be allocated for the construction of kitchen sheds and improvement of infrastructure and other facilities for the delivery of the midday meal.

References

Abramovich, Victor E. 2005. "Courses of Action in Economics, Social and Cultural Rights: Instruments and Allies." *Sur – International Journal on Human Rights* 2: 194–232. https://doi.org/10.1590/S1806-64452005000100009.

ACHC. 2012. "La Cartera Hospitalaria Sigue Creciendo, Ya Supera Los 4 Billones de Pesos." Bogotá: Asociación Colombiana de Clínicas y Hospitales.

ACIJ, and Junta Vecinal de Villa Inflamable. 2012. "Villa Inflamable: Donde Comenzó El Caso 'Mendoza' Los Derechos Siguen Esperando." Buenos Aires.

ACUMAR. 2022, April 8. *Basurales remanentes de la Línea de Base, por tipología*. ACUMAR. www.acumar.gob.ar/indicadores/basurales-remanente-linea-base/

ADC. 2008. *La Corte y los derechos: 2005–2007*. Buenos Aires: Siglo Veintiuno.

Albarracín, Mauricio. 2022. "Moviendo La Constitución: Reconocimiento Del Matrimonio Igualitario En Colombia." In *Activismo Judicial: Como Deciden Los Tribunales Constitucionales de América Latina. Un Análisis a Partir Del Matrimonio Igualitario*, edited by Marie-Christine Fuchs and Mônia Clarissa Hennig Leal, 181–232. Bogotá: KAS/Temis.

Albisa, Cathy, and Amanda Shanor. 2017. "United States: Education Rights and the Parameters of the Possible." In *Social Rights Judgments and the Politics of Compliance: Making It Stick*, edited by Malcolm Langford, César Rodríguez Garavito, and Julieta Rossi, 255–86. New York: Cambridge University Press.

Alizada, Nazifa, Rowan Cole, Lisa Gastaldi, et al. 2021. "Autocratization Turns Viral: Democracy Report 2021." V-Dem Institute, University of Gothenburg, Gothenburg.

Andreassen, Bård-Anders, and Gordon Crawford. 2013. *Human Rights, Power and Civic Action: Comparative Analyses of Struggles for Rights in Developing Societies*. Routledge Research in Human Rights 5. Abingdon: Routledge.

Ansolabehere, Karina. 2013. "More Power, More Rights? The Supreme Court and Society in Mexico." In *Cultures of Legality: Judicialization and Political Activism in Latin America*, edited by Javier Couso, Alexandra Huneeus, and Rachel Sieder, 78–111. New York: Cambridge University Press.

Ansolabehere, Karina, Sandra Botero, and Ezequiel González Gonzalez-Ocantos. 2022. "Conceptualizar y medir la cultura legal. Evidencia a partir de una encuesta a Jueces Federales Mexicanos." *Política y gobierno* 29 (2). www.politicaygobierno.cide.edu/index.php/pyg/article/view/1497.

Attrill, Martin. 1998. *A Rehabilitated Estuarine Ecosystem: The Environment and Ecology of the Thames Estuary*. Dordrecht: Kluwer.

Auditoría General de la Nación, Argentina. 2016. "Informe de Auditoría."

Banik, Dan. 2010. "Governing a Giant: The Limits of Judicial Activism on Hunger in India." *Journal of Asian Public Policy* 3 (3): 263–80. https://doi.org/10.1080/17516234.2010.536343.

Barrera, Leticia, and Jimena Sáenz. 2020. "Corte Suprema y participación ciudadana: reflexiones a partir de una audiencia pública de la Corte argentina." *Estudios Socio-Jurídicos* 22 (1): 263–91. https://doi.org/10.12804/revistas.urosario.edu.co/sociojuridicos/a.8069.

Barreto Valderrama, Francisco. 2012. "La Crisis Del Sistema UPAC Como Crisis Social y Su Dimensión Jurídica: Política, Regulación y Neoconstitucionalismo." In *Los Actores En La Crisis Económica de Fin de Siglo*, edited by Miguel Urrutia and Jorge Llano, 101–62. Bogotá: Universidad de Los Andes.

Baviskar, Amita. 2012. "Public Interest and Private Compromises: The Politics of Environmental Negotiation in India." In *Law against the State: Ethnographic Forays into Law's Transformations*, edited by Julia M. Eckert, 171–201. Cambridge Studies in Law and Society. Cambridge: Cambridge University Press.

Benedetti, Miguel Ángel, and Jimena Sáenz. 2016. *Las Audiencias Públicas de la Corte Suprema: Apertura y límites de la Participación Ciudadana en la Justicia*. Derecho y Política Ser. Buenos Aires: Siglo XXI Editores.

Bergallo, Paola. 2006. "Justicia Y Experimentalismo: La Función Remedial Del Poder Judicial En El Litigio de Derecho Publico En Argentina." In *Derecho Y Pobreza*, edited by Roberto Saba. Buenos Aires: SELA.

2014. "La Causa Mendoza: Una Experiencia de Judicialización Cooperativa Sobre El Derecho a La Salud." In *Por Una Justicia Dialógica: El Poder Judicial Como Promotor de La Deliberación Democrática*, edited by Roberto Gargarella, 245–91. Buenos Aires: Siglo XXI Editores.

Bertranou, Fabio, Oscar Cetrángolo, Carlos Grushka, and Luis Casanova. 2011. *Encrucijadas En La Seguridad Social Argentina: Reformas, Cobertura y Desafíos Para El Sistema de Pensiones*. Buenos Aires: CEPAL/Organización Internacional del Trabajo.

Bhuwania, Anuj. 2017. *Courting the People: Public Interest Litigation in Post-Emergency India*. Cambridge: Cambridge University Press.

2018. "The Case That Felled a City: Examining the Politics of Indian Public Interest Litigation through One Case." *South Asia Multidisciplinary Academic Journal* 17 (March): 1–25. https://doi.org/10.4000/samaj.4469.

Birchfield, Lauren, and Jessica Corsi. 2009. "Between Starvation and Globalization: Realizing the Right to Food in India." *Michigan Journal of International Law* 31: 691.

Bonilla Maldonado, Daniel. 2013. *Constitutionalism of the Global South: The Activist Tribunals of India, South Africa, and Colombia*. Cambridge: Cambridge University Press.

Botero, Sandra. 2018. "Agents of Neoliberalism? High Courts, Legal Preferences and Rights in Latin America." In *Latin America since the Left Turn*, edited by Tulia Falleti and Emilio Parrado, 214–40. Democracy, Citizenship, and Constitutionalism. Philadelphia: University of Pennsylvania Press.

2020. "Confianza, Apoyo a La Democracia y Corrupción: Una Mirada a La Corte Constitucional Colombiana En La Opinión Pública." *Latin American Law Review* 4 (January): 25–47. https://doi.org/10.29263/lar04.2020.02.

Botero, Sandra, and Daniel M. Brinks. 2023. "The Politics of Judicial Impact in Social and Economic Rights Cases." In *The Oxford Handbook of Economic and Social Rights*, edited by Malcolm Langford and Katharine Young. Oxford: Oxford University Press (online edn, Oxford Academic, 18 Aug. 2022). https://doi.org/10.1093/oxfordhb/9780197550021.013.15, accessed 9 June 2023.

Botero, Sandra, Daniel M. Brinks, and Ezequiel A. Gonzalez-Ocantos, eds. 2022. *The Limits of Judicialization: Progress and Backlash in Latin American Politics*. New York: Cambridge University Press.

Brinks, Daniel M., and Abby Blass. 2018. *The DNA of Constitutional Justice in Latin America: Politics, Governance, and Judicial Design*. Cambridge. New York: Cambridge University Press. https://doi.org/10.1017/9781316823538.

Brinks, Daniel M., and William Forbath. 2014. "The Role of Courts and Constitutions in the New Politics of Welfare in Latin America." In *Law and Development of Middle-Income Countries: Avoiding the Middle-Income Trap*, edited by Randall P. Peerenboom and Tom Ginsburg, pp. 221–245. New York: Cambridge University Press.

Brinks, Daniel M., Siri Gloppen, and Bruce Wilson. 2012. "Transforming Environmental Conflicts through Law: A Framework for the Study of Water, Rights, and the Politics of Human Development." In *Paper Presented at the Annual Conference of the Law and Society Association, Honolulu, HI, June 5–8, 2012*.

Brinks, Daniel M., M. V. Murillo, and S. Levitsky, eds. 2020. *The Politics of Institutional Weakness in Latin America*. Cambridge: Cambridge University Press.

Bryerley, Alissa. 2019. "PUCL v. Union of India Political Mobilization and the Right to Food." In *A Qualified Hope: The Indian Supreme Court and Progressive Social Change*, edited by Gerald N Rosenberg, Sudhir Krishnaswamy, and Shishir Bail, 212–42. Cambridge ; New York: Cambridge University Press.

Bustamante, Thomas, and Emilio Peluso Neder Meyer. 2022. "The Brazilian Federal Supreme Court's Reaction to Bolsonaro." *Verfassungsblog* (blog). September 26, 2022. https://verfassungsblog.de/the-brazilian-federal-supreme-courts-reaction-to-bolsonaro/.

Calderón Lopez, José Miguel. 2002. "El Rol Político de Los Jueces En El Trazado de La Regulación Económica: El Caso Del Sistema UPAC." MA Thesis, Bogota: Universidad Javeriana.

Cano Blandón, Luisa Fernanda. 2017. "Constitucionalismo Experimental y Protección Judicial Del Derecho al Agua En Colombia." PhD Dissertation, Bogotá, Colombia: Universidad de Los Andes.

2021. "Los límites de la justicia dialógica en la protección de los derechos sociales en Colombia." *Revista Derecho del Estado*, 49 (April): 131–58. https://doi.org/10.18601/01229893.n49.08.

Castillo-Ortiz, Pablo. 2019. "The Illiberal Abuse of Constitutional Courts in Europe." *European Constitutional Law Review* 15 (1): 48–72. https://doi.org/10.1017/S1574019619000026.

Cavanagh, Ralph, and Austin Sarat. 1980. "Thinking about Courts: Toward and Beyond a Jurisprudence of Judicial Competence." *Law & Society Review* 14 (2): 371–420. https://doi.org/10.2307/3053318.

CELS. 2004. *Derechos humanos en Argentina: Informe 2004*. Buenos Aires: CELS and Siglo XXI.

Derechos humanos en la Argentina: Informe 2007. Buenos Aires: Siglo XXI Editores.

"En Busca de Soluciones Judiciales Para Mejorar La Calidad de Vida de Los Habitantes de La Cuenca Matanza-Riachuelo." In *Derechos Humanos En Argentina: Informe 2009*. CELS/Siglo XXI.

"El Modelo de La Prisión Depósito. Medidas Urgentes En Los Lugares de Detención En La Argentina." In *Derechos Humanos En La Argentina: Informe 2012*, 183–255. Buenos Aires: Siglo XXI Editores.

Cepeda, Manuel José. 2011. "Social and Economic Rights and the Colombian Constitutional Court." In Texas Law Review Symposium, Latin American Constitutionalism, Social and Economic Rights Panel, University of Texas at Austin, March 4.

Chandra, Shekhar. 2018. "Why Delhi's Air Pollution Problem Never Gets Solved." June 20, 2018. www.livemint.com/Opinion/Cq1XFnxfqjkKyA8mRIsg2M/Why-Delhis-air-pollution-problem-never-gets-solved.html.

CIPPES. 2013. *Pobreza E Indigencia En Argentina*. Buenos Aires: Centro de Investigaciones Participativas en Políticias Económicas y Sociales.

Clavijo, Sergio. 2007. "Impacto Económico de Algunas Sentencias de La Corte: El Caso de La 'Mesada Pensional 14' y de Las Regulaciones En Vivienda." In *Dialogo Entre Abogados y Economistas Sobre Aspectos Económicos de La Constitución*. Bogotá: Ministerio de Hacienda.

Colombia, Corte Constitucional. 2017. T-302 2017. M.P. Aquiles Arrieta.

Comité contra la Tortura. 2007. *El Sistema de La Crueldad. Informe Sobre Violaciones a Los Derechos Humanos En Los Lugares de Detención de La Provincia de Buenos Aires. 2006–2007*. La Plata: Comité Contra la Tortura, Comisión por la Memoria de la Provincia de Buenos Aires.

Comité contra la Tortura. 2012. *Informe Anual 2012*. La Plata: Comité contra la Tortura.

Comité por la Memoria. 2018. "Informe Anual 2018. El Sistema de La Crueldad XII." Comité por la Memoria.

Corte Constitucional de Colombia, Sala de Seguimiento de la T-760 2008. n.d. "Seguimiento Al Cumplimiento de La Sentencia T-760 de 2008."

CSR. 2010. "Pacto Social Por El Derecho a La Salud."

Cuerpo Colegiado. 2016. "Cuerpo Colegiado: Sobre El Proceso de Saneamiento Del Riachuelo."

Cuellar, Maria Mercedes. 2006. *¿A la Vivienda quien la ronda?* Tomo I. Bogota: Universidad Externado.

Defensoría del Pueblo, Colombia. 2010. "La Tutela y El Derecho a La Salud 2009." Bogota: Defensoría del Pueblo.

"La Tutela y El Derecho a La Salud 2010." Bogota: Defensoría del Pueblo.

"La Tutela y El Derecho a La Salud 2011." Bogota: Defensoría del Pueblo.

Defensor del Pueblo de la Nación. 2014. *Residuos y basurales: Escrito presentado en el Expediente Causa Matanza Riachuelo N° 311/05*. http://dpn.gob.ar/articulo.php?id=3109&pagN=6.

Defensor del Pueblo de la Nación, Asociación Vecinos de la Boca, CELS, Defensoría Adjunta de la CABA, FARN, Fundación Ciudadano, and Universidad Tecnologica Nacional. 2003. "Informe Especial Sobre La Cuenca Matanza – Riachuelo." Buenos Aires.

Dixon, Rosalind. 2007. "Creating Dialogue about Socioeconomic Rights: Strong-Form versus Weak-Form Judicial Review Revisited." *International Journal of Constitutional Law* 5 (3): 391–418.

Dixon, Rosalind, and Rishad Chowdhury. 2019. "A Case for Qualified Hope? The Supreme Court of India and the Midday Meal Decision." In *A Qualified Hope: The Indian Supreme Court and Progressive Social Change*, edited by Gerald N Rosenberg, Sudhir Krishnaswamy, and Shishir Bail, 243–68. Cambridge; New York: Cambridge University Press.

Dreyfus, Magali. 2013. "The Judiciary's Role in Environmental Governance." *Environmental Policy and Law* 9: 167.

Drèze, Jean. 2006. "Universalisation with Quality: ICDS in a Rights Perspective." *Economic and Political Weekly* August: 3706–15.

Drèze, Jean, and Aparajita Goyal. 2003. "Future of Mid-Day Meals." *Economic and Political Weekly* 38 (44): 4673–83. https://doi.org/10.2307/4414222.

Drèze, Jean, and Reetika Khera. 2013. "Rural Poverty and the Public Distribution System." *Economic and Political Weekly* XLVIII (45–46): 55–60.

Dugard, Jackie. 2022. "Water Rights Struggles in Johannesburg and Detroit Revisited: Looking Beyond Courts at the Politics and Power of Rights-Based Legal Mobilization in a Neoliberal Global Order: A 'Powerpack' Analysis." *Journal of Human Rights Practice* 15 (1): 1–23. https://doi.org/10.1093/jhuman/huac011.

Epp, Charles R. 1998. *The Rights Revolution: Lawyers, Activists, and Supreme Courts in Comparative Perspective*. Chicago: University of Chicago Press.

Epstein, Lee, and Jack Knight. 2013. "Reconsidering Judicial Preferences." *Annual Review of Political Science* 16 (1): 11–31. https://doi.org/10.1146/annurev-polisci-032211-214229.

Epstein, Lee, Jack Knight, and Olga Shvetsova. 2001. "The Role of Constitutional Courts in the Establishment and Maintenance of Democratic Systems of Government." *Law & Society Review* 35 (1): 117. https://doi.org/10.2307/3185388.

FARN. 2014. "Boletin FARN No. 28." Fundación Ambiente y Recursos Naturales.

FARN, CELS, Greenpea, ACDH, and Vecinos de la Boca. 2017. "9 Años Del Fallo de La Corte. Una Política de Estado Todavía Ausente."

Feeley, Malcolm. 1998. *Judicial Policy Making and the Modern State: How the Courts Reformed America's Prisons*. Cambridge: Cambridge University Press.

Ferraz, Octavio. 2011. "Brazil : Health Inequalities, Rights, and Courts : The Social Impact of the Judicialization of Health." In *Litigating Health Rights: Can Courts Bring More Justice to Health*, edited by Alicia Ely Yamin and Siri Gloppen, 76–102. Human Rights Program Practice Series. Cambridge, MA: Human Rights Program, Harvard Law School: Harvard University Press.

Fillipini, Leonardo. n.d. "Superpoblación Carcelaria y Hábeas Corpus Colectivo." Buenos Aires.

Forero Alba, Sofia, and Juan Carlos Rodriguez Raga. 2022. "Courting Judicial Legitimacy: An Experimental Study of the Colombian Constitutional Court." In *The Limits of Judicialization: Progress and Backlash in Latin American Politics*, edited by Sandra Botero, Daniel M. Brinks, and Ezequiel A. Gonzalez-Ocantos, 164–94. Cambridge: Cambridge University Press.

Forero, Efraín. 2014. "Evolution of the Mortgage System in Colombia: From the UPAC to the UVR." *Housing Finance International* 18 (3): 32–41.

Fundación Metropolitana. 2018, July. *La cuenca del Matanza Riachuelo a 10 años del fallo Mendoza*. Fundación Metropolitana. https://metropolitana.org.ar/idm/la-cuenca-del-matanza-riachuelo-a-10-anos-del-fallo-mendoza/.

Galanter, Marc. 1974. "Why the Haves Come out Ahead: Speculations on the Limits of Legal Change." *Law & Society Review* 9: 95.

Gargarella, Roberto. 2014a. "Deliberative Democracy, Dialogic Justice and the Promise of Social and Economic Rights." In *Social and Economic Rights in Theory and Practice*, edited by Helena Alviar Garcia, Karl Klare, and Lucy A. Williams, 105–20. New York: Routledge.

2014b. "El nuevo constitucionalismo dialógico frente al sistema de los frenos y contrapesos." In *Por una justicia dialógica: el poder judicial como promotor de la deliberación democrática*, edited by Roberto Gargarella, 119–58. Buenos Aires: Siglo XXI Editores Argentina.

Gauri, Varun, and Daniel M. Brinks, eds. 2008. *Courting Social Justice: Judicial Enforcement of Social and Economic Rights in the Developing World*. Cambridge; New York: Cambridge University Press.

Gauri, Varun, Jeffrey K. Staton, and Jorge Vargas Cullell. 2015. "The Costa Rican Supreme Court's Compliance Monitoring System." *The Journal of Politics* 77 (3): 774–86. https://doi.org/10.1086/681260.

George, Alexander L., and Andrew Bennett. 2005. *Case Studies and Theory Development in the Social Sciences*. Cambridge, MA: MIT Press.

Gerring, J., and L. Cojocaru. 2016. "Selecting Cases for Intensive Analysis: A Diversity of Goals and Methods." *Sociological Methods & Research* 45 (3): 392–423.

Gianella-Malca, Camila, Siri Gloppen, and Elisabeth Fosse. 2013. "Giving Effect to Children's Right to Health in Colombia? Analysing the Implementation of Court Decisions Ordering Health System Reform." *Journal of Human Rights Practice* 5 (1): 153–76. https://doi.org/10.1093/jhuman/hus035.

Gianella-Malca, Camila, Oscar Parra Vera, Alicia Ely Yamin, and Mauricio Torres Tovar. 2009. "¿Deliberación Democrática O Mercadeo Social? Los Dilemas de La Definición Pública En Salud En El Contexto Del Seguimiento de La Sentencia T–760 de 2008." Health and Human Rights.

Gibson, James L., Gregory A. Caldeira, and Vanessa A. Baird. 1998. "On the Legitimacy of National High Courts." *American Political Science Review* 92 (2): 343–58. https://doi.org/10.2307/2585668.

Gillman, Howard. 1999. "The Court as an Idea, Not a Building (or a Game): Interpretive Institutionalism and the Analysis of Supreme Court Decision-Making." In *Supreme Court Decision-Making: New Institutionalist Approaches*, edited by Cornell W. Clayton and Howard Gillman, 65–87. Chicago: Chicago University Press.

Gloppen, Siri. 2008. "Litigation as a Strategy to Hold Governments Accountable for Implementing the Right to Health." *Health and Human Rights* 10 (2): 21–36.

2011. "Litigating Health Rights: Framing the Analysis." In *Litigating Health Rights: Can Courts Bring More Justice to Health*, edited by Alicia Ely Yamin and Siri Gloppen. Human Rights Program Practice Series, 17–42. Cambridge, MA: Human Rights Program, Harvard Law School: Harvard University Press.

Gloppen, Siri, Roberto Gargarella, and Elin Skaar, eds. 2004. *Democratization and the Judiciary the Accountability Function of Courts in New Democracies*. London/Portland: Frank Cass.

Goertz, Gary. 2006. *Social Science Concepts: A User's Guide*. Princeton: Princeton University Press.

Gonzalez Velez, Ana Cristina, and Isabel Cristina Jaramillo Sierra. 2020. *La Batalla Por El Derecho al Aborto*. Bogota: Siglo del Hombre Editores | Universidad de Los Andes | La Mesa por la Vida y la Salud de las Mujeres.

Gonzalez-Ocantos, Ezequiel A. 2016. *Shifting Legal Visions: Judicial Change and Human Rights Trials in Latin America*. Cambridge: Cambridge University Press.

Greenpeace Argentina. 2013. "Las Aguas Siguen Bajando Turbias: Análisis Sobre La Calidad Ambiental de Las Aguas Superficiales En La Cuenca Matanza-Riachuelo. Campañas ACUMAR 2008–2012." Buenos Aires: Greenpeace.

Guha-Khasnobis, Basudeb, and S Vivēkānanda. 2007. *Rights-Based Approach to Development Lessons from the Right to Food Movement in India*. Helsinki, Finland: UNU World Inst. for Development Economics Research (UNU/WIDER).

Gutiérrez Beltrán, Andrés Mauricio. 2018. *El Amparo Estructural de Los Derechos*. Madrid: Centro de Estudios Políticos y Constitucionales.

Gutiérrez, Ricardo, and María Gabriela Merlinsky. 2011. "En Los Confines de La Política Ambiental: Gestión Municipal y Articulación Interjurisdiccional En La Región Metropolitana de Buenos Aires." In X Congreso Nacional de Ciencia Política Argentina, Córdoba, Argentina.

Guttikunda, Sarath K., and Rahul Goel. 2013. "Health Impacts of Particulate Pollution in a Megacity—Delhi, India." *Environmental Development* 6 (April): 8–20. https://doi.org/10.1016/j.envdev.2012.12.002.

Hall, Peter. 2003. "Aligning Ontology and Methodology in Comparative Research." In *Comparative Historical Analysis in the Social Sciences*, edited by James Mahoney and Dietrich Rueschemeyer, 373–404. Cambridge: Cambridge University Press.

Hernández Álvarez, Mario, and Mauricio Torres Tovar. 2010. "Colombia's New Health Reform: Helping Keep the Financial Sector Healthy." *Social Medicine* 5 (4): 177–81.

Herrero, Álvaro. 2011. "La incidencia de la Corte Suprema de Justicia en la formulación de políticas públicas: una exploración empírica del caso argentino." *Política. Revista de Ciencia Política* 49 (1): 71/106. https://doi.org/10.5354/rp.v49i1.16311.

Hertel, Shareen. 2015. "Hungry for Justice: Social Mobilization on the Right to Food in India: Social Mobilization on the Right to Food in India." *Development and Change* 46 (1): 72–94. https://doi.org/10.1111/dech.12144.

Hibbing, John R., and Elizabeth Theiss-Morse. 2002. *Stealth Democracy: Americans' Beliefs About How Government Should Work*. Cambridge: Cambridge University Press.

Hilbink, Lisa. 2011. *Judges beyond Politics in Democracy and Dictatorship: Lessons from Chile*. New York: Cambridge University Press.

Hirschl, Ran. 2004. *Towards Juristocracy: The Origins and Consequences of the New Constitutionalism*. Cambridge, MA: Harvard University Press.

Hirschl, Ran, and Evan Rosevear. 2011. "Constitutional Law Meets Comparative Politics: Socio-Economic Rights and Political Realities." In *The Legal Protection of Human Rights: Sceptical Essays*, edited by Tom Campbell, K.D. Ewing, and Adam Tomkins, 207–228. New York: Oxford University Press.

Horowitz, Donald L. 1977. *The Courts and Social Policy*. Washington: Brookings Institution.

Howse, Robert, and Ruti Teitel. 2010. "Beyond Compliance: Rethinking Why International Law Really Matters: Beyond Compliance." *Global Policy* 1 (2): 127–36. https://doi.org/10.1111/j.1758-5899.2010.00035.x.

Huq, Aziz Z. 2018. "Democratic Erosion and the Courts: Comparative Perspectives." *New York University Law Review* 93 (21): 21–31.

Jackson, Michael, and Armin Rosencranz. 2003. "The Delhi Pollution Case: Can the Supreme Court Manage the Environment?" *Environmental Policy and Law* 33 (2): 88–91.

Jayaraman, Rajshri, and Dora Simroth. 2011. "The Impact of School Lunches on Primary School Enrollment: Evidence from India's Midday Meal Scheme." https://papers.ssrn.com/sol3/papers.cfm?abstract_id=1969396.

Jimenez Gil, William. 2010. *Pierre Bourdieu y La Racionalidad Jurídica Como Instrumento de Subyugación: Análisis de La Crisis de Los Deudores Individuales de Créditos Hipotecarios En UPAC a La Luz de La Teoriética Del Campo Jurídico*. Bogota: Universidad La Gran Colombia.

Kapiszewski, Diana. 2012. *High Courts and Economic Governance in Argentina and Brazil*. Cambridge: Cambridge University Press.

Kapiszewski, Diana, and Matthew M. Taylor. 2013. "Compliance: Conceptualizing, Measuring, and Explaining Adherence to Judicial Rulings." *Law & Social Inquiry* 38 (4): 803–35.

Kathuria, Vinish. 2004. "Impact of CNG on Vehicular Pollution in Delhi: A Note." *Transportation Research Part D: Transport and Environment* 9 (5): 409–17. https://doi.org/10.1016/j.trd.2004.05.003.

Keck, Thomas M. 2009. "Beyond Backlash: Assessing the Impact of Judicial Decisions on LGBT Rights." *Law & Society Review* 43 (1): 151–86.

2014. *Judicial Politics in Polarized Times*. EBSCOhost EBook Collection. Chicago: The University of Chicago Press.

Khera, R. 2011. "Revival of the Public Distribution System: Evidence and Explanations." *Economic and Political Weekly* XLVI (44–45), 36–50.

Klarman, Michael J. 2004. *From Jim Crow to Civil Rights: The Supreme Court and the Struggle for Racial Equality*. New York: Oxford University Press.

Krishnan, Preethi, and Mangala Subramaniam. 2014. "Understanding the State: Right to Food Campaign in India." *The Global South* 8 (2): 101–18.

Kureshi, Yasser. 2022. "To Reinforce or Replace: Judicial Roles and Democratic Backsliding." Manuscript.

Landau, David. 2012. "Landau (2012) The Reality of Social Rights Enforcement." *Harvard International Law Journal* 53: 190–247.

Langford, Malcolm. 2014a. "Housing Rights Litigation: Grootboom and Beyond." In *Socio-Economic Rights in South Africa: Symbols or Substance?*, edited by Malcolm Langford, Ben Cousins, Jackie Dugard, and Tshepo Madlingozi, 187–225. New York: Cambridge University Press.

2014b. "Introduction." In *Socio-Economic Rights in South Africa: Symbols or Substance?*, edited by Malcolm Langford, Ben Cousins, Jackie Dugard, and Tshepo Madlingozi, 1–32. New York: Cambridge University Press.

2021. "The Impact of Public Interest Litigation: The Case of Socio-Economic Rights." *Australian Journal of Human Rights* 27 (3): 505–31. https://doi.org/10.1080/1323238X.2022.2030039.

Langford, Malcolm, Ben Cousins, Jackie Dugard, and Tshepo Madlingozi, eds. 2014. *Socio-Economic Rights in South Africa: Symbols or Substance?* New York: Cambridge University Press.

Langford, Malcolm, and Steven Kahanovitz. 2017. "South Africa: Rethinking Enforcement Narratives." In *Social Rights Judgments and the Politics of Compliance: Making It Stick*, edited by Malcolm Langford, César Rodríguez Garavito, and Julieta Rossi, 315–350. New York: Cambridge University Press. https://doi.org/10.1017/9781316673058.

Langford, Malcolm, César Rodríguez Garavito, and Julieta Rossi, eds. 2017. *Social Rights Judgments and the Politics of Compliance: Making It Stick*. New York: Cambridge University Press. https://doi.org/10.1017/9781316673058.

Larkins, Cristopher. 1998. "The Judiciary and Delegative Democracy in Argentina." *Comparative Politics* 30 (4): 423–43.

Leal, Fernando, and Thomaz Pereira. 2022. "The Court, the Text, and the Struggle for Constitutional Fidelity in Brazil." *Verfassungsblog* (blog). September 26, 2022. https://verfassungsblog.de/the-court-the-text-and-the-struggle-for-constitutional-fidelity-in-brazil/.

Liebenberg, Sandra. 2014. "Participatory Approaches to Socio-Economic Rights Adjudication: Tentative Lessons from South African Evictions Law." *Nordic Journal of Human Rights* 32 (4): 312–30. https://doi.org/10.1080/18918131.2015.957462.

Linzer, Drew A., and Jeffrey K. Staton. 2015. "A Global Measure of Judicial Independence, 1948–2012." *Journal of Law and Courts* 3 (2): 223–56. https://doi.org/10.1086/682150.

López Sánchez, Ericka. 2021. “Las cortes supremas y los derechos LGBT en América Latina.” *Revista de Estudios Políticos* 194 (December): 157–88. https://doi.org/10.18042/cepc/rep.194.06.

Madlingozi, Tshepo. 2014. “Post-Apartheid Social Movements and Legal Mobilisation.” In *Socio-Economic Rights in South Africa: Symbols or Substance?*, edited by Malcolm Langford, Ben Cousins, Jackie Dugard, and Tshepo Madlingozi, 92–130. New York: Cambridge University Press.

Mahoney, James. 2003. “Strategies of Causal Assessment in Comparative Historical Analysis.” In *Comparative Historical Analysis in the Social Sciences*, edited by James Mahoney and Dietrich Rueschemeyer, 337–72. Cambridge: Cambridge University Press.

2012. “The Logic of Process Tracing Tests in the Social Sciences.” *Sociological Methods & Research* 41 (4): 550–97.

Mahoney, James, and Dietrich Rueschemeyer, eds. 2003. *Comparative Historical Analysis in the Social Sciences*. Cambridge: Cambridge University Press.

Mander, Harsh. 2012. “Food from the Courts: The Indian Experience.” *IDS Bulletin* 43 (s1): 15–24.

Mathur, Kuldeep. 2004. “Battling for Clean Environment: Supreme Court, Technocrats and Populist Politics in Delhi.” Working Paper, #1, Working Paper Series, Centre for the Study of Law and Governance Jawaharlal Nehru University, New Delhi.

McAdam, Doug, and Richard Scott. 2005. “Organizations and Movements.” In *Social Movements and Organization Theory*, edited by Gerald F. Davis, Doug McAdam, William Richard, Scott Mayer, and Nathan Zald, 4–40. Cambridge Studies in Contentious Politics. Cambridge; New York: Cambridge University Press.

McCann, Michael. 1994. *Rights at Work: Pay Equity Reform and the Politics of Legal Mobilization*. Language and Legal Discourse. Chicago: University of Chicago Press.

1996. “Causal versus Constitutive Explanations (or, On the Difficulty of Being so Positive…).” *Law & Social Inquiry* 21 (2): 457–82.

McCubbins, Mathew D., and Thomas Schwartz. 1984. “Congressional Oversight Overlooked: Police Patrols versus Fire Alarms.” *American Journal of Political Science* 28 (1): 165. https://doi.org/10.2307/2110792.

Menon, Nivedita. 2014. “Environment and the Will to Rule: Supreme Court and Public Interest Litigation in the 1990s.” In *The Shifting Scales of Justice: The Supreme Court in Neo-Liberal India*, edited by Mayur Suresh and Siddharth Narrain, 59–78. New Delhi: Orient BlackSwan.

Merlinsky, María Gabriela. 2009. “Atravesando El Rio: La Construcción Social y Política de La Cuestión Ambiental En Argentina.” PhD Dissertation, Paris/Buenos Aires: Facultad de Ciencias Sociales, Universidad de Buenos Aires / Paris 8.

2016. “Efectos de las causas estructurales en el largo plazo: la causa Riachuelo.” *Revista Direito e Práxis* 7 (14): 397–420. https://doi.org/10.12957/dep.2016.22954.

Ministerio de Justicia, Provincia de Buenos Aires. 2010. “Informe Casal (Respuesta a La Resolución de La Corte Suprema de Justicia de La Provincia de Buenos Aires).” La Plata.

Moog, Robert. 2019. “Implementation in the Delhi Pollution Case.” In *A Qualified Hope: The Indian Supreme Court and Progressive Social Change*, edited by Gerald N Rosenberg, Sudhir Krishnaswamy, and Shishir Bail, 269–92. Cambridge; New York: Cambridge University Press.

Muñoz, Andrea Juliana, Bonnie Dayana García, and Rosa Angélica Lara. 2007. “Derecho Del Medio Ambiente y Mecanismos de Participación Ciudadana En El Canal Bogotá (San José de Cúcuta).” Cucuta: Universidad Libre.

Nader, Esteban. 2022. *Constitución, Justicia Ambiental y Derechos*. Instituto de Estudios Constitucionales del Estado de Queretaro.

Napoli, Andres. 2009. "Una Política de Estado Para El Riachuelo. Informe Ambiental FARN." Buenos Aires: FARN.

Napoli, Andres, and Javier García Espil. 2011. "Riachuelo: Hacer Hoy Pensando En La Cuenca Del Mañana. Informe Ambiental FARN." Buenos Aires: FARN.

Narain, Urvashi, and Ruth Greenspan Bell. 2005. "Who Changed Delhi's Air? The Roles of the Court and the Executive in Environmental Policymaking." 05–48. Washington DC: Resources for the Future.

Nigam, A. 2014. "Embedded Judiciary: Or the Judicial State of Exception?" In *The Shifting Scales of Justice: The Supreme Court in Neo-Liberal India*, edited by M. Suresh and S. Narrain, 28–38. New Delhi: Orient BlackSwan.

Nunes, Rodrigo M. 2010. "Ideational Origins of Progressive Judicial Activism: The Colombian Constitutional Court and the Right to Health." *Latin American Politics and Society* 52 (3): 67–97.

O'Donnell, Guillermo. 1999. "Polyarchies and the (Un)Rule of Law in Latin America: A Partial Conclusion." In *The (Un) Rule of Law and the Underprivileged in Latin America*, edited by Juan E Méndez, Paulo Sérgio de Moraes Sarmento Pinheiro, and Guillermo A O'Donnell, 303–37. Notre Dame, IN: University of Notre Dame Press.

Orduz Salinas, Natalia. 2014. "La Consulta Previa En Colombia." 3. Documentos de Trabajo ICSO. Instituto de Investigación en Ciencias Sociales UDP.

Pande, Suchi, and Peter P. Houtzager. 2016. "Food Fight: Civil Society Innovation and Resilience in the Struggle for the Right to Food in India." IDS Working Paper, Brighton: IDS. www.researchgate.net/profile/Peter_Houtzager/publication/303406624_Food_Fight_Civil_Society_Innovation_and_Resilience_in_the_Struggle_for_the_Right_to_Food_in_India/links/5741e46408ae9f741b37541a.pdf.

Parra Vera, Oscar, and Alicia Ely Yamin. 2013. "La Sentencia T-760 de 2008, Su Implementación e Impacto: Retos y Oportunidades Para La Justicia Dialógica." In *Salud: Sobre (Des)Igualdades y Derechos*, edited by Laura Clérico, 2191–649. Buenos Aires: Abelardo Perrot.

Peruzzotti, Enrique, and Catalina Smulovitz. 2006. *Enforcing the Rule of Law: Social Accountability in the New Latin American Democracies*. Pitt Latin American Series. Pittsburgh: University of Pittsburgh Press.

Pierson, Paul. 2004. *Politics in Time: History, Institutions, and Social Analysis*. Princeton: Princeton University Press.

Puga, Mariela. 2012. *Litigio y Cambio Social En Argentina y Colombia*. Buenos Aires: CLACSO.

Rajamani, Lavanya. 2007. "Public Interest Environmental Litigation in India: Exploring Issues of Access, Participation, Equity, Effectiveness and Sustainability." *Journal of Environmental Law* 19 (3): 293–321. https://doi.org/10.1093/jel/eqm020.

Ravindra, Khaiwal, Eric Wauters, Sushil K. Tyagi, Suman Mor, and René Van Grieken. 2006. "Assessment of Air Quality After the Implementation of Compressed Natural Gas (CNG) as Fuel in Public Transport in Delhi, India." *Environmental Monitoring and Assessment* 115 (1): 405–17. https://doi.org/10.1007/s10661-006-7051-5.

Rich, Jessica. 2019. *State-Sponsored Activism: Bureaucrats and Social Movements in Democratic Brazil*. Cambridge: Cambridge University Press.

Roa, Jorge Ernesto. 2019. "Justicia constitucional, deliberación y democracia en Colombia: Jeremy Waldron reflexivo en Bogotá." *Revista Derecho del Estado* 44: 57–98.

Robertson, Graeme B. 2011. *The Politics of Protest in Hybrid Regimes*. New York: Cambridge University Press.

Rodríguez Garavito, César. 2010. "Beyond the Courtroom: The Impact of Judicial Activism on Socioeconomic Rights in Latin America." *Texas Law Review* 89: 1669.

2012. "La Judicialización de La Salud: Síntomas, Diagnósticos y Prescripciones." In *La Salud En Colombia: Logros, Retos y Recomendaciones*. edtied by Oscar Bernal and Catalina Gutiérrez, 507–60, Bogota: Universidad de Los Andes.

ed. 2022. *Litigating the Climate Emergency: How Human Rights, Courts, and Legal Mobilization Can Bolster Climate Action*. Globalization and Human Rights. Cambridge: Cambridge University Press. doi:10.1017/9781009106214.

Rodríguez Garavito, César, and Diana Rodríguez Franco. 2010. *Cortes y cambio social cómo la Corte Constitucional transformó el desplazamiento forzado en Colombia*. Bogotá: Dejusticia.

2015. *Radical Deprivation on Trial: The Impact of Judicial Activism on Socioeconomic Rights in the Global South*. Cambridge: Cambridge University Press.

Rodríguez, Gloria Amparo. 2008. "Contexto: La Participación y Consulta Previa." *Semillas* 36/37.

Rodríguez, Gloria Amparo, Andrés Gómez, and Carlos Lozano. 2011. *Protección Jurídica Del Agua En Colombia*. Bogotá: Grupo Editorial Ibañez.

Rodriguez, Peñaranda, Maria Luisa. 2021. "¿Logran las decisiones judiciales emancipar? Metodologías en el seguimiento del cumplimiento de las decisiones judiciales." In *Altas cortes y transformación social. (Des) obediencia a las órdenes judiciales*, edited by Maria Luisa Rodriguez Peñaranda, Daniel Ricardo Jimenez Estevez, and Fabián Andrés León Peñuela, 11–66. Bogotá: Universidad Nacional de Colombia.

Rodriguez, Peñaranda, Maria Luisa, Daniel Ricardo, Jimenez Estevez, and Fabián Andrés, León Peñuela. 2021. *Altas cortes y transformación social. (Des) obediencia a las órdenes judiciales*. Bogotá: Universidad Nacional de Colombia.

Rofman, Rafael. 2002. "The Pension System and the Crisis in Argentina: Learning the Lessons."

Rofman, Rafael, Eduardo Fajnzylber, and Germán Herrera. 2008. "Reforming the Pension Reforms: The Recent Initiatives and Actions on Pensions in Argentina and Chile." http://ssrn.com/abstract=1992438.

Romero-Prada, Martín, Rubén Marrugo-Figueroa, Germán Acero, Carlos Arango Bautista, and Nelson Alvis-Guzman. 2014. "Impacto En El Acceso a Medicamentos En La Población Colombiana Después de La Actualización Del Plan de Beneficios En El 2012." *Gerencia y Políticas de Salud* 13 (27): 228–41. https://doi.org/10.11144/11969.

Rosenberg, Gerald N. 2008. *The Hollow Hope: Can Courts Bring about Social Change?* Chicago; London: The University of Chicago Press.

Rosenberg, Gerald N, Sudhir Krishnaswamy, and Shishir Bail, eds. 2019. *A Qualified Hope: The Indian Supreme Court and Progressive Social Change*. Cambridge; New York: Cambridge University Press.

Rossi, Francisco, Luz Marina Umbacía, and Edna Sanchez. 2012. "Inclusiones de Medicamentos Incorporados En El Plan Obligatorio De Salud (POS) – Acuerdo 029 de 2011." IFARMA.

Ruibal, Alba. 2009. "Self-Restraint in Search of Legitimacy: The Reform of the Argentine Supreme Court." *Latin American Politics and Society* 51 (3): 59–86.

2014. "Movement and Counter-Movement: A History of Abortion Law Reform and the Backlash in Colombia 2006–2014." *Reproductive Health Matters* 22 (44): 42–51. https://doi.org/10.1016/S0968-8080(14)44803-1.

Rutledge, Jennifer Geist. 2012. "Courts as Entrepreneurs: The Case of the Indian Mid-Day Meals Programme." *Asian Politics & Policy* 4 (4): 527–47.

Ryan, Daniel, Cecilia Larivera, and Andres Napoli. 2017. "Relocalizaciones Urbanas y Riesgos Ambientales: Un Análisis de Los Casos de Magaldi y Villa 26 En La Cuenca Matanza Riachuelo (Argentina)." WP19DR1SP. Working Papers. Lincolns Institute of Land and Policy.

Ryan, Daniel, and Andres Napoli. 2017. "Legal Mobilization and the Politics of Water Pollution: The Case of the Matanza-Riachuelo Basin in Argentina." In *The Politics of Fresh Water Access, Conflict and Identity*, edited by Catherine Ashcraft and Tamar Mayer, 28–40. Abingdon: Routledge.

Sabel, Charles F., and William H. Simon. 2004. "Destabilization Rights: How Public Law Litigation Succeeds." *Harvard Law Review* 117 (4): 1015–1101. https://doi.org/10.2307/4093364.

Sahu, Geetanjoy. 2008. "Implications of Indian Supreme Court's Innovations for Environmental Jurisprudence." *Law, Environment and Development Journal* 4 (1): 1–23.

Sanchez Botero, Esther. 2012. "La Consulta Previa En La Práctica." *Razón Pública* 2012. https://razonpublica.com/la-consulta-previa-en-la-practica/.

Sánchez Urribarrí, Raul. 2022. "Populism, Constitutional Democracy, and High Courts – Lessons from the Venezuelan Case." In *Anti-Constitutional Populism*, edited by Adam Czarnota, Martin Krygier, and Wojciech Sadurski, 185–219. Cambridge Studies in Law and Society. Cambridge: Cambridge University Press. https://doi.org/10.1017/9781009031103.008.

Sandoval Rojas, Nathalia. 2021. "Institutional Conversion from Below: Free, Prior and Informed Consultation in Latin America." PhD Dissertation, Austin: The University of Texas at Austin.

Siegel, Reva B. 2006. "Constitutional Culture, Social Movement Conflict and Constitutional Change: The Case of the De Facto Era. 2005–2006 Brennan Center Symposium Lecture." *California Law Review* 94 (5): 1323. https://doi.org/10.2307/20439068.

Sigal, Martín, Julieta Rossi, and Diego Morales. 2017. "Argentina: Implementation of Collective Cases." In *Social Rights Judgments and the Politics of Compliance: Making It Stick*, edited by Malcolm Langford, César Rodríguez Garavito, and Julieta Rossi, 140–75. Cambridge: Cambridge University Press.

Slater, Dan, and Daniel Ziblatt. 2013. "The Enduring Indispensability of the Controlled Comparison." *Comparative Political Studies* 46 (10): 1301–27. https://doi.org/10.1177/0010414012472469.

Srinivasan, V., and S. Narayanan 2007. *Food Policy and Social Movements: Reflections on the Right to Food Campaign in India* [Case Study #1 of the program: "Food Policy for Developing Countries: The Role of Government in the Global Food System"].

Staton, Jeffrey K. 2010. *Judicial Power and Strategic Communication in Mexico*. New York: Cambridge University Press.

Staton, Jeffrey K., and Georg Vanberg. 2008. "The Value of Vagueness: Delegation, Defiance, and Judicial Opinions." *American Journal of Political Science* 52 (3): 504–19.

Stone, Diane. 2000. "Non-Governmental Policy Transfer: The Strategies of Independent Policy Institutes." *Governance* 13 (1): 45–70.

Sturm, Susan. 1990. "Resolving the Remedial Dilemma: Strategies of Judicial Intervention in Prisons." *University of Pennsylvania Law Review* 138 (3): 805–912. https://doi.org/10.2307/3312269.

Thiruvengadam, Arun K. 2014. “Swallowing a Bitter PIL?: Reflections on Progressive Strategies for Public Interest Litigation in India.” In *The Shifting Scales of Justice: The Supreme Court in Neo-Liberal India*, edited by Mayur Suresh and Siddharth Narrain, 120–38. New Delhi: Orient BlackSwan.

Torres Tovar, Carlos Alberto. 2009. *Ciudad Informal Colombiana*. Bogotá: Universidad Nacional de Colombia.

Torres Tovar, Mauricio. 2011. “Diez Años Por Un Movimiento Social En Salud.” *Le Monde Diplomatique*, November 2011.

Tushnet, Mark V. 2008. *Weak Courts, Strong Rights: Judicial Review and Social Welfare Rights in Comparative Constitutional Law*. Princeton: Princeton University Press.

Uprimny, Rodrigo. 2003. “The Constitutional Court and Control of Presidential Extraordinary Powers in Colombia.” *Democratization* 10 (4): 46–69. https://doi.org/10.1080/13510340312331294027.

Uprimny, Rodrigo, and Mauricio García Villegas. 2004. “Corte Constitucional y Emancipación Social En Colombia.” In *Emancipación Social y Violencia En Colombia*, edited by Boaventura De Sousa Santos and Mauricio García Villegas, 463–514. Bogotá: Norma.

Vaca, Claudia. 2015. “El Plan de Beneficios de Colombia: ¿Que Lecciones Nos Deja?” Breve 8. Serie de Políticas y Métodos Basados En Presentaciones a Expertos. Inter-American Development Bank.

Vanberg, Georg. 2001. “Legislative-Judicial Relations: A Game-Theoretic Approach to Constitutional Review.” *American Journal of Political Science* 45 (2): 346. https://doi.org/10.2307/2669345.

Vasquez Alfaro, Mónica. 2014. “La Crisis Del UPAC a Través de La Mirada de Los Jueces. Un Estudio de Caso En La Ciudad de Barranquilla (Colombia).” *Revista de Derecho*. www.redalyc.org/resumen.oa?id=85131029006.

Velandia Caicedo, Fernando. 2002. *Del Rio Pamplonita al Rio Zulia. Historia Del Acueducto y Alcantarillado de La Ciudad de Cucuta*. Cucuta: Litografia Nueva Granada.

Verbitsky, Horacio. 1993. *Hacer La Corte: La Construcción de Un Poder Absoluto Sin Justicia Ni Control*. Buenos Aires: Planeta.

Verón, René. 2006. “Remaking Urban Environments: The Political Ecology of Air Pollution in Delhi.” *Environment and Planning A: Economy and Space* 38 (11): 2093–2109. https://doi.org/10.1068/a37449.

Villareal, Evelyn, and Bruce Wilson. 2022. *El Agua Como Derecho Humano: Reconocimientos y Disputas En Costa Rica*. San José: Programa Estado de la Nación.

Vishwanath, Apurva. 2017. “What Are the Lessons Learnt from the Right to Food Case?” *Livemint*, March 20, 2017. www.livemint.com/Politics/IEBWhfvkvPCaQW6xky5TjO/What-are-the-lessons-learnt-from-the-Right-to-Food-case.html.

Waldron, Jeremy. 2005. “The Core of the Case against Judicial Review.” *Yale Law Journal* 115: 1346–1406.

Wilson, Bruce. 2009. “Institutional Reform and Rights Revolutions in Latin America: The Cases of Costa Rica and Colombia.” *Journal of Politics in Latin America* 1 (2): 59–85.

Wilson, Bruce, and Juan Carlos Rodríguez Cordero. 2006. “Legal Opportunity Structures and Social Movements: The Effects of Institutional Change on Costa Rican Politics.” *Comparative Political Studies* 39 (3): 325–51. https://doi.org/10.1177/0010414005281934.

Wilson, Stuart. 2011. “Litigating Housing Rights in Johannesburg’s Inner City: 2004–2008.” *South African Journal on Human Rights* 27 (1): 127–51. https://doi.org/10.1080/19962126.2011.11865008.

Yamin, Alicia Ely, and Siri Gloppen, eds. 2011. *Litigating Health Rights: Can Courts Bring More Justice to Health*. Human Rights Program Practice Series. Cambridge, MA: Human Rights Program, Harvard Law School : Harvard University Press.

Zemans, Frances Kahn. 1983. "Legal Mobilization: The Neglected Role of the Law in the Political System." *The American Political Science Review* 77 (3): 690–703.

Index

Printed in the USA
CPSIA information can be obtained
at www.ICGtesting.com
CBHW071915260824
13723CB00004B/37

9 781009 281997